The
MANIAC

ALSO BY BENJAMÍN LABATUT

When We Cease to Understand the World

The
MANIAC

Benjamín Labatut

Pushkin Press

Pushkin Press
Somerset House, Strand
London WC2R ILA

The MANIAC was first published in 2023 by Pushkin Press (UK) and Penguin Press (US)

1 3 5 7 9 8 6 4 2

Hardback ISBN 13: 978-1-78227-981-5
Trade Paperback ISBN 13: 978-1-80533-067-7

Offset by Tetragon, London
Printed and bound in the United Kingdom by Clays Ltd, Elcograf S.p.A.

www.pushkinpress.com

To Juana, Julieta, Kali and Pina

I saw a queen, wearing a gold dress, and her dress was full of eyes, and all the eyes were transparent, like fiery flames and yet like crystals. The crown she wore on her head had as many crowns, one above the other, as there were eyes in her dress. She approached me dreadfully fast and put her foot on my neck, and cried out in a terrible voice: "Do you know who I am?" And I said: "Yes! Long have you caused me pain and woe. You are my soul's faculty of reason."

HADEWIJCH OF BRABANT,

THIRTEENTH-CENTURY POET AND MYSTIC

(ADAPTED BY ELIOT WEINBERGER IN *ANGELS & SAINTS*)

PAUL

or

The Discovery of the Irrational

On the morning of the twenty-fifth of September 1933, the Austrian physicist Paul Ehrenfest walked into Professor Jan Waterink's Pedagogical Institute for Afflicted Children in Amsterdam, shot his fifteen-year-old son, Vassily, in the head, then turned the gun on himself.

Paul died instantly, while Vassily, who suffered from Down syndrome, was in agony for hours before being pronounced dead by the same doctors who had cared for him since his arrival at the institute, in January of that same year. He had come to Amsterdam because his father had decided that the clinic where the boy had spent the better part of a decade, located in Jena, in the heartland of Germany, was no longer safe for him with the Nazis in power. Vassily—or rather Wassik, as almost everyone called him—had to endure severe mental and physical disabilities during his short life; Albert Einstein, who loved the boy's father as if they were brothers and was a regular houseguest at the Ehrenfests' home in Leiden, nicknamed Wassik "patient little crawlikins," for he had such trouble getting around, and would sometimes feel so much pain in his knees that he could not stand. And yet, even then, the child did not lose his seemingly boundless enthusiasm, dragging himself along the carpet, with his useless legs trailing behind, to meet his favorite "uncle" at the door. Wassik spent most of his life institutionalized, but he was a cheerful child nonetheless, often sending postcards to his parents in Leiden featuring quaint German landscapes, or letters with accounts of his daily life, written in his unsure hand, telling them what new things he had learned, how his best friend had fallen ill, how hard he was trying to be a good boy, just as they had taught him, and how in love he was with not one but two girls in his class, as well as his teacher, Mrs. Gottlieb, who was the most caring and wonderful person he had ever met, a thought that would bring tears to his father's eyes, as Paul Ehrenfest was, first and foremost, a teacher.

Paul had suffered from extreme melancholy and bouts of crippling depression all his life. Like his son, he had been a weak boy, often ill. When he was not nursing nosebleeds, coughing due to his asthma, or dizzy and wheezing from lack of breath after escaping the bullies who teased and taunted him at school—*Pig's ear, donkey's ear, give 'em to the Jew that's here!*—he would feign some other ailment, a fever perhaps, a cold, or an unbearable stomachache, just to stay at home in his mother's arms, hidden from the outside, safely wrapped in her embrace, as if deep down, in some way, little Paul, the youngest of five brothers, could foretell that she would die when he was ten, and all his prior suffering was nothing but a premonition, an anticipation of loss that he dare not speak of, to himself or to others, afraid that if he said it out loud, found the courage to put it into words, her death would somehow hasten forward to meet him; so he remained silent, fearful, and sad, shouldering a weight that no child should bear, a dark foreknowledge that haunted him past her death, past his father's demise six years after hers, and that would follow behind him like the toll of a bell up to the day of his undoing, by his own hand, at fifty-three years of age.

However much he was at odds with himself and the world, Paul was the most gifted member of his household and the best student of any class he ever took part in. He was well liked by his friends, highly esteemed by his classmates, and appreciated by his teachers, but nothing could convince him of his self-worth. Yet he was by no means an introvert; on the contrary, he would pour out everything he took in, delighting those around him with fabulous displays of knowledge and his uncanny ability to translate the most complicated ideas into images and metaphors that anyone could understand, threading together concepts from disparate fields that he drew from the ever-growing number of books he fed on with ravenous, spongelike intelligence. Paul was capable of absorbing everything around him while making no differentiations. His mind was fully porous, lacking, perhaps, some essential membrane; he was not so much interested in the world as he was invaded by its many forms. With nothing to keep him safe, he felt raw and exposed to the information flowing constantly back and forth across his blood-brain barrier. Even when he obtained his PhD and became firmly established as a distinguished professor, after succeeding the great Hendrik Lorentz in the theoretical physics chair at the University of Leiden, the only thing that really sparked joy in Paul was giving himself to others, to the point that, as one of his many beloved students remarked, "Ehrenfest distributed all that was living and active in him," such that sometimes it looked like "he gave away everything he had found or observed, without building up a reserve, a kind of stronghold, within himself."

As a physicist, he made no earth-shattering discoveries, but he enjoyed the full respect of such towering figures as Niels Bohr, Paul Dirac, and Wolfgang Pauli. Albert Einstein wrote that, no more than a few hours after having met Paul, he felt "as though our dreams and aspirations were meant for each other." These friends of Paul's admired

5

not only his critical and intellectual capacities but something rather different, a virtue that is usually lacking among giants: ethics, character, as well as a deep, some would say overwhelming, desire to understand, to grasp the core of things. Ehrenfest sought relentlessly what he called *der springende Punkt*, the leaping point, the heart of the matter, as for him deriving a result by logical means was never enough: "That is like dancing on one leg," he would say, "when the essence lies in recognizing connections, meanings and associations in every direction." For Ehrenfest, true understanding was a full-body experience, something that involved your entire being, not just your mind or reason. He was an atheist, a doubter and a skeptic with such a rigid standard for truth that he sometimes became a figure of fun among his peers: in 1932, at the end of a meeting of three dozen of Europe's best physicists at the Niels Bohr Institute in Copenhagen, a parody of *Faust* was staged to celebrate the centennial of Goethe, and Paul was cast as the great scholar Heinrich Faust himself, unwilling to be convinced by the demon Mephistopheles, portrayed by Wolfgang Pauli, of the existence of the neutrino, a newly postulated fundamental particle. They called him the Conscience of Physics, and while there was a hidden barb in that nickname due to Ehrenfest's undeterred opposition to the road that not only physics but the whole of the exact sciences seemed to be taking during the first decades of the twentieth century, many of his colleagues would visit him regularly at his home in Leiden, just across the river from the university, to try their ideas on him, and on his wife, since Tatyana Alexeyevna Afanassjewa was an accomplished mathematician in her own right. She coauthored some of Ehrenfest's most important scientific papers, including the one that first made his name (though it did almost nothing for her career) and eventually led to his appointment as successor to the much-revered Lorentz: it was a summary article on statistical mechanics, a favored subject of his mentor, the ill-fated Ludwig Boltzmann. Boltzmann was one of the strongest advocates of the atomic hypothesis, a veritable trailblazer who first discovered the role that probability plays in the behavior and properties of atoms. Like Ehrenfest, Boltzmann also suffered greatly during his restless and unhappy life, crippled as he was by severe bouts of uncontrollable mania and abysmal depression, the effects of which were compounded by the vicious antagonism that his revolutionary ideas bred among his peers. Ernst Mach, a staunch positivist who contended that physicists should not speak of atoms as anything but theoretical constructs—since, at the time, there was no direct evidence for their existence—hounded and mocked Boltzmann without end, interrupting one of his lectures on atoms with the mean-spirited question: "Have you ever seen one?" The Bull, as his friends called Boltzmann due to his corpulence and his stubborn tenacity, despaired at the ferocity of his critics, and even though he laid down one of the fundamental equations of modern physics, his statistical interpretation of the second law of thermodynamics, in his personal life he could not escape the slow and constant advance of his mental disorder, which seemed, like the entropy of the universe he had so wonderfully captured in his equation, to be constantly and irreversibly increasing, leading to inevitable randomness and decay. He admitted to his colleagues that he lived in perpetual fear that he might suddenly lose his mind during a lecture. Toward the end of his life he could hardly breathe from his asthma, his eyesight dimmed to the point where he could no longer read, and his headaches and migraines became so utterly unbearable that his physician ordered him to completely abstain from any scientific activity. In September 1906, Boltzmann hanged himself with a short rope from the crossbars of the window frame in a room at the Hotel Ples, during a summer holiday in Duino, near Trieste, while his wife and young daughter were out swimming in the calm, turquoise waters of the Adriatic.

Speak the truth, write with clarity, and defend it to your very end was Boltzmann's personal motto, and Paul, his disciple, took it to heart. The weight of the respect that Ehrenfest carried among so many outstanding physicists was due to his capacity to bring other people's ideas into sharp focus and capture their fundamental essence, transmitting this knowledge with such passion and vim that his audience was brought in to his thinking as if under a spell. "He lectures like a master. I have hardly ever heard a man speak with such fascination and brilliance. Significant phrases, witty points and dialectic are all at his disposal in an extraordinary manner. He knows how to make the most difficult things concrete and intuitively clear. Mathematical arguments are translated by him into easily comprehensible pictures," wrote the great German theoretical physicist Arnold Sommerfeld, who both appreciated and feared Ehrenfest's fame as the grand inquisitor of physics. Paul did not shy away from pointing out flaws in other people's arguments with the same pitiless criticism with which he would chastise himself; that role of his was particularly important during the fateful Solvay Conference of 1927, when classical physics and quantum mechanics faced off, forever changing the foundations of that branch of science. Ehrenfest mediated between the two major players—Einstein, who abhorred the weight that chance, indeterminacy, probability, and uncertainty were given in the new science of the quantum, and Bohr, who sought to enthrone a fundamentally different type of physics for the subatomic world. At one point, Ehrenfest took to the stage among the gaggle of some thirty-odd Nobel Prize winners screaming over each other in French, English, German, Dutch, and Danish and scribbled a couple of verses from the Bible on the blackboard: *The Lord did there confound the languages of all the Earth.* Everyone laughed, but the arguments continued to rage on for days, with quantum mechanics coming out victorious over the classical scheme of physics, in spite of, or perhaps due to, the fact that it was completely opposed to common sense. Although Ehrenfest was firmly on the side of the new, and much more open than his friend Einstein to the revolutionary principles coming from Bohr, Heisenberg, Born, and Dirac, he could not shake the feeling that a fundamental line had been crossed, that a demon, or perhaps a genie, had incubated in the soul of physics, one that neither his nor any succeeding generation would be able to put back in the lamp. If one were to believe the novel rules governing the inner realm of the atom, suddenly the entire world was no longer as solid and real as it once was. "Surely there is a special section in purgatory for professors of quantum mechanics!" Paul wrote to Einstein when he returned from Solvay to Leiden, but all his attempts at humor could not slow his descent into the dark pit toward which he seemed to be spiraling down at a faster and faster pace, not least due to the strange direction that his hallowed discipline was taking, filled as it now was with logical contradictions, uncertainties, and indeterminacies that he could no longer explain to his beloved students, as he had no way of understanding them himself. In May 1931, Ehrenfest confessed his fears to Niels Bohr in a letter: "I have completely lost contact with theoretical physics. I cannot read anything anymore and feel myself incompetent to have even the most modest grasp about what makes sense in the flood of articles and books. Perhaps I cannot at all be helped anymore. Every new issue of the *Zeitschrift für Physik* or the

Physical Review immerses me in blind panic. I know absolutely nothing!"
Bohr wrote back to console his friend, pointing out that it was not just
Ehrenfest, but the whole of the physics community that was having problems dealing with the latest discoveries, only to receive an even longer
letter in return, in which Paul decried that he felt like a dog that, totally exhausted, was running after a streetcar carrying his master out of
sight. Where some saw the quantum revolution as a protean fire spark-
ing novel results at an unrelenting pace, Ehrenfest saw mostly stagna-
tion and even degeneration: "Those awful abstractions! That incessant
focus on tricks and techniques! The mathematical plague that erases
all powers of imagination!" he cried out bitterly before his students in
Leiden. The direction in which theoretical physics was heading went
completely against his grain: real, physical intuition was being replaced
with brute-force artillery, and mathematical formulae were set in place
of matter, atoms, and energy. Paul detested the likes of John von Neumann, that Hungarian wunderkind, with his "terrifying mathematical guns and unreadably complicated formula apparatus," as much as
he despised the indigestion that the "infinite Heisenberg-Born-Dirac-
Schrödinger sausage-machine factory" caused him. He lamented the
attitude of his younger students, who "no longer noticed that their heads
had been turned into relays in a telephone network for communicating
and distributing sensational physics messages" without realizing that,
like almost all modern developments, mathematics was hostile to life:
"It is inhuman, like every truly diabolic machine, and it kills everyone whose spinal marrow isn't conditioned to fit the movement of its
wheels." His already excruciating self-criticism and inferiority complex
became truly unbearable, for although he knew mathematics, it was not

simple for him. He was not a computer. He could not calculate with ease, and his inability to keep up with the times fueled a self-destructive streak that was his constant companion and torturer, an inner voice that whispered to him, and continuously betrayed him. By 1930, his letters to his friends spoke of nothing but death and despair: "I clearly feel I'll destroy my life if I don't succeed in pulling myself together. Every time I have a chance to review my affairs, I see some sort of chaos in front of me—a gambler or alcoholic has to see similar pictures when sober." His inner turmoil mirrored the economic and political turbulence that was beginning to tear Europe apart. Paul was officially nondenominational; Jews were not allowed to marry Christians in the Austro-Hungarian empire, and both he and Tatyana had given up their respective religions to marry each other back in 1904. But with anti-semitism growing on all sides, he began to entertain increasingly morbid thoughts. In 1933, he wrote to his friend Samuel Goudsmit with a macabre plot to shock German society out of its Nazi-induced trance: "What if a group of eminent, elderly Jewish academics and artists collectively commit suicide, without any demonstration of hatred or issuance of demands, in order to prick the German conscience?" Goudsmit wrote back in a fury, sick of his friend's obsession with suicide and disgusted by the utter absurdity of his idea: "A group of dead Jews can do nothing, and their deaths would merely delight *das teutonische Volk*." Three days before Ehrenfest wrote that letter, Hitler's regime, barely two months old, had enacted the Law for the Restoration of the Professional Civil Service, putting all Jews who held government jobs at risk, a move that convinced Ehrenfest that "the remarkably open and care fully planned extermination of the Jewish 'plague' from German art, science, jurisprudence, and medicine would quickly be 90 percent effective." During the last year of his life he used his contacts and influence to help Jewish scientists find work outside of Germany, even though he had lost all faith in a possible future for himself. His thoughts went around in a furious circle, with money never far from his mind: his Leiden home was mortgaged many times over. He longed to put an end to his own suffering, but he could not bear to leave his wife with the care of poor Wassik—she had lost all her investments in Russian stock in the aftermath of the First World War and the Russian Revolution—or inflict such a lifelong burden of charge on his two eldest daughters, Tatyana and Galinka, or his older son, Paul Jr. His suicidal fantasies, which up to that point had been exclusively centered on his own death, began to include his youngest child: "Surely you understand my wish that Galinka and Tanitschka should not in the future have to work themselves to the bone simply to keep their idiot brother alive?" he wrote to Nelly Posthumus Meyjes, an art historian with whom he was having an intense love affair that brought him a small measure of joy and happiness, but also inflamed his already disordered mental state.

The affair began with his wife's tacit permission: at the onset of the relationship, Tatyana would even send Nelly her regards. She was as worried as anybody else about her husband's mental breakdown, and thought that an extramarital adventure, while clearly a risk, could perhaps soothe his mind and turn him away from his obsession with chess and the never-ending list of hobbies—the model aircraft he built, the now-rotting herb garden, the abandoned stamp collection, the home-made telescope, the artisanal brewery in his basement—on which Paul fretted away his time to avoid finishing his physics investigations and long-overdue articles, because the mere thought of sitting down to work on them would often send him into a spiraling panic. Up to that point, Tatyana had been all that Paul had ever wanted, and while she would spend long seasons away, staying in Russia with her family, their marriage had always been a happy one, based as it was on a profound mutual understanding and many shared intellectual interests. Tatyana had a keen mind and was respected and admired by all of Paul's colleagues. His lover, Nelly, however, was not only smart, she had a dark side that rivaled Ehrenfest's own death wish, but she appeared to be fully able to control it. The first time he saw her was during one of her lectures in the Teylers Museum in Haarlem: Paul was smitten by her intelligence and good looks, and by the subject of her talk, an old Pythagorean myth that spoke of the disharmony of the world and the discovery of the irrational, which became the prime focus of his obsessions during the final year of his life, and a perfect counterpoint to his increasing worries about the rise of the Nazis in Germany.

In nature, Nelly said, there are such things that surpass proportion and cannot be likened to any other. They obey no measure and refuse categorization, because they exist outside the order that encompasses all phenomena. These outliers, these singularities, these monstrosities, will not be governed or compared by means of a number, because they lie at the root of what is disharmonious, chaotic, and unruly about the world. For the Greeks, she explained, the discovery of the irrational was a heinous crime, an act of unforgivable impiety, and the divulgence of that knowledge, an offense punishable by death. Nelly spoke of the two surviving accounts of the Pythagorean sage who defied this fundamental commandment: in one version, the man who discovered the irrational was banished from his community, and his friends erected a tomb for him, as though he were already dead; in the other, he was drowned at sea by members of his own family, or perhaps by the gods themselves dressed as his wife and his two children. If you discovered something disharmonious in nature, Nelly explained, something that negates the natural order entirely, you should never speak of it, not even to yourself, but instead do everything within your means to remove it from your thoughts, purge your memory, watch your speech, and even stand guard against your own dreams, lest the wrath of the gods fall upon you. The harmony of nature was to be preserved above all things, as it was older than the Titans, wiser than the Oracle, more sacred than Mount Olympus, and as sacrosanct as the lifeblood that animates this and all other worlds. To acknowledge even the possibility of the irrational, to recognize disharmony, would place the fabric of existence at risk, since not just our reality, but every single aspect of the universe—whether physical, mental, or ethereal—depended on the unseen threads that bind all things together. This taboo was not merely a concern for the ancients, Nelly explained, but lies at the heart of western philosophy and science: Kant had written that science demands that we be able to think of nature as a totality. You start by classifying the simplest aspects of the world—the shimmering tendrils of a creeping vine, the iridescent body of a beetle—and follow by ordering these phenomena in species, then genus, then family, order, class, phylum, kingdom, and domain, working, all the while, under the premise that every conceivable wing, feather, root, rivulet, coil, and appendage will fall somewhere in that order, occupying its rightful place in a system that encompasses the entire universe, fruit of a wisdom so profound that it underlies and upholds the manifest and unmanifested forms of existence. But perhaps that wasn't really the case, Nelly warned her audience; it may well be that nature is utterly chaotic, with no law able to subsume the apparent heterogeneity, no concept capable of whittling down its ever-increasing complexity. What if nature cannot be cognized as a whole? Our civilization had yet to come to terms with this terrifying possibility, and she very much doubted that it could, for it would be a death blow to science, philosophy, and rationality. Meanwhile, Nelly said, artists had already fully embraced it; she believed that the rediscovery of the irrational was the driving force behind all vanguard movements, movements that, even to a lay observer, were evidently suffused with a Faustian, boundless energy, a haste, a tragic fall in which everything was permitted. For modern art recognized no laws, no method, no truth, just a blind, uncontainable surge, a rush of madness that would not stop for anyone or anything but drive us onward even to the ends of the Earth.

Paul was entranced. He approached Nelly and bombarded her with questions before she even had the time to pick up her papers, and they talked all through the day, increasingly fascinated by each other's intelligence. They spent that night together at a nearby hotel. Perhaps due to the strange chemical effects of new love, or owing to the consequences of his lifelong depression, which can wreak havoc on the brain, Paul became convinced that he was somehow related to the Pythagorean sage from the legend that Nelly had spoken about, and he began seeing disharmony and turbulence everywhere. He could no longer distinguish any type of reasonable order to the universe, no natural laws, no repeating patterns, just a vast, sprawling world without measure, riddled with chaos, infected by nonsense, and lacking any sort of meaningful intelligence behind it; he could perceive the rise of the irrational in the mindless chants of the Hitler Youth spewing over the radio waves, in the rants of warmongering politicians, and in the blind proponents of endless progress, but he could also distinguish it, ever more

15

clearly, in the papers and lectures of his colleagues, brimming over with supposedly revolutionary ideas that he regarded as nothing but the industrialization of physics. He wrote of his dismay to Einstein—whose youngest son, Eduard, was schizophrenic and had been institutionalized on several occasions, so Paul felt his friend was weighed down by part of his same burdens—decrying in his letter what he saw as a dark, unconscious force that was slowly creeping into the scientific worldview, one in which rationality had become somehow confused for its very opposite: "Reason is now untethered from all other deeper, more fundamental aspects of our psyche, and I'm afraid it will lead us by the bit, like a drunken mule. I know that you see it as well as I do, but most of the time I feel alone, as if I were the only human being bearing witness to how far we have fallen. We lie on our knees, praying to the wrong god, a childish deity who hides at the center of a corrupted world that he can neither govern nor understand. Or is it that we have made him ourselves, in our own fetid image, but then forgotten we have done so, as young boys birth the monsters and demons who haunt their dreams, without ever realizing that they have only themselves to blame?" Afraid of what she now saw in him, Nelly encouraged Paul to write down all recollections of his childhood, an exercise meant to find the driving force behind his depression, but he could not manage to do so, as he felt increasingly disconnected, from others and from himself. His memories, his past, his family and friends, all those ties and treasured reveries now belonged to some other person, a man whom he would sometimes catch a glimpse of in the mirror—pint-sized, bespectacled, and heavyset, with spiky hair cut short and a thick mustache over buckteeth that looked as if they were shying away from each other—and whom he failed to recognize. He was torn between the sincere devotion he felt for his wife and the painful euphoria that Nelly kindled in him, but neither of those women could steer him away from the path that some unknown force seemed to have chosen for him, with a bullet waiting at the end. "Why are people like me condemned to continue living?" he wrote to his lover during his last summer. "If you or Tatyana were to ask me whether I love you, there's only one answer, and Tatyana knows it already: in utter helplessness I crave your proximity, and if that craving gives me neither warmth nor strength, then I am overcome by desolation. Love is such a mightily divisive element. All the suffering it brings! Surely it's one's duty to put an end to one's life as soon as possible, before causing hideous destruction." Seeing that Paul could make no headway against his demons, Tatyana asked for a divorce. Paul begged her to take him back, and she finally agreed to stop the proceedings, which were already in their final stage, on the condition that he leave Nelly. Paul agreed but did not have the strength to stop seeing his lover, nor could he restore his relationship with his wife. Whatever had held them steadfast during more than three decades had been lost in the space of a few months. Finally, Paul gave up and filed for divorce himself, without confessing to Tatyana that he had already written—though not yet sent—his suicide note, a letter that his closest friends would receive a couple of days after the hideous tragedy at the Waterink Institute had taken place: "My dear friends: Bohr, Einstein, Franck, Herglotz, Joffé, Kohnstamm, and Tolman! I absolutely do not know any more how to carry further during the next few months the burden of my life which has become unbearable. I cannot stand it any longer to let my professorship in Leiden go down the drain. I must vacate my position here. Perhaps it may happen that I can use up the rest of my strength in Russia . . . If, however, it will not become clear rather

17

soon that I can do that, then it is as good as certain that I shall kill my-self. And if that will happen sometime, then I should like to know that I have written, calmly and without rush, to you whose friendship has played such a great role in my life . . . In recent years it has become ever more difficult for me to follow the developments in physics with under-standing. After trying, ever more enervated and torn, I have finally given up in desperation. This made me completely weary of life . . . I did feel condemned to live on mainly because of the economic cares for the children. I tried other things but that helped only briefly. Therefore I concentrate more and more on the precise details of suicide. I have no other practical possibility than suicide, and that after having first killed Wassik. Forgive me . . . May you and those dear to you stay well."

In May 1933, he took a train from Leiden to Berlin. There, he saw Nazi Brownshirts storming trade unions, labor banks, and coopera-tives. He read the news reports describing the mob of morally outraged students who had attacked the Institute of Sex Research, and he walked through the ashes left in front of the State Opera, where the pages of twenty thousand books had gone up in flames, illuminating the faces of giddy boys and girls, members of the Deutsche Studentenschaft, who had raided the libraries of their universities in search of all "un-German" publications, journals, and magazines, singing, chanting, and swearing oaths as they fed an enormous bonfire, while senior members of the Nazi Party murmured incantations, and Goebbels screamed to a crowd of thousands, *No to decadence and moral corruption! Yes to decency and morality in family and state!* Paul saw soldiers on the streets, marching to the sound of the military music that blared from all radio stations, interrupted by the shrieks of Germany's newly appointed chancellor, Adolf Hitler, who endorsed Roosevelt's world disarmament proposal and demanded an immediate revision of the Treaty of Versailles. By the end of May, Germany had legalized eugenic sterilization, and less than two months later, when the Nazi Law for the Prevention of Offspring with Hereditary Diseases was approved, allowing the State to *render incapable of procreation by means of a surgical operation any person suffering from a hereditary disease, if the experience of medical science shows that it is highly probable that his descendants would suffer from some serious physical or mental hereditary defect*, a dictum that included not only those afflicted with congenital mental deficiency, schizophrenia, manic-depressive insanity, hereditary epilepsy, Huntington's, hereditary blindness, deafness, or any other hereditary deformity, but even those who suffered from severe alcoholism, Paul traveled to the Johannes Trüper Youth Sanatorium, in Jena, and took young Wassik to Amsterdam, where he began to receive care at the Waterink Institute. During the first year of the law, more than sixty-four thousand people were forcibly sterilized, after being deemed unfit by Genetic Health Courts composed of a judge, a medical officer, and a medical practitioner.

In July, as the light of summer started to brighten the skies above his home in Leiden, Paul's dark mood lifted enough for him to outline the beginning of a new investigation with Hendrik Casimir on one of the great unsolved mysteries of classical physics: turbulence, that sudden phenomenon by which any smooth-flowing liquid breaks down into a wild chaos of eddies within eddies within eddies, racing in so many directions at the same time that their movement cannot be predicted by any known model. Turbulence is ubiquitous in nature, so common, in fact, that even young children playing in the white waters of a brook have some unconscious knowledge of its mechanisms, even if they are unaware that it is also present in the torrent of blood their puppy hearts rush through their veins; it can be seen in the most mundane substances, invoked by a drop of milk in a coffee cup or a simple puff of smoke, and yet, mathematically, it is both bewildering and profound. Some of the most brilliant minds have tried to tame it, but all have failed, so Paul was very surprised to discover that his own mind, frenzied and fractured as it was, had suddenly developed a wondrous affinity for fluid equations, so powerful that it not only took over his waking hours but also seeped into his dreams. At night, he would see dark water all around him, his naked body pounded by savage currents, sucked in by a colossal maelstrom that spun around an unfathomable void. While these nightmares hounded him, he would wake strangely transfixed, not by images of ocean horror but by a remarkable feeling of enlightened calm, a gripping certainty that, deep down, for reasons that went beyond his understanding, his wife and lover, his sons and daughters, his friends, colleagues, and students, even his home country would all be well, because however hopeless his own situation seemed at the time, things were protected, safe and sound, each in its place, shielded by a force that wed pain to pleasure, darkness to light, and order to chaos, with life and death caught up in the same dizzying spiral, intertwined in so many ways that we could not tell them apart. As soon as he woke, he would jump out of bed, covered in sweat as if he were the sole survivor of a shipwreck, and work feverishly in his study, sending off such a flood of letters to Casimir that he knew his colleague would find it impossible to follow his train of thought, because one missive was quickly contradicted by the next, and then replaced by another in which his argument had turned around and swallowed its own head. He tried to calm down and develop his ideas serenely, but his enthusiasm, and the joy of working once more, free from the heavy fog of melancholia, was simply too much for him to contain. It was this work, and this alone, that would tie his name to history: a solution to the irregular and unpredictable behavior of turbulence, a law behind its irreducible randomness. On the verge of the one thing that he had been denied his entire career, he could think of nothing else, and abandoned himself completely. But even in the midst of his ecstasy, he continued to worry. Why had he suddenly been granted this strange gift? Why him, why now? He had done nothing to deserve it. The last years of his life had been a waste, and ever since he had met Nelly, his entire consciousness had been consumed by the many trivial worries of romantic love. Though perhaps that was the key to all of this: possession, a sudden invasion from without, work that was not the product of thought or will but, as the Greeks knew well, of rapture and ardor. He needed to get out of the way, to let things pass through him, and be changed. He wiped tears from his eyes as his pen flew across the page, each term in his equations flowing softly into the next, all ideas not considered but inspired by this force that had come into him, this strength that went beyond any he had known, but that left him as abruptly as it had come. His mania spent, he ordered the jumble of papers strewn across his study but dared not approach them for days. The horror of his false epiphany was so apparent to him that he did not need to sit down before his desk to know that his mistakes were too many to tally, his ambitions too large to anchor in reality, and his equations so flawed and incomplete that they could never be redeemed by experiment.

When August came, he spent a couple of days wandering alone in the national park on the island of Schiermonnikoog, and in the beginning of September he visited Niels Bohr in Copenhagen, where he mediated a conference, at the end of which he opened up about his depression and suicidal thoughts to the least likely person imaginable, the English physicist Paul Dirac, a wild, unworldly genius who was portrayed by one of his colleagues as "the strangest man alive," utterly unequipped to understand the intricacies and contradictions of Ehrenfest's character. Paul opened up to him nonetheless, and spoke about his fears for the future of his family, and especially of young Wassik, for surely the influence of Nazism, with its loathing of Jews, eugenic pseudoscience, and murderous hate for all things "other," would soon pour out from Germany and spread to all its neighboring countries, fueled, as it no doubt was, by a dark, unconscious impulse that was driving us to a future where our species would have no place, substituted, sooner than later, by something completely monstrous. There was nowhere to run, Paul said, no place to hide, because although he had rescued his boy from the claws of his would-be assassins, already sharpening their axes to cut down and prune back what they considered to be the sickened limbs of Deutschland's Great Oak, he felt, nevertheless, unable to protect him from his own reckless drive toward death and self-destruction, and knew of no way to keep him safe from the strange new rationality that was beginning to take shape all around them, a profoundly inhuman form of intelligence that was completely indifferent to mankind's deepest needs; this deranged reason, this specter haunting the soul of science, which Paul could almost see as an incorporeal wraith, an unholy spirit hovering over his colleagues' heads at meetings and conferences, peering over their shoulders, or nudging their elbows, ever so slightly, as they wrote down their equations, a truly malignant influence, both logic-driven and utterly irrational, and though still fledgling and dormant it was undeniably gathering strength, wanting desperately to break into the world, preparing to thrust itself into our lives through technology by enrapturing the cleverest men and women with whispered promises of superhuman power and godlike control. Paul sensed its budding influence, could hear the faint stirring of its tendrils as it slowly crawled toward us, and yet he could not name or place it, and hardly dared to speak of it out loud, for how could he tell if this morbid imagining, this inexplicable bane that he felt it was his duty to arrest, was the fruit of genuine foresight, or just another malignant growth of the delusion that was slowly overcoming his mind? A confounded Dirac listened to Ehrenfest's confession without knowing what to say and finally blurted out some meaningless words of encouragement, praising Paul's invaluable role as a mediator in physics, a modern-day Socrates without whose questioning, something fundamental would surely be lost. Dirac tried being as supportive as he could while quietly shying away from the Austrian physicist who had grasped him firmly by the arm, his face soaked in tears, telling him that he could not imagine what such praise meant to a man who had lost all will to live.

At first light on September 25, 1933, Paul opened his eyes, served himself a sparse breakfast, donned his hat and coat, and walked from his home to the Leiden train station with a gun in his pocket. He bought a ticket to Amsterdam, but since the train left at nine thirty, he still had an hour to kill, so he dropped by the house of Arend Rutgers, one of his former PhD students, who lived close by. They drank water (Paul abhorred liquor and even refused to drink coffee or tea) and talked physics and religion, Paul confessing that, although he himself had lost faith as a very young boy, he had always appreciated pious men such as Rutgers, and would have been unable to survive without constant congress with actively religious individuals, for in their belief in a sacred order upholding the entire world, however naïve and misplaced, he found a small measure of hope. Ehrenfest not only cherished their proximity but thought that all searchers of truth formed a community for lost souls, a refuge of sorts, the hearth, he said, of the home that we have lost due to reason's destructive influence, which has ruined our capacity for living. Paul, who had placed all his faith in physics, now felt let down, cast out from a paradise that, due to the increasing influence of quantum mechanics and the unstoppable spread of the mathematical plague, was retreating into a darkness deeper than the abyss within atoms. Rutgers tried his best to console him—Would he not consider staying for lunch?—but Ehrenfest replied that it was much too late for him, and left in a hurry, almost sprinting out the door, leaving his hat behind.

In truth he still had time, perhaps too much of it, and when he arrived at the train station and sat down to wait, he felt a sudden urge to turn back, to return to his friend's house, or to his own home, to escape to any moment other than the present. As he looked at the clockface on the opposing side of the rails, its hands appeared to stop and stick in place. Paul closed his eyes and could almost see the gears frozen inside the mechanism; when he was a child, his grandmother, the old woman who had given him the love and attention that his father had denied him, would hand him a chest full of broken clocks when he came to visit her, discards from a shop that had gone out of business, and Paul, that thin, nervous, polite, and inquisitive little boy, would spend the whole afternoon playing with cogs, springs, and coils, trying to put them back together again, a game he endlessly enjoyed, even though he never succeeded in repairing a single one. Those few blissful days stuck out in his memory and gnawed at him like fleas on a dog, each one an example of an irreversible process, little windows through which he could see his former self sketching out the floor plan of his family's apartment after his older brother, Arthur, who seemed to know everything there was to know about the world, showed him how to do so, in the winter of 1896, when he was the same age that Vassily, poor little Wassik, poor little crawlikins, was now, an age when Paul had gone through his "calendar craze," collecting all the almanacs, yearbooks, and calendars that he could lay his hands on, or drawing them himself on pieces of scrap paper and food wrappers, arranging the days in neat rows, flicking the corners of the pages to make the months and years pass by in fractions of a second, time flowing on and on and on, in a never-ending series that reminded him of "Chad Gadya," the Passover song he was taught by the rabbis in school, one he would sing to himself in the many nights during which sleep felt like something that only others could enjoy, a nursery rhyme that tells the story of a father who buys a young goat for two farthings, but then the kid—who the wise men said represented Israel in its purest, most innocent state—is killed by a cat, which is bitten by a dog, which is wounded by a stick, which is burned by fire, which is quenched by water, which is drunk by an ox, which is slaughtered by a man, in an unbroken chain of cause and effect, sin and penance, crime and punishment, that reaches all the way to heaven, where the Mighty Lord himself, the Holy One, Blessed be He, smites the angel of death, establishing the Kingdom of God, a rhyme the true meaning of which Paul had never been able to understand till then, when the hands on the clock started moving again and he felt shaken, strangely chilled, as he checked his pocket to make sure it was still there, afraid, or perhaps hoping, that his ticket had been lost somewhere along the way; but it was there, all things were in their place, exactly where they should be, waiting for the train to arrive, now, now, now, at any moment now, even though he could not hear it, could not feel its faint rumbling in the distance, he still knew that it would come, there was no way of stopping it, in fact it had just arrived, he could see it rolling slowly into the platform, smoke billowing all around him as the whistle shrieked, but even then he still had time to turn back, the dog, the stick, to stand, take stride, the cat, the angel of death, and walk away, he still had time, and yet he stood, machinelike, propelled by a force he neither recognized nor understood, and took five steps with his legs as stiff as an automaton's, to board the wagon and take his place among the rest.

He would be there by ten.

JOHN

or

The Mad Dreams of Reason

One afternoon in the 1840s, as George Boole walked across a field near Doncaster, a thought flashed into his head that he believed was a religious vision. Boole suddenly saw how you could use mathematics to unlock the mysterious processes of human thought. The same symbols that were used in algebra could be used to describe what went on inside people's heads as they followed a train of thought, expressing all the twists and turns in simple binary form. If this, then that. If that, then not this. And in 1854, Boole wrote a book that caused a sensation. It was called *An Investigation of the Laws of Thought.* Its aim, "to investigate the fundamental laws of those operations of the mind, by which reasoning is performed" . . . Boole was driven by an almost messianic belief that he had been allowed a glimpse, by God, into the truth of the human mind. But there were those who doubted this; the philosopher Bertrand Russell was astonished by the brilliance of Boole's mathematics, but he didn't believe that what Boole had discovered was anything to do with human thought. Human beings, Russell said, do not think like that. What Boole was really doing was something else . . .

ADAM CURTIS, *CAN'T GET YOU OUT OF MY HEAD*

He was the smartest human being of the 20th century.

An alien among us.

David Hilbert, pope of 20th-century mathematics, sat in for his doctorate examination, and was so stunned by him that when his turn came to interrogate the twenty-two-year-old Hungarian student, he had just one question: "Pray, who is the candidate's tailor?"

When cancer spread to his brain and began to destroy his mind, he was sequestered by the United States military and confined to the Walter Reed Army Medical Center. Two armed guards stood outside his door. No one was allowed to see him without express permission from the Pentagon. An Air Force colonel and eight airmen with top secret clearance were assigned to assist him full-time, even though there were days he could do nothing but rage like a madman. He was a fifty-three-year-old Jewish mathematician who had emigrated from Hungary to America in 1937, and yet at his bedside, hanging on his every word, sat Rear Admiral Lewis Strauss, Chairman of the Atomic Energy Commission; the Secretary of Defense; the Deputy Secretary of Defense; the Secretaries of Air, Army, and Navy; and the military Chiefs of Staff—all waiting for a final spark, one more idea from the individual who had birthed the modern computer, laid down the mathematical foundations of quantum mechanics, written the equations for the implosion of the atomic bomb, fathered the Theory of Games and Economic Behavior, heralded the arrival of digital life, self-reproducing machines, artificial intelligence, and the technological singularity, and promised them godlike control over the Earth's climate, now wasting away before their eyes, screaming in agony, lost in delirium, dying, just like any other man.

His name was Neumann János Lajos.

A.k.a. Johnny von Neumann.

PART I

The Limits of Logic

Eugene Wigner

Only he was fully awake

There are two kinds of people in this world: Jancsi von Neumann and the rest of us.

He was in the class below me at the Fasori Gimnázium, a Lutheran secondary school in Budapest, perhaps the most rigorous high school in the world at the time, part of a brilliant national education system designed specifically for the elite, that produced several scientists, musicians, artists, and mathematicians of the highest caliber, and one true genius. I clearly remember the first time I saw him, because he arrived in 1914, the same year that the war broke out, and so those two things—Jancsi and war—are inseparably tied together in my memory. That luciferin boy hit us like a comet, as though he were a harbinger of something grand and terrible, just like those celestial messengers that wander around the darkness of our solar system, and that the superstitious have always associated with great calamities, disasters, plagues, or social cataclysms. I remember how, when Halley's Comet passed in

1910, so bright that we could see it with our naked eyes, my own mother, a deeply religious woman who was, in all other matters, a staunch rationalist, shut certain doors in our house (the one that led down to the cellar and the door of the room that used to be our nursery, and that my father had converted into his study) and did not let anybody open them for days, refused to eat anything that had been brought in from the outside, and took just the tiniest sips of water till the comet finally disappeared from the sky, because she feared that it was pouring pestilent vapors down onto the earth. She was so convinced of this that she actually tried to force my father to buy gas masks for all of us, a petition that he, of course, refused. Curiously enough, my mother never took a liking to Jancsi either, not even after we became the closest of friends, and I'm sure that she died unaware of the fact that our friendship was, at least in part, her fault, because she was the one who first told me about him: one of my senior teachers, Gábor Szegő, a very well-known and respected Hungarian mathematician, and a close friend of my mother, had been hired by Jancsi's parents (in the old country, Johnny was still called Janos, or Jancsi to his friends) to give the boy private lessons before the school term began. According to the story that my mother related over dinner (quite incapable of holding back her admiration or disguising the jealousy she felt for Jancsi's mother, who had birthed that wondrous child), when Szegő came home after meeting the young prodigy he had tears in his eyes; he slumped down in his armchair and called out to his wife, who found him there, weeping, holding the crumpled folios where that ten-year-old had solved, with no apparent effort, questions that Gábor had labored over for months, and that would have racked the brains of any competent adult mathematician, staring at them without blinking, poring over every symbol and number as if those pages had been torn directly from the holiest Torah. I always thought that was just another legend—there are so many tall tales about Jancsi—but many years later, I had the chance to talk to Szegő, and he confessed to me, rather sheepishly, that he still had those pages, written by Jancsi on his father's bank stationery. He told me that he had known, right there and then, that von Neumann would change the world, even if he could not imagine how. I asked him what had led him to believe something so outlandish, and he said that no sooner had he laid eyes on my friend's enormous head than he had felt in the presence of something completely Other.

So there was an alien among us, a true wunderkind, and nobody at school could stop talking about him. They said that he had learned to read by age two. That he was fluent in Latin, Ancient Greek, German, English, and French, that he could divide two eight-digit numbers in his head by the time he was six, and that, during one summer, bored out of his mind after being locked in his father's library because he had set his fencing teacher's hair on fire, he had taught himself calculus and then committed to memory all forty-five volumes of Wilhelm Oncken's General History. It turned out that all those things were true, but you can imagine my disappointment when I finally saw him waddle across the schoolyard in my direction, nowhere near as plump and chubby as he would later become, and yet still moving about in a rotund and dawdling manner, like an extremely lively duck who had been fattened ahead of some fancy dinner; he advanced by taking small steps, accelerating randomly, and then came to a sudden halt in front of me, as if he were deeply involved in an elaborate game with players that nobody else could see. Thinking back on him now, it seemed almost like he was doing his best impression of the way a regular human being walked, but having never seen one before. He introduced himself, very politely, and told me that Szegő had suggested that we meet and talk, because we had shared interests, and while my immediate instinct was to shy away from him—I was a year older, just having turned eleven, and was very wary of being ostracized by becoming friends with this strange boy—I found myself taking an immediate liking to him nonetheless, because his quirks and mannerisms, the many, many strange things that separated him from the rest of our classmates, made him completely endearing to me.

There was something not quite right about Jancsi. That was immediately apparent, but I did not suspect just how different he was till decades later, when his mind began to unravel and he started to entertain ideas that were not just completely irrational but also very dangerous. I'm not sure if anyone really knew who he was. His father and mother certainly didn't. His first wife, Mariette, loved him, but they were like cousins, really, more like a pair of drinking buddies than a husband and a wife. His daughter, Marina, was as stubborn as he was, and incredibly talented, so they butted heads right to the end. She somehow managed to get out from under his shadow, but although I know that he respected her immensely, I am just as sure that he never let her see inside of himself. That leaves his two brothers, Michael, who came after him, poor boy, and the youngest—Nicholas—whom he loved like a son. And then there is Klari, of course, beautiful, tormented Klari, who fell in love with him in an instant, married him, and then suffered for it to her last day. Those two tortured each other in so many ways that it is a wonder to me that they could have stayed together for as long as they did. I know for a fact that Johnny was a terrible husband, but although she was one of the smartest, most passionate, and beguiling women I ever met, she was also profoundly melancholic, and as mysterious, closed-off, and distant as he was. Did I know what went on inside the mind of Janos von Neumann? No, I can't say that I did; all I can say is that I was tied to him by a strange kinship right from the start with a bond that still holds fast, even after his death. Back in school, I was his only friend. Jancsi was never "one of the boys," although he did try, awfully hard, to fit in. Many of the other children felt uneasy around him. And you really can't blame them, because he would sometimes behave as if he had been sent to school not to learn, like the rest of us, but to study and observe us. There was an eeriness to him, an aura of intelligence that radiated out from his big brown eyes and that even the dullest person could distinguish, because Jancsi was unable to mask it behind his awful, base comments, or drown it out with his choice selection of inane Yiddish jokes.

Although I would later devote my entire life to physics, in school I was an aspiring mathematician, so I knew just barely enough to intuit Jancsi's unbelievable talent: he explained set theory to me—the basis of modern mathematics—in such a simple and clever way that I still find it hard to believe that he could have had such a profound understanding before he had even begun to shave. In the very few moments when he dropped his facade and spoke honestly, I could tell just how driven he was. He was almost consumed by his passion for logic, and during his entire life, that strange gift of his let him see things with remarkable clarity, granting him a vision so blinding that to others, whose focus is smeared by emotional considerations and prejudices, his point of view seemed completely incomprehensible. Jancsi was trying to make sense of the world. He was searching for absolute truth, and he really believed that he would find a mathematical basis for reality, a land free from contradictions and paradoxes. To do so, he was determined to suck understanding out of everything. He read voraciously and studied day and night. I once saw him take two books to the toilet, for fear that he might finish the first one before he was done. At school he was a bane to our more mediocre teachers and a godsend to others, who used him as their assistant in their classes, but he was never one to show off. Quite the contrary, he seemed ashamed of his talents. On more than one occasion, I saw him feign ignorance and pretend not to know something, just to make whoever he was talking to feel more at ease. He became involved in university-level mathematics early on, and published his first paper on minimal polynomials and the transfinite diameter in the *Mathematische Zeitschrift* while still in school—he coauthored it with Michael Fekete, who later dedicated his entire career to the ideas they developed—but he would happily put those things aside to study beginner's algebra with the rest of his classmates, and actually seemed to enjoy it! His powers of concentration, when fully engaged, were a spectacle: if someone asked him an interesting question, he would slink off into a corner and turn his back on whoever he had been speaking to, compelled, as it were, by the same instinct that drives animals to take shelter, and there he would fall into a trance, his chin buried against his neck and his shoulders hunched down, as if he were about to disappear into himself. He would remain muttering under his breath, staring at the ground, shifting his weight from one foot to the other, and then whip around like a magician to deliver a complete, precise, and carefully worded answer. After witnessing several of these spells—during which Jancsi's features would take on a disturbingly mechanical, almost inanimate quality—I estimated that he usually took less than three minutes, and never needed more than five, to reach a result, no matter how complicated or convoluted the subject. When not fully involved, however, his mind was always wandering and never dwelled on any particular topic for too long. And there was also his extreme forgetfulness: at forty, he could quote back a book that he had read when he was six, word for word, but he could easily forget a friend's or a colleague's name, and be completely stumped by someone asking what he had for breakfast. To me, it was clear that Jancsi simply couldn't stop thinking. His mind was in a state of constant hunger. During his career he flitted from one branch of the exact sciences to the next, never coming to a rest, like those wretched hummingbirds who must eat incessantly or die.

It was a burden growing up so close to him. I often wonder if my horrific inferiority complex, which not even the Nobel Prize has diminished in the slightest, is a product of having known von Neumann for the better part of my life. What made it worse is that he was so nice to me, so eager to please, because, if I were to tell the whole truth, I would have to admit that what first drew me toward him, and then kept me bound to him, was a sense of pride: the vanity of knowing that this special being, this one-of-a-kind little rich boy, had taken such an intense interest in me that he would follow me around school wherever I went, almost like a pet. Growing up he was not shy, introverted, or ill at ease in his own body, and in that sense he was unlike any other genius I ever met, but as a child the most unusual things confounded him, things that would never bother a normal boy: he confessed that he could not understand how he had learned to ride a bicycle—a veritable feat of balance, equilibrium, and coordinated motor function—without once having had to use his reason. How could his body think by itself? How could it figure out the complicated motions that it had to execute so as not to fall flat on his face? These simple activities, in which you actually had to *stop thinking* to fully accomplish them, would fascinate him for his entire life, and even though he loved sports when he was a boy, he avoided all forms of physical exertion when he became a man. Klari took him on a skiing trip once. She had been a champion figure skater in her youth in Budapest and moved about with such grace that Jancsi looked like a tiny chauffeur or a bellboy following her around. He said yes to the invitation and went along tamely enough, but after going down the first run he threatened divorce and spent the rest of that weekend getting drunk and working out some fantastic scheme to heat the planet's weather and ensure a tropical climate all over the world, with Inverse, a wretched little mutt that Jancsi taught how to count to five, twitching on his lap as it slept.

I have often wondered about the consciousness of animals, how it must be more shadowy than ours, more dreamlike and fleeting, small thoughts like half-burned candles, their outlines never fully formed. And perhaps that is also the case for many of us who must strain to think with clarity. I have known a great many intelligent people in my life. I knew Planck, von Laue, and Heisenberg. Paul Dirac was my brother-in-law, Leo Szilard and Edward Teller have been among my closest friends, and Albert Einstein was a good friend too. But none of them had a mind as quick and acute as Janos von Neumann. I remarked on this in the presence of those men, several times, and no one ever disputed me.

Only he was fully awake.

Margit Kann von Neumann

Spoiled, savage

Born three days after Christmas 1903 different from the beginning

Did not cry after doctor's slap

Unnerving

Looked more like middle-aged man not newborn

Smiled right at me

When four-five saw me smoking at window staring out, asked, *Mommy, what are you calculating?*

Precocious

Happy but lonely

Makes own toys cars/trains/guns

Not shy but always at my side

No friends then too many

Clown

Loves little brother

Strong/healthy but fever spells vomiting confusion. Everything had to be repeated. *Tell me what you said, mama. Say it
like you said before. Say it again! Say it again! Like before, like before!
Like you said before!* Endless loop

Loves bugs dogs cats

Polite too generous: brought home poor boy gave father's
watch

Sometimes sleeps in servants' rooms

Jealous

Flirtatious

In love with all maids/cousins

Nickname: Little Prince

Eats all day reads all night

Reckless

Nosy

Mischievous

Spoiled

Strange

Savage?

Nicholas Augustus von Neumann
At the head of his horde

I t all began with a mechanical textile loom, and I must tell you, that thing was a monstrous device. It looked exactly like the machine that Franz Kafka dreamed up to stitch prisoners' sins on their backs in that story of his, "In the Penal Colony": a giant metal insect with ten thousand legs, gobbling up instructions and excreting silken threads like a deformed and aged spider. Father brought it home for us to see. He explained that it was an automated machine that could weave tapestries, brocade, and knitted fabrics by following patterns that were stored as sets of holes punched into cards. He allowed us to feed a couple of those cards—dotted with tiny perforations, as if they had been attacked by ravenous caterpillars—into the mechanism, but as it was turned off, nothing came out the other end and I got bored pretty quickly. Janos, however, was bewitched by it and accosted Father with an endless string of questions. How could holes transmit information?

How could the cards become fabric? Could he keep it, please? Could he have the loom? Did it work for just certain types of patterns? Did the process go in reverse? Could he have a carpet or a rug or a curtain to try it out for himself? My brother would later use the same punched-card method for the memory of his computers, but even before he figured out how it worked—at least theoretically—that gargantuan contraption took hold of him, and we had to ask the help to move several chairs, sofas, desks, and carpets out of the way because he wanted to play with it in the biggest room in our town-house apartment, which, of course, he did, for two days straight. Father usually brought home whatever his bank was investing in, and we would all discuss commercial strategies, the pros and cons of new technologies, business ventures, and other such projects at the dinner table, but this one—the loom— was surely the most extravagant of them all. According to Father, it took roughly four thousand punched cards to manufacture a single textile; he told us that he had seen a portrait of the gadget's inventor, a Frenchman by the name of Joseph-Marie Jacquard, which had taken over twenty-four thousand cards to weave. The magic of it all, he said, is that once it had been set up with the proper instructions, a single Jacquard loom could produce unlimited copies of a pattern, without the intervention of human workers, so its impact on the weaving industry had been enormous. Janos squealed with delight when Father said that Jacquard had been nearly lynched by an angry mob, as hundreds of thousands of laborers had been suddenly put out of work. He told us that many of the original looms had been hacked to pieces, burned, and destroyed, and this only served to incite my older brother's desire all the more. I really could not see why Father was making such a fuss about a machine invented at the beginning of the nineteenth century, but Janos was transfixed, and could not stop staring and fondling its various parts with that awful single-minded focus of his, something he usually reserved for Lili, our eldest and most beautiful cousin. He tinkered and toyed with it, taking it apart piece by piece, becoming so completely engrossed that on the second day he skipped tea and then dinner, and was still working on it, crawling beneath the main mechanism on his hands and knees, when I gave up trying to convince him to leave it and come out and play with me before bedtime. That night he woke me up in a state of panic. Try as he might, he could not piece it back together again, and was deadly afraid that, if he could not fix it by morning, if he could not figure out how to undo what he had done, Father would surely take it away from him and return it to the bank, and he might never see it again. That thought was completely unbearable to Janos. He said that he simply could not part with the machine, so I comforted him, wiped away his tears, and we stayed up till dawn fiddling with its million cogs and springs, pulls and levers and chains, in what seemed, at least to me, an obviously impossible task for two boys our age. I stayed with him even though I could hardly keep my eyes open, because Janos was always there for me when I needed him—during my entire life, he was there when I needed him the most. He really was the best brother I could have hoped for, incredibly protective and so much fun to be around. I felt safe with him, in part because he was the only person I ever met who seemed to know everything, who could understand and solve any problem I brought him, and always had an answer, no matter what I asked. I felt protected at his side, there was no harm that could come to me when I was next to him, even when we were doing the silliest things, truly dangerous things, like chasing trains on horseback, or setting off those homemade explosives that he somehow put together with match heads and chemicals from the garden shed in our summer residence, or shooting down the ancient war-scarred hills of Buda in a modified bicycle that he had removed the brakes from—because why would we ever want to go slower—speeding past horse-drawn drosh-kies carrying silk-gowned women and hussars in red uniforms who cursed at us when we tried to knock off their furred hats with a barrage of tightly packed snowballs. That night, to distract from the thought that Father would chastise him (Janos was as afraid of him as he was in love with our mother, and even though they were both supportive and incredibly proud of him, Mother found it hard to deal with his intensity and would shy away from what she referred to as his "excessive famil-iarity," while Janos would immediately drop his eyes to the ground and hunch his shoulders ever so slightly when Father called on him or looked in his direction, like those stray dogs that have suffered violence as pup-pies and that walk around slinking, with their tails tucked between trembling legs, never rid of their original trauma), I asked him to ex-plain how the loom worked, because, of course, he had already deduced it by then. Janos told me about Leibniz, who back in the seventeenth century had demonstrated that all you needed to realize the operations of logic and arithmetic were ones and zeros. My brother said that, by using this profound but simple process of abstraction, any pattern, nat-ural or man-made, could be broken down and translated into the "lan-guage" of the loom, a language that was embedded in the little holes punched into the cards, and that determined which threads the mecha-nism would pull up and thread through more than four hundred hooks, to weave each successive line of the tapestry. Those cards, brother said, stored all the relevant information about the finished work in its purest and most abstract form, and it worked in such a way that the machine did not have to be altered in any way to produce a new pattern, all you needed to do was to change the cards. While I know that this is true, and that it has transformed the world since then, I still cannot believe that with a hole—and the absence of one—you can give life to the many garlands and roses, lions and lambs, angels and devils that adorned the walls and floors of the most lavish homes in Europe, homes like the one we grew up in, or that a loom, which is rudimentary, primitive machinery by modern standards, could have contained within its working the seed of another technology that would transform every aspect of the human experience, for good and evil. Because, what other things could be done with such a mechanism? I asked my brother as the first rays of the morning sun shone between the heavy curtains that kept us safe from the cold outside, a question that back then went unanswered, but that I believe that he—who rushed upstairs to cower in his bed, sheets pulled above his head, while I was left sitting with a handful of screws in my palm, already prepared to take the blame for him—did more than almost any other person to resolve. We could not have known then what was to come, or the role that he would play in it all, but I believe that somehow, upon seeing the loom, he suffered a vague yet intense foreshadowing of the future, a vision that gripped him with ferocity and that kindled in him the same macabre attraction that he only ever felt toward games and explosions. I sensed nothing so specific, of course, and yet I could not help but feel slightly repulsed by the remains of the loom scattered around my feet, a sensation that has followed me ever since. For reasons that I cannot fully understand, as I have no conscious fear of that particular device, or a general aversion to technology of any kind, I have had a recurring nightmare that has haunted me for much of my adult life, one in which that very loom comes alive and rushes madly at me across the living room floor, with its tangle of legs and sharp hooks, bloodred threads trailing behind, and my older brother riding atop, like a Mongol conqueror at the head of his horde.

Mariette Kövesi

The devil at your door

I rode into his life on a tricycle when I was just two and a half years old and he must have been, what, no more than eight at the time. I was a rich brat, but then again he was too, so we had that in common. I saw him once or twice while we were growing up, before Europe tore itself apart in the Great War, a conflict that, mind you, caused neither him nor me much suffering. I could swear that he spent all those dreadful years moving imaginary troops, tanks, and artillery positions around on maps, re-creating the senseless carnage of the Battle of the Somme, or the horrors of the gas-filled trenches at Ypres, on his Kriegsspiel board, using such information as he could glean from the papers. That awful war game was a veritable obsession for him, and it was no surprise that he always won, because its outcomes were determined by mathematical calculations. It had been adopted by the Prussian military a century before, and had such a large following at the beginning of the century among our empire's intelligentsia that I have often thought that there must be some connection between those trivial ersatz war simulations and the enthusiasm with which Central Europe threw itself into armed conflict. Jancsi and his brothers would spend weeks with their noses against the board, wearing mock German uniforms, almost as if those tiny cardboard replicas of bloodshed and warfare were more important than the real onslaught taking place across the continent. I find it embarrassing to admit that I envied their capacity to become so immersed in their imaginations, for I was simply willfully ignorant of the larger world around me, and while I knew that the continent was catching fire, I was far too busy enjoying the many pleasures that my coddled existence as a rich teenager in Budapest offered me to worry myself over the fate of the war. Yes, it was terrible, but no major battles were fought inside our country. Hungary was the breadbasket for Austria-Hungary, and wartime shortages boosted wheat prices so much that the rich actually became richer. So many of us acted as if nothing was happening. This might seem shocking, I know, but it taught me a simple human truth that I learned very early on, which is that you can dance even with the devil knocking at your door. Because that is what I did, what a lot of us did. And could you really blame us? The Hungary that I was born in was a plutocracy going through a belle epoque. Budapest was the fastest-growing city in Europe. We had six hundred coffeehouses, the first underground subway on the continent, and an opera house that rivaled Vienna's. Industrialization was exploding all around us, but our city still smelled like violets in the spring. We had everything at our disposal. It seemed as if every day there was something new. A new discovery, a new record in agricultural production, a new product to buy, a new fashion to wear. Always the thrill of the new. So we did what we had to do. We had fun. We played. We got drunk and danced from one war to the next. What else were we supposed to do? We all knew that the wonderful world that had been built for us was coming to an end. So our games were urgent. Necessary. We simply *had* to have fun. There was nothing else for us. Because we knew what was coming. I don't know how, we just did. All of us. Men and women. Rich and poor. Jews and goyim. All knew. So we behaved like children and did what children do best. Pretend that there was nothing wrong and continue to play. The world would have to take care of itself.

As thriving members of the highly assimilated Jewish haute bourgeoisie, Johnny's family lived in an apartment that occupied the entire top floor of a building in the heart of Pest, on Váci Boulevard in the elegant Lipótváros neighborhood, no less lavish than my own family's home. Both our families would spend the summer in massive country houses in the hills near the capital, to which we would travel in a sprawling caravan that included maids, butlers, cooks, tutors, pets, and governesses, lugging huge trunks and wardrobes bursting with dresses, swimsuits, evening wear, fancy costumes, and enough food and wine for a two-week journey across a barren desert, even though our promised land was not more than five miles away from our apartments in the city. But that was about as far as the similarities between our early lives went: I was an only child, he had two younger brothers; his mother was a wafer-thin chain-smoker whom Johnny adored all his life, mine was a hypochondriac who would feign sickness and remain in bed for weeks whenever I so much as raised my voice at her; his father was headstrong but kind and supportive, I was brought up by a chronic womanizing drug addict whom I rarely saw, a violent man, always busy at his job heading the Jewish Hospital in Budapest, and who would not touch me unless it was to slap me across the face with a surgeon's precision if I came home a minute after curfew. So I feel no shame regarding the life I have lived, or the enormous amount of fun that Johnny and I had while we were married. Nor do I feel the least bit guilty for having left him for a younger man when we moved to the United States. We remained on good terms and even shared custody of our daughter, Marina, bless her little soul, according to an arrangement that was all Johnny's idea, mind you, one that gave me a degree of freedom that, back then, was very uncommon for any woman: Marina lived with me while she was young, and moved in with him when she turned sixteen, which I think greatly benefited her—she became a gifted economist and the first female officer of General Motors, she was an adviser to presidents, a director at the Council on Foreign Relations, and headed more committees and boards than I care to remember—even if it meant that she had to suffer Johnny's second wife, that madwoman Klari, and her hysterical outbursts. I never loved him for his brains. That was her mistake. I married Johnny because, idiot that he was, he made me laugh, and we remained in lust during our entire lives, even if that drove our spouses crazy. But I could not have stayed married to that man. Ay, yes, the great von Neumann. What a mensch! God of science and technology! King of consultants! Father of computers! Makes me laugh. If they only knew him like I did. That man could not tie his shoes. Useless. Worse than a baby. I swear that if I had left him home by himself for a couple of days he would have starved in front of the stove. Perhaps that is why I always cared and worried about him so much, right to the day he died on us. I even thought about keeping his surname after I remarried. Johnny's father, grand old Max, had been awarded a hereditary title by Emperor Franz Joseph himself, for "meritorious services in the financial field." A not too subtle way of thanking him for his money, which they used to finance Hungary's participation in World War I. That honor allowed him to add the "von" to his last name, something that my late husband kept when we arrived in Princeton, even though he switched from Janos to "Johnny." He relished the German association, in spite of his undying hatred for the Nazis, because the "von" got him great service in restaurants and retail stores. Johnny loved to poke fun at himself, even if most of his jokes failed to amuse his audience. There was one that he always told, past the point when it was funny: In a small village in Poland, a terrifying rumor was spreading. A Christian girl had been found murdered. Fearing swift retaliation, the Jewish community gathered in the shul to plan whatever defensive actions were possible under the circumstances. Just as the emergency meeting was being called to order, in ran the president of the synagogue, out of breath and all excited. *Brothers*, he cried out. *Brothers, I have the most wonderful news! The murdered girl—the murdered girl is Jewish!*

After our brief childhood encounters, we met again at the end of the twenties, when he was making a name for himself in Germany. I was bored out of my mind and could not wait to get away from my parents, so I said yes to his marriage proposal even before I knew what I was getting into. My parents demanded that he convert to Catholicism before the wedding, as they had done a couple of years earlier, for all the good that did them. I was furious. Not because I cared much for my Jewish origins, but because of how terribly overbearing they were.

Johnny couldn't care less. He was completely secular, neither proud nor ashamed of being Jewish. I could swear that his only real attachment to our people was his seemingly boundless store of Yiddish jokes, which he often directed at the goyim, and his all-time favorite put-down for anyone who was being a bore or saying something that he considered stupid, which, of course, could be any number of things—*Nebbish!*

George Pólya

What kind of a boy is this?

I will never forget the first time I laid eyes on him. Never. If I close them, if I close my eyes, I can still see him, even now I can see him. So sharp, so clear that memory is, in spite of the time, in spite of the years. How many now? Twenty? Thirty? *Forty*? That, I forget. That, I know not. But him, him I will always remember. I will never forget, forever I will remember.

I was teaching a seminar in Budapest, a very special seminar, only for particularly gifted students. And there he was, Janos von Neumann, sitting in the back of my class. Already Gábor Szegő had told me, but I was still unprepared. I was not ready, not ready for how quick he was. At first he was quiet, quiet but smiling, always smiling that one. But then, I came to an important theorem. This, I said, this was exceedingly difficult. Not proven yet. Not by anyone. Lots had tried, yes, tried and failed. I myself was trying, for decades, using the class to test my proofs. I was getting close, I knew it. I could feel it. That is mathematics, see? A feeling. You feel, even before the answer you have the feeling.

Ah! you say. *Yes!* This *feels* right! But you don't know, not till the very end. And even at the end, sometimes you don't know. Or you don't understand. So I showed the problem to the class, showed the theorem and what I had done, and how it did not work, not yet. And then I told everyone, *Discuss, discuss!* Bright boys, very bright boys, all of them, all talking out loud. That is how I teach, you see? Some people cannot, but I like the noise, the questions, the fights! It's how I do my best work. But von Neumann did not participate. Not a word. Not him. He just closed his eyes and then he raised his hand. When I called on him, he walked to the blackboard and wrote down a completely stunning proof. In a second. With no effort. No thinking even, only doing. I could not believe it. Years, all my years of work, passed by in a second. And this thing he did . . . it was so beautiful, so elegant, I remember asking myself, What is *this*? This boy . . . What *kind* of a boy is this? I still don't know, but after that, I was afraid of von Neumann.

In the early 1920s, David Hilbert proposed a wildly ambitious program to determine whether the entire mathematical universe could be built up from a unique set of axioms. It sought to establish a complete and consistent foundation that could avoid the unsolvable paradoxes that were being unearthed as new and radical ideas vastly expanded the mathematical landscape but threatened to bring down its entire edifice.

Hilbert's program proved irresistible to a young von Neumann, not just because he was convinced that the principles of science should rest on the immutable truths of mathematics, but because he feared that a dangerous unreason was slowly beginning to well up from the bedrock into which his colleagues had dug during their frantic search for truth.

Theodore von Kármán

Some lost their minds

A well-known Budapest banker came to see me with his son. He had a very unusual request. He wanted me to dissuade his firstborn from becoming a mathematician. "Mathematics," he declared, "is a breadless art." I did not understand at first, but then I talked to the boy. He was spectacular. Not seventeen yet and already involved in studying the different concepts of infinity, one of the deepest problems of abstract mathematics, on his own, with no help. I completely identified with him. When I was thirteen, my own father had forbidden me from even thinking about mathematics, for which I showed a great deal of precocious talent, not because he did not care about my mental development, he said, but because he did not want me to turn into a freak, with a lopsided intellect. So I did not even see an advanced equation again until university. I thought it would be a shame to influence that young man away from his natural bent, but I could see that it was useless to argue with his father, who was not only very wealthy but also a lawyer, so I did my best to get them to reach a compromise. The boy would become a chemist *and* a mathematician. He joined the chemical engineering program of the Eidgenössische Technische Hochschule in Zurich (an institution so demanding that Albert Einstein failed to pass its entrance exam), but he also enrolled as a student of mathematics at the University of Berlin and the University of Budapest, at the same time. I know of no other person who could have placed such a heavy burden on himself and succeeded, but it took that boy just four years to obtain a degree in chemical engineering and a doctorate in mathematics. Pólya, one of his professors in Budapest, told me that he graduated summa cum laude while hardly attending a single class, because he spent most of his time in Germany working under David Hilbert. It is no wonder then that he became the youngest privat-dozent in that country's history, a professor by age twenty-two. To thank me for my intervention on his behalf, von Neumann sent me his doctoral thesis. It couldn't have been more ambitious. He had aimed at the holy grail.

What von Neumann had tried to do was to find the purest and most basic truths of mathematics, and to express them as unquestionable axioms, statements that could not be denied, disproven, or contradicted, certainties that would never fade or become distorted and so would remain—like a deity—timeless, unchangeable, and eternal. On this solid core, mathematicians could then construct all their theories, unfolding the diverse beauty of quantity, structure, space, and change without fear that they might encounter a monster, some awful chimera born of paradox and contradiction that, once awakened, could tear their tidy, ordered cosmos apart. Von Neumann's grandiose—and, at least to my mind, slightly foolish—attempt to capture mathematics in a formal system of axioms was, of course, the essence of Hilbert's program, which the young man had clearly taken up as his own.

Absolutist and extreme, Hilbert's program was really a symptom of its time, a desperate attempt to find security in a world that was spinning out of control. It took shape during an era of maximal change. Fascism was emerging all around us, quantum mechanics was unsettling our ideas about how matter behaved inside atoms, and Einstein's theories were revolutionizing our concepts of space and time. But what Hilbert, von Neumann, and many others like them were after was perhaps even more primordial, because then as now, an ever-growing proportion of knowledge and technology rested on the exactitude and sanctity of the queen of the natural sciences. What else can we put our trust in? There are as many gods as there are people who believe in them, and the so-called human sciences are no better than philosophy, just mindless games played with meaningless words. Mathematics is different. It has always been held up as a torch, the true light of reason, blinding and unquestionable. But things started to change at the beginning of the twentieth century. Many mathematicians feared that the queen's throne would start to wobble, and that her once-firm crown was now balanced precariously on her head. As more and more discoveries were made, it became apparent that mathematics did not really have a foundation everyone could agree upon. This nagging suspicion—that their entire kingdom rested on nothing—came to be known as the "crisis of the foundations of mathematics," and it was the most profound questioning of the discipline since the time of the Greeks. The crisis was a strange affair that involved some of the most original thinkers and brightest minds on this planet, but when I look back on it, it seems no more than an Arthurian quest, one where reason strayed past its limits only to find itself holding an empty chalice.

The mathematical universe is built much like the pyramids of the ancient pharaohs. Each theorem rests on a deeper and more elementary substrate. But what supports the bottom of the pyramid? Is there anything solid to be found there, or does it all float on the void, like an abandoned spiderweb blowing in the morning wind, already unraveling at the edges, held together merely by frail and thinning strands of thought, custom, and belief? I remember talking to some of my friends about it. Logicians? They were having nervous breakdowns! Completely traumatized. Paradoxes, everywhere they looked. The most basic concepts behind geometry seemed completely inadequate when faced with the inexplicable shapes of non-Euclidean space, populated with bizarre objects that suggested the impossible: parallel lines—which should never intersect—would meet at a point of infinity. It made no sense. Suddenly, mathematicians could no longer trust their own arguments and this made them see, much in the way that a simple mason is never aware of the grand design of the cathedral that he is working on, and so must simply trust the solidity of the pillars established by others before him, that they could either keep working on faith or delve down to the very heart of mathematics to try to find the cornerstones that upheld the entire structure. But uncovering foundations is always dangerous, for who can tell what lies in wait among the fault lines in the logic of our universe, what creatures sleep and dream amid the tangle of roots from which human knowledge grows? The crisis of the foundations of mathematics was a risky undertaking. It cost some men their reputations, while others, like Georg Cantor, lost their minds.

Cantor was an extraordinary man. He was the creator of set theory, an essential part of modern mathematics, but he also greatly contributed to the foundational crisis when he achieved something that should have been impossible: he expanded infinity. Before him, infinity was regarded purely as a mental construct, with no real correspondences in nature. Boundless and endless, larger than any number, the notion of infinity was a very useful (if somewhat fanciful) abstraction, and it had proven to be an incredibly powerful mathematical tool. Armed with it, we could study infinitesimal changes, we could consider scenarios that were simply intractable without the beguiling mathematics of the infinite, and yet, scientists felt a natural distrust when dealing with it. Both Plato and Aristotle abhorred the notion of infinity, and that was pretty much the state of things among mathematicians until Cantor came along at the end of the nineteenth century and showed us that there was not just one type of infinity, but a great variety of them. Cantor's thesis threw the whole of mathematics into pandemonium, as his enormously expanded theoretical landscape—where each new infinity seemed to be vaster than anything we had known before—was teeming with dangerous, self-contradictory notions, and logical absurdities that appeared to have sprung from some mad god's deranged imagination. By using his new ideas, Cantor could apparently demonstrate that there were as many points in a one-inch line as there were in all of space. He had taken a giant leap into the unknown and found something unique, something that nobody had ever considered before him, but his critics, who were many and varied, argued that he had simply gone too far. His infinities, while undoubtedly interesting, could never be considered objects for serious mathematical study. However, Cantor was armed with a proof that seemed completely airtight. "I see it, but I don't believe it!"

he wrote to a close friend when he had finished it, and his biggest problem, from then on, was that so many others were equally unable to accept this new and confounding article of faith.

Cantor was born and raised in Russia, a nation whose inhabitants have become famous for their depth of feeling, the intensity of their religious and political beliefs, and a certain inclination for all things tragic, and while one could argue that these things are nothing but cultural clichés, easily discarded, in Cantor they all appeared to come alive, and they help in part to explain the complex and tortuous relationship he had with his own ideas. According to all accounts, he was a very pious Lutheran and an extremely sensitive soul. While he defended his theory in public, privately he could hardly deal with the consequences of his undeniably brilliant discovery, or what it appeared to be saying about the world. In some way, he confided to his daughter, he felt that his enormously expanded infinities put God into question. Or, at the very least, the outdated concept we had of Him and of His creation. These theological dialectics, in which he played the accuser and the accused, pained him as much as the vicious attacks that he received from so many of his peers. The great Henri Poincaré called his work *"un beau cas pathologique,"* a disease from which mathematics would eventually be cured, while others dismissed it as mathematical insanity, utter nonsense, or "no more than fog on a fog." They went so far as to label him a scientific charlatan and a corrupter of youth. It was not only those insults that pained him but also the excessive admiration that his ideas garnered from others. "Not even God will expel us from the paradise which Cantor has created," Hilbert wrote. Cantor, who should have felt supported and appreciated by the applause and recognition of someone of Hilbert's stature, felt this praise unwelcome and unnecessary, because he was not working for fame or money, nor to put his name down in history. No, he was answering to a higher calling, one that was its own reward, something important enough to be an end in itself. Ever since he was a boy, Cantor had heard what he called "an unknown, secret voice" compelling him to study mathematics. He later became convinced that he had been able to develop his infinities through divine intervention. As with all true revelations, he believed that they would lead the human race toward a greater, transcendent certainty. But the exact opposite was taking place. No one could make head or tail of his infinities, and his opponents did everything they could to stunt his career and thwart his investigations. While undoubtedly worthy of a professorship in any of Prussia's leading universities, Cantor languished in the backwaters of Halle, venting his frustration to a diminishing circle of friends and colleagues. "The fear my work inspires in some," he wrote, "is a form of myopia that destroys the possibility of seeing what is really infinite, even though, in its highest and most perfect form, it is the infinite that has created and sustained us. I was recently shocked to receive a letter from Mittag-Leffler in which he writes, to my great amazement, that, after serious consideration, he regarded my intended publication as 'approximately 100 years ahead of time.' If so, I would have to wait until 1984, and that seems too much to ask of any man! No matter what they say, my theory stands as firm as a rock; every arrow directed against it will quickly return to wound the heart of its would-be assassin." Trying to silence his opponents by making his theory complete, Cantor developed an entire hierarchy of infinities, but he struggled with increasingly strong episodes of uncontrollable mania, attacks that were followed by deep melancholy and the darkest possible depression. These spells became so regular that he was unable to work on mathematics; as a substitute, he devoted his boundless manic energy to try to prove that Shakespeare's plays had actually been written by the English philosopher Francis Bacon, and that Christ was the natural son of Joseph of Arimathea, views that only helped to give more credence to the arguments of those who said that he was slowly going insane. In May 1884, he had a massive mental breakdown and had to be institutionalized at a sanatorium in Halle. According to his daughter, during these crises his entire personality would be transformed. He would shriek and yell uncontrollably at the doctors and nurses, and then fall stone-still and remain completely silent. One of his psychiatrists noted that, when he was not consumed by rage, he would give in to paranoid fantasies of persecution, imagining a devilish cabal that was working to undermine him and his work. During the periods between breakdowns, he continued to teach mathematics and kept toiling away at his infinities, but he was haunted by his own results, and became caught in a strange loop from which he could not extricate himself: he would first prove that the grand hypothesis that he was chasing after—the now infamous continuum hypothesis—was true, and then, a couple of months or even just weeks later, he would prove that it was false. This vicious cycle of truth and falsehood, truth and falsehood, truth and falsehood repeated again and again, compounding the misery that became the hallmark of his later years. Finally, on January 6, 1918, after suffering the death of his youngest son, numerous illnesses, bankruptcy, and severe malnutrition during the First World War, Cantor died from a heart attack in the Halle Nervenklinik, a university psychiatric institution where he had spent the last seven months of his life.

Cantor's death was a tragedy for mathematics, but it did nothing to quell the arguments that his infinities had spawned. As the victim of an incomprehensible idea, he suffered for the great gift that he gave us, but he was certainly not the only one who agonized over the foundational crisis. In 1901, Bertrand Russell, one of Europe's foremost logicians, discovered a fatal paradox in set theory, and it became a veritable obsession for him. It would not let him rest, even when he was sound asleep, because he would dream of it, again and again. To try to excise it, Russell and his colleague Alfred North Whitehead wrote a massive treatise intended to reduce all of mathematics to logic. They did not use axioms as Hilbert and von Neumann did, but an extreme form of logicism: to them, the foundation of mathematics had to be logical, and so they went about it, building mathematics from the ground up. This was not an easy task by any measure: the first seven hundred and sixty-two pages of their gargantuan treatise—*Principia Mathematica*—were dedicated solely to proving that one plus one equals two, at which point the authors dryly note, "The above proposition is occasionally useful." Russell's attempt to establish all of mathematics on logic also failed, and his paradox dreams were replaced by a new and recurring nightmare, which expressed the insecurities he felt regarding the value of his own work: In his reverie, Russell would stride along the halls of an endless library, with spiral staircases winding down into the abyss, and a high vaulted ceiling that rose up to meet the heavens. From where he was standing, he could see a young, gaunt librarian pacing the rows of books with a metal pail, such as one would use to draw water from a well, hanging from his arm, an undying fire burning within it. One by one, he would pick up the volumes from the shelves, open their dust-covered jackets, and flip through their pages, placing them back or tossing them into the bucket, to be consumed by the flames. Russell would watch him advance, knowing, with that certainty that we can only fully experience in dreams, that the young man was edging toward the last extant copy of his *Principia Mathematica.* When he picked it up, Russell would strain to try to make out the expression on the man's face as he leafed through his book. Was that the beginning of a smile he could see creeping over his features? Was it disgust? Boredom, perhaps? Confusion? Disdain? The young man would put down the bucket, its flames licking at his fingertips, and stay there, unmoving, holding the book with both of his hands, his muscles taut from its excessive weight, and then he would suddenly look at the old logician, who would wake up in his bed, screaming, not knowing the fate of his work.

Russell and Whitehead covered more than two thousand pages with dense notations and obscure logical schemes to try to create a consistent and complete foundation for mathematics, while von Neumann's doctoral thesis was so concise, his set of axioms could be written down on a single sheet of paper. Although it later turned out that his attempt was also unsuccessful, his audacity and succinctness did not go unnoticed, and he soon became famous for it among his peers. His thesis was an early demonstration of the style that he applied to all of his later work: he would pounce on a subject, strip it down to its bare axioms, and turn whatever he was analyzing into a problem of pure logic. This otherworldly capacity to see into the heart of things, or—if viewed from its opposing angle—this characteristic shortsightedness, which allowed him to think in nothing *but* fundamentals, was not merely the key to his particular genius but also the explanation for his almost childlike moral blindness.

Gábor Szegő

A god-shaped hole

He was a little devil, that one, but also an angel to those of us who saw the madness that was coming and fled from Germany before it was too late. I'm glad that I taught him when he was only a boychik, because he was very different as a grown man. A mathematical behemoth, yes indeed, but Hashem knows he was also a fool, and a dangerous one at that! Such a contradiction. It was like talking with two different people at the same time. Brilliant but childish, insightful yet incredibly shallow. Always gossiping that one. Always drinking! Wasting his time with idiotic friends, spending his money on high-priced whores, and morbidly interested in the stupidest things imaginable, like what cousin this or that baron had married, and how many legitimate and illegitimate children they had. I never understood his need for all that farkakteh small talk. He once spent half an hour explaining the many advantages of having a small Pekinese versus a Great Dane, and he was still going on about it when I got up and left. This, from the same person who made countless contributions to group, ergodic, and operator theory, and published thirty-two major papers in less than three years. But I came to him for help, nonetheless, because I knew that he was someone you could count on for important things. Janos was only twenty-seven and already a full professor in Princeton, constantly traveling back and forth between America and Budapest, Göttingen and Berlin. I was teaching mathematics at the University of Königsberg and living very comfortably, but I had learned enough from the two years of White Terror in Hungary, after Béla Kun's short-lived communist government, when so many of my people were executed, hanged in public, tortured, imprisoned, or raped, just because some of the communist leaders had been Jewish, to know what to expect when the Nazis began to speak openly against us. I wrote to him, and we agreed to meet in Berlin, where I hoped to ask him if he could use his contacts so that my family and I could migrate to America. And where do you think he invited me to lunch? To Horcher, no less! The lavish, wood-paneled restaurant where the senior members of the Nazi Party would dine on crab to celebrate the political purge and butchery of the Night of the Long Knives just four years later. That was quintessential von Neumann. So accustomed to privilege that nothing but the best would do. Horcher was the finest restaurant in Berlin, so naturally that was where we should eat. When I arrived, I felt completely underdressed and out of place, but as soon as I mentioned his name, I was treated with the utmost respect and taken to one of the best tables in the house, where Janos was waiting for me smoking a thick cigar, illuminated by the autumn glow that shone through a pair of tall windows veiled by intricately woven lace curtains. Even if the Nazis only had a couple of seats in parliament at the time, I can't help but shiver at the memory of the two of us sitting in that lion's den at the corner of Lutherstrasse—the same spot that would become Himmler's favorite place to dine—making escape plans while completely surrounded by royals, diplomats, spies, movie stars, politicians, moguls, and other wretched members of the German aristocracy.

We spoke about mathematics first, of course, and I could immediately sense the perverse influence that arrogant nudnik Hilbert was having on my former pupil. Janos had developed a strange compulsion, the same single-minded obsession with logic and formal systems that I have seen eat away at other great men. I was taken aback at how completely overzealous he had become. But then again, fanaticism was the norm in Mitteleuropa, even among us mathematicians. When he told me that he was close to realizing his dream of capturing the essence of mathematics in axioms that were consistent, complete, and totally free from contradictions, I scoffed. You should grow like an onion, I said, with your head in the ground! How could such a strict reduction—which creates as many problems as it solves—guide humanity toward anything resembling the paradise of rigorous clarity that he was dreaming of? And what kind of an Eden would that be? I wondered. Surely not a place where plants and trees could grow. He kept on ordering more food and drink, not even noticing that I did not touch mine. I told him that he should stay in America, and never return to Germany, but there was no way to convince him. He said he was working on something very important. He could feel an idea taking shape in the back of his mind, and feared that if he could not interact with Hilbert and other members of the Göttingen circle, he might lose it. I told him that it was better to lose an idea than to lose his life, but he looked at me in a way that made it clear that he saw it the other way round. Did I not know what was happening in quantum physics? It is all numbers, he said to me, these things do not behave like particles, they are not like bundles of matter or energy . . . They behave like numbers! And who better than us to comprehend that new reality? For Janos, it was not chemistry, industry, or politics that would shape the future of our world. It was mathematics. And that was why we needed to understand it to the deepest level. I had no way of imagining what he was talking about, because the tools and technology that he would later develop did not exist yet, but he became so uncharacteristically serious that, for reasons I cannot fathom, I began to shiver as if a gust of cold air had blown in from the outside. I believe he noticed it, because he immediately changed the subject and told me that I did not have to worry. America would welcome us with open arms. He spoke with such absolute confidence that I felt immediately relieved, but when I asked him for details, wanting to know to whom he would talk, and where he thought I might end up, he simply made a toast in my name and said that he would take care of it all. And he did, to his credit, but—to my shame—in that moment I did not believe him. I even felt angry, because I could tell that he was already bored with the subject, so bored, in fact, that when I continued to insist on answers he simply ignored me and began to flirt with three tall blonde ladies who had sat down at the table next to us. I got up and went to the toilet.

When I think of the things he did later in life, I despair. Was there any way I could have warmed his heart? Could I have swayed his will, strong as it was, or just planted a tiny seed that might have sprouted and saved some part of his soul? But I did nothing, said nothing, not a word. I did not even try, because I was so afraid for myself. And that, that still pains me, though I'm sure that anything I could have said would have been met with ridicule. One of his tasteless jokes, no doubt. Yes, I can hear him now. A rabbi, a priest, and a horse walk into a bar. Oy vey! How much difference could I have made? We mustn't forget that it was not just he who played with fire. His entire generation set loose the hounds of hell. Even so, I cannot help but feel guilty, because I was his first teacher. He was a pup when I met him, a child in my care, and the habits we develop in youth are what we follow in old age. So I failed him, failed him miserably in what is most important: I was unable to communicate the sanctity, the holiness of our discipline. I did not teach him what the "pure" in "pure mathematics" really means. It is not what people think. It is not knowledge for its own sake. It is not a search for patterns, nor is it a series of abstract, intellectual games completely unconnected from the real world and its many troubles. It is something quite other. Mathematics is the closest we can come to the mind of Hashem. And so, it should be practiced with reverence, because it has true power, a power that can be easily used for evil, as it is born from a faculty that only we possess, and that the Lord, blessed be He, gave us instead of teeth, claws, or talons, but that is equally dangerous and lethal. Of this, I taught him nothing. Whatever judgment awaits me, I cannot deny that I saw it before anyone else. What he could do. It was so rare and beautiful that to watch him was to weep. Yes, I saw that, but I also saw something else. A sinister, machinelike intelligence that lacked the restraints that bind the rest of us. Why did I remain silent, then? Because he was so superior. To me, to all of us. I felt slightly ashamed in his presence. Belittled and debased. Nothing but a foolish old man with foolish ideas. And now, older still, I recognize that, in spite of his callousness, he was trying to understand this world at its deepest level. He had a burning vision, an inner fire that I never felt, though I have chased after it. Spiritually, he was an ignoramus, yes, but he did have unquestionable faith in logic. Ah, but that type of faith is always dangerous! Especially if it is later betrayed. Nothing should be beyond question. Moses even questioned the Almighty! And while the Lord, blessed be He, does not answer, the questions themselves may save us. Lost faith is worse than no faith at all, because it leaves behind a gaping hole, much like the hollow that the Spirit left when it abandoned this accursed world. But by their very nature, those god-shaped voids demand to be filled with something as precious as that which was lost. The choice of that something—if indeed it is a choice at all—rules the destiny of men.

As I was making my way back from the toilet, I heard a very loud ruckus, men and women screaming and shouting, followed by the unmistakable thud of a body landing heavily on the floor. When I walked into the dining hall and looked at our table, I saw Janos being picked up by two waiters, while a massive, uniformed man was being dragged outside by three other soldiers who could hardly hold him back as he strained against them, rampant, his neck bulging out of his shirt collar like a bull's, the veins of his forehead ready to explode. And Janos? He was laughing! Cackling maniacally while wiping a trickle of blood from the corner of his mouth and smiling at the maître d', who kept apologizing to him, over and over. What the hell had happened? I stood there, frozen in place, feeling—why, why do I always feel that way?— that the entire restaurant was looking not at him but at me, turned pale as a ghost, trembling while the soldiers hauled their comrade out the front door. As the calm returned and the usual mindless chatter and noise of plates, knives, and forks reigned once again, Johnny waved me over and offered me his drink to calm down, because he could clearly see just how upset I was, but I refused. I just wanted to get out of there, as quickly as possible, so he called over one of the waiters, who informed us that the bill had already been settled, of course, of course, and kept on begging for our forgiveness as he helped Janos and me retrieve our hats and coats. It took me a great deal of time to put mine on, not just because my hands kept shaking, but also because I did not want to bump into the soldiers, if they were still outside. I asked Janos what had happened. He just giggled to himself, remarked that idiots always lacked a sense of humor, but refused to say another word except that it had been completely worthwhile. When we finally left Horcher and stepped out into the cold, I could not figure out if he was truly fearless or just reckless and irresponsible, but as we walked through the dead leaves of the Tiergarten and headed toward the Technische Hochschule, where I would meet up with a colleague, I saw a sign of the true nature of his character, and of just how far he would fall.

The roads were closed because of a military parade and there was a large crowd of onlookers. I realized that we would have to make a very long detour to get past it, so I grabbed Janos by the arm and tried to pull him away, but he was spellbound. We had only caught the tail end of it, thank the Lord, but he insisted that we stay and watch the armored division of the Reichswehr. I told him that I did not want to go anywhere near those wretched things, but as the first giant tank came rumbling down the avenue, I could swear that he began to salivate like a dog who hears his master emptying leftovers into its bowl. It was a gruesome sight, this grown man jumping up and down trying to see over the heads of the crowd as if he were a young boy, wringing his hands while he gawked at those instruments of death, perhaps one of the very same vehicles that later thundered across Europe, crushing the bones of the living and the dead, spearheads of the iron storm the Nazis unleashed upon the continent before enslaving, starving, torturing, and exterminating so many of our people in such ungodly ways. Looking at him there, entranced by that mechanical contraption, and knowing what he was capable of, I realized that there was very little hope for him, indeed very little hope for any of us, and surely none for me.

· Eugene Wigner

A mathematician's nightmare

J ancsi was outsmarted by only one person during his entire life.
But it changed him.

It happened in Königsberg, where he had traveled to attend
the Second Conference on the Epistemology of the Exact Sciences, a
scientific gathering on matters so profound that they bordered on the
esoteric. He was there to represent Hilbert's program, with its underly-
ing assumptions, and to fight it out against those he considered his enemies, during a three-day debate on the many philosophical questions
that were arising from quantum mechanics, Wittgenstein's ideas about
linguistics, and the crisis of the foundations of mathematics. That meeting included titans like Werner Heisenberg—already lauded as a genius
for his discovery of matrix mechanics and the uncertainty principle—
but Jancsi was the golden boy, preceded by such a sterling reputation
that it had given rise to a saying: *Most mathematicians prove what they can.
Von Neumann proves what he wants.* It was September 1930, and he was at
the peak of his powers. He was exceeding everyone's expectations; his

output during his years in Germany had been terrifying. We met in Budapest the day before the conference, early, for breakfast, and walked arm in arm to the train station. He told me that he was helping Szegő find work in America, and since he knew that I had also been approached by Princeton, he asked me to intervene on Szegő's behalf as well. I was preparing my own plans to emigrate, but he made me promise that we would leave together. I agreed, but I did not understand why he was putting it off. So I asked him, point-blank, why he felt that he needed to stay in Europe and to travel so often to Germany. He was so close, he said, so close to the foundations of mathematics that he could feel a tingle in his brain! That month, the Nazis had become the second-strongest political force in Germany, and Jancsi's wife, Mariette, kept nagging me to convince him to stop traveling there, to stay with her in Hungary. It was pointless, really, we both knew how stubborn he was, so I did not even try. I was just as worried as she was, but I trusted him more: Jancsi was obsessed with history—especially with the fall of ancient empires—and though his hatred for the Nazis was essentially boundless, he was also convinced that he would know exactly when to leave. I now shudder at the accuracy of some of his prognoses, prophecies that no doubt came from his incredible capacity to process information and to sift the sand of the present through the currents of history. That gave him a certain sense of security, an overconfidence that would no doubt have betrayed a lesser man. But Janos was many moves ahead; he behaved as if he was looking back at things that had already happened. As we waited for the train to pull into the station, he patted me on the shoulder and told me that I needn't worry, because there was still time. We will enjoy Europe, he announced, and especially Germany, to the very last, because he doubted that there would be much left if the Nazis continued to gain power. I trusted his judgment, like I always did, even though I knew that SS groups were already terrorizing their political opponents, and that parades of the Hitler Youth could be seen marching through the streets of Prussia, spitting at people like me and Jancsi. I told him that things had become so dark and hopeless that I could no longer imagine a future; he smiled at me and softly said that it was precisely then, in the darkest times, when one could see furthest. I insisted that we should go, and go quickly, but Janos was adamant: he had important work to do, the paradoxes that Cantor and others had introduced to mathematics had to be rooted out and expunged. I could not comprehend that particular obsession of his. Was it just academic ambition, or did it stem from a deeper and more personal need? When I finally put him on the train to Königsberg, and watched him smile and wave his hat at me from the window as the carriage slowly picked up speed, I could not have suspected that his grand dream regarding mathematics would be ripped away from him by a twenty-four-year-old graduate student who has come to be regarded as the greatest logician of all time.

It was during the final moments of the last day of the conference, which was an adjunct session of the Sixth Congress of German Physicists and Mathematicians. Rudolf Carnap had already spoken in favor of Russell and the logicists, Heyting had defended Brouwer's intuitionist school, and Reichenbach had conveyed the need to replace a strict two-value logic by probability when dealing with quantum systems; the meeting was formally over and some participants were already walking out the door, when a skeletal and extremely odd-looking young man raised his voice, ever so slightly, and made a comment that was to change mathematics forever. He was an Austrian by the name of Kurt Gödel, and nobody expected much of him: he had been invited to present a paper on the completeness of the logical calculus, which he had delivered the day before, to little effect. Because of that, no one really paid any attention when he began to speak with a stutter, so low and so awkwardly that the conference notetaker failed to record his words, which should rightly be famous, but are lost to history, since they were not included in the meeting's final report. As such, his monumental discovery could have gone completely unnoticed at the time were it not for Jancsi, who was the only person there who realized what had just happened. "I b-believe that we can p-p-postulate, within any consistent f-formal system, a statement that is t-t-true but that can never be pr-proven within the rules of said system." That is the gist of what Gödel said, according to Jancsi. His remark was met with silence, because those who did not simply ignore him couldn't wrap their heads around what they had heard. How could a statement be considered true if there was no way of proving it? It did not make sense to anyone, except for Janos, who suddenly broke out in a sweat and had trouble breathing. He felt so dazed that he remained completely still, unable to move from his seat, trying to comprehend what had happened, and when he finally managed to get up, the young man was nowhere to be found. Jancsi ran out of the building and found Gödel two blocks away, speaking to himself, and without making any sort of introduction he began to badger him with a barrage of questions that at first confused but then, apparently, delighted the young Austrian.

It was the end of Hilbert's program.

Jancsi understood it immediately, but he could hardly accept it at first. If what Gödel was saying was correct, no matter what he did—no matter what anyone ever did—there would be no way to axiomatize mathematics, no way to unearth the logical foundations that he so desperately wanted to find. Gödel had shown him that if someone succeeded in creating a formal system of axioms that was free of all internal paradoxes and contradictions, it would always be incomplete, because it would contain truths and statements that—while being undeniably true—could never be proven within the laws of that system. Gödel had found what appeared to be an ontological limit, something that we could not think past. An unprovable truth is a mathematician's nightmare, and it was a personal catastrophe for Jancsi, because it opened up a monumental rift that no future knowledge or theory could patch up. The philosophical implications of Gödel's logic were astonishing, and his incompleteness theorems, as they later came to be known, are now considered a fundamental discovery, one that hints at the limits of human understanding. Of course, that was not the case when the Austrian first shared his ideas. When Gödel published them, his logic seemed so ludicrous and counterintuitive that Bertrand Russell could not accept it: "Are we to think that 2 plus 2 is not 4, but 4.001?" he remarked, and when he finally capitulated and accepted what Janos had been so quick to understand, he confessed, rather bitterly, that he was very glad indeed not to be working on fundamental logic any longer. It is not surprising that it took a brain like Jancsi's to grapple with the Austrian's concepts, but, true to form, as soon as he had understood the essence of the logical operations involved, he began to expand on them, his mind racing as he rode the train back from Königsberg to Budapest, where I gather he holed himself up for two months and worked on nothing else, day and night, to the point that Mariette worried that he had come down with something. Jancsi, as obsessive as he could be, was never one to get stuck on a problem like that; he was not one of those scientists who forget to brush their teeth or change their clothes. Quite the contrary, it was always a joy for him to work out his ideas. His intelligence was playful, not tortured, and his insights were usually immediate, practically instantaneous, not labored. But Gödel had broken something in him, so he locked himself up and Mariette would hear him scream in six different languages. When he finally emerged in late November, sporting a patchy beard that she would later make fun of whenever she wanted to humiliate him, he walked straight to the post office to send a letter to Gödel, informing him that he had developed an even more remarkable corollary to his already outstanding theorem: "Using the methods you employed so successfully . . . I achieved a result that seems to me to be remarkable; namely, I was able to show that the consistency of mathematics is unprovable." Jancsi had basically turned Gödel's argument on its head. According to the Austrian, if a system was consistent—free from contradictions—then it would be incomplete, because it would contain verities that could not be proven. Janos, meanwhile, had demonstrated the opposite: if a system was complete—if you could use it to prove every true statement—then it could never be free of contradictions, and so it would remain inconsistent! An incomplete system was not satisfactory, for obvious reasons, but an inconsistent one was much worse, because with it you could prove anything you liked: the wildest imaginable conjecture and its opposite, an impossible statement *and* the negation of that impossibility. When you combined Gödel's and von Neumann's ideas, the outcome defied logic itself: from here to eternity, mathematicians would have to choose between accepting terrible paradoxes and contradictions, or work with unverifiable truths. It was an almost intolerable dilemma, but there appeared to be no way around it. Gödel's logic, however mysterious, was airtight. Something pulled from a madman's dreams. And what my dear friend had proven was just as strange. It was his first real stroke of genius, the one thing that would have cemented his name among those of the greatest mathematicians of his or any other age. But Jancsi had finally met his match: Gödel replied politely, saying yes, indeed, Janos was absolutely right, but that he had developed the same result himself, and formalized it as the argument of his second incompleteness theorem, which was soon to be published. He even offered Janos an advance copy of the full proof, which he enclosed in the letter that he sent him from Vienna.

Janos never worked on the foundations of mathematics again. He remained in awe of Gödel for the rest of his life. "His achievement in modern logic is singular and monumental . . . a landmark which will remain visible far in space and time. The result is remarkable in its quasi-paradoxical 'self-denial': it will never be possible to acquire with mathematical means the certainty that mathematics does not contain contradictions . . . The subject of logic will never again be the same," he wrote ten years after they had met for the first time, when he was doing everything he could to rescue Gödel from Nazi Germany, by trying to convince the United States government to grant him a visa. By then, we were both established in America, and from there we received word that Gödel had been badly beaten by Brownshirts in the streets of Vienna. They had thought him to be Jewish, and he might have been killed were it not for his wife, Adele, a strong-willed woman whom he had met while she was working as a receptionist and dancer at a nightclub in Austria, who rescued him by attacking the bastards with the metal tip of her umbrella. "Gödel is absolutely irreplaceable; he is the only mathematician alive about whom I would dare to make this statement. Salvaging him from the wreck of Europe is one of the greatest single contributions anyone could make," Jancsi said in a letter that he circulated widely at the highest diplomatic levels, and that finally did the trick: a full year after the war broke out, Gödel made his way to the United States, after taking a tortuous route through Siberia and across the Pacific to avoid crossing a U-boat–riddled Atlantic, but he never grew accustomed to his adoptive country, and though he remained the most respected and admired mathematician in the entire world, in the decades that followed he slowly began to exhibit the undeniable signs of mental derangement.

Kurt Gödel enjoyed an almost godlike status among scientists. Albert Einstein confided near the end of his life that his own work no longer meant much to him, and he went to his office at the Institute for Advanced Study—where Gödel had been offered a professorship thanks largely to Jancsi's interventions on his behalf—merely to have the privilege of walking to his office with the Austrian logician by his side. They were bound by a tremendous affinity for each other. Gödel was probably the only man alive who felt entitled to question the greatest physicist of the twentieth century: as a gift for Albert's birthday, he came up with a solution to the field equations of general relativity that modeled a universe where it was actually possible to travel back in time, an idea that greatly appealed to Gödel, because he had only been truly happy and carefree when he was a very young boy. His bouts of paranoia had begun in his adolescence, but it was only in America that his mind began to warp and twist until all that he could see was a deformed view of reality. He developed a severe eating disorder, and subsisted solely on a diet of butter, baby formula, and laxatives. He also started seeing ghosts, and became convinced that other mathematicians were intent on killing him, to take revenge for the insoluble uncertainty that he had brought into their world; he believed that they would use the gases from his own refrigerator to do him in, or that they would poison his food, so he refused to eat anything that was not prepared by his wife, or tried by her beforehand. His descent into madness was a slow and painful process that his few friends witnessed in despair. In 1977, Adele underwent surgery and was hospitalized for months. During her convalescence, Gödel stopped eating altogether. Those who saw him then said that he looked like a living corpse: he was five feet, four inches tall and weighed less than seventy-nine pounds. By the time Adele recovered sufficiently to come back home, he had starved himself to death.

A lot has been written about Gödel's mental decline, but most people agree that his particular form of paranoia was not just the cause of his downfall, but also lay at the root of his incredible mathematical achievements. One of his professors from the University of Vienna, who met him when he was a very young man, said that he could not figure out if it was the nature of his work that made him unstable, or if you actually had to *be* unstable to think in the way that Gödel did. I believe there is truth in both views. The few times I spoke to him, I could sense how logic and logical thinking were inextricably bound to his mounting derangement, because, in some sense, paranoia is logic run amok. "Every chaos is a wrong appearance," wrote Gödel; he was of the firm belief that there was a reason for everything. If you think that way, it's a small step to begin to see hidden machinations and agents operating to manipulate the most common, everyday occurrences. But it was not just a psychological imbalance that undid him, he was also affected by the ideas that he brought into the world, ideas from which we have yet to recover. Truths that cannot be proven, contradictions that cannot be avoided—these self-referential nightmares of logic preyed on him as powerful demons that, once called down upon us, could never be truly banished, demons that also gnawed away at my dear friend Janos.

There are many secret ties between Janos and Gödel. Even in death, they are still connected, buried in the same cemetery, a few feet apart from each other. Jancsi's reaction to the great Austrian's ideas was hardly noticeable at first. After all, even if his grand project had been ruined, it was not in his character to get depressed. He went along with things almost as if nothing had happened. But the affair had affected him, in a very profound way. I don't know if others noticed it, but I certainly did. He was never the same. After he came back from Königsberg, I soon realized that there was something missing in him, something lost, and this injury, this sudden sense of emptiness, did not remain limited to his ideas about mathematics, but began to permeate his entire world-view, which became darker and darker as the years went by. It did not help, of course, that soon after he met Gödel the Nazis came to power and began to persecute us, but to him that was not really a surprise, only the starkest confirmation of his total disillusionment with human decency and the ultimate proof of the sway that irrationality held over the human race. Little by little, the strange boy I knew from school, that being destined for greatness, became more alien still, and in just a couple of years, he completely upended his life: he resigned his professorship in Berlin even before the Nazis began dismissing Jews from German universities in 1933, and then, two years later, he publicly renounced his membership in the German Mathematical Society. Jancsi, more than anyone else I know, took it as a most personal affront that any nation, group of people, or individual could possibly choose the base and unsophisticated philosophy of Nazism over the minds of Einstein, Hans Bethe, Max Born, Otto Frisch, and many, many others, including, last but not least, Jancsi himself.

We traveled to America on the same boat. He changed his name from Janos to Johnny (I became Eugene instead of Jenő) and things were happy for both of us at first, but after his daughter was born his marriage fell apart, Mariette left him, and though he met and quickly married Klari, their intense love affair turned sour as soon as their honeymoon was over. Outwardly, his life in the United States was almost as magnificent as it had been in the old country; after teaching at Princeton University, he was recruited to the newly created Institute for Advanced Study, an institution that quickly replaced Göttingen as the world's preeminent center for mathematics, by giving sanctuary to others who had also fled from Europe, like Hermann Weyl, James Alexander, Wolfgang Pauli, and André Weil. Jancsi was given free rein there to dedicate himself to whatever he pleased, with no obligation to teach, in a completely exceptional intellectual environment. The great Oppenheimer headed the institute for a while, and Alan Turing almost became Jancsi's assistant, but he decided to return to England when the war broke out. Janos continued forward at the same breakneck speed, but I could see that inwardly he was suffering, casting about randomly, deprived of direction and unable to find something to which he could dedicate his full attention. And that pained him. It's not just that it bothered him psychologically—I think he actually experienced real, physical discomfort. He felt a craving or an itch, like a tiger pacing about scratching his mange against the bars of a cell. Jancsi was dying to break out, and he did, eventually, but in doing so he entered uncharted territory, a treacherous wilderness where he ranged beyond what was reasonable, until he finally lost himself. From Gödel onward, I was always afraid for him, because once he abandoned his juvenile faith in mathematics he became more practical and effective than before, but also dangerous. He was, in a very real sense, set free.

In the United States, von Neumann became a renegade mathematician, a mind for hire, increasingly seduced by power and by those who could wield it. He would charge exorbitant fees to sit with people from IBM, RCA, the CIA, or the RAND Corporation, sometimes for no longer than a couple of minutes, and worked on so many private and government projects that he seemed to possess the ability to be in many places at the same time.

As soon as he was granted citizenship, he applied for a commission in the Army Reserve as a lieutenant, but was rejected due to an age cutoff. That did not deter him; when the United States entered World War II, he was one of the mathematicians and physicists who disappeared into the West, quietly making their way to a top-secret laboratory located in the high desert of northern New Mexico, under the shadow of the Sangre de Cristo Mountains, to become part of the Manhattan Project.

PART II

The Delicate Balance of Terror

We were all little children with respect to the situation which had developed, namely, that we suddenly were dealing with something with which one could blow up the world.

JOHN VON NEUMANN

We knew the world would not be the same. A few people laughed, a few people cried, most people were silent. I remembered the line from the Hindu scripture, the Bhagavad Gita: Vishnu is trying to persuade the prince that he should do his duty, and to impress him takes on his multiarmed form and says, "Now I am become Death, the Destroyer of Worlds." I suppose we all thought that, one way or another.

J. ROBERT OPPENHEIMER

Richard Feynman

I could see nothing but light

We fought over the chessboard in Los Alamos, you know? Then someone brought in a Go board and we started playing on that too. Vicious, endless games with no time limit against some of the smartest guys I ever met. It was nerve-wracking. It ate away at me. 'Cause I'm competitive, see, I like to play and I like to win, so I couldn't help myself. We had nothing better to do! I really felt like I was losing my mind stuck there in the middle of the desert. Especially at the beginning, when the place was still being built and the labs weren't ready, I think I went a little crazy. But nobody noticed, 'cause it was all crazy. The scale of the project, the speed of things happening, the actual weapon we were building, all of it. Wasn't like people imagine, though. Hot New Mexico desert, yeah, but so, so beautiful. Los Alamos was high up on a mesa with tall cliffs carved in dark red earth, lots of trees and shrubs all around. The landscape was breathtaking, the most beautiful place I'd ever seen. Coming from New York, I'd never traveled out to the West before, so I really felt like I was in another world. In Mars or something. It had the strange energy of a sacred space, a haven far away from the civilized world, away from prying eyes, farther than God could see. The perfect spot to do the unimaginable. And it had to be like that, you know, remote and uninhabited, 'cause the lab had to be beyond the range of airplanes and bombers, so at least two hundred miles away from the coastline or any national border. We also needed fair weather year-round, so construction would never have to stop. And there weren't really many places like that, we had to build one from scratch. An entire town from nothing. It was Oppenheimer who found the place, his folks had a cabin near there, and the main thing is that the land was so empty, there was almost nothing there but a rich boys' school, a ranch school that Gore Vidal and William Burroughs went to, and they built the thing around it, all of Los Alamos, they came and bulldozed the entire plateau and the town began mushrooming around the school. It just appeared there, from nothing, almost overnight. I was one of the first to arrive. Riding a truck, climbing up a slow winding road, I looked out at the country, at that landscape, and I just blurted out like an idiot, "There must be Indians here," and then the driver, this thin, wiry fellow, one of the few soldiers that I ever got along with, just stops the truck dead, jumps out, walks a few meters, and ducks behind a large boulder without saying anything. So I bolted right after him and left the rest of the passengers sitting there, waiting under the sun. When I got past the boulder he shows me the entrance to a cave, and on both sides of it these terra-cotta drawings of antelopes and buffalo and whatnot, right there, just off the side of the road. It was real wilderness, wild, wild country, pristine until we got there. And then it changed, completely, in an instant. The structures went up so fast it was hard to believe, all those labs, administration and security buildings, barracks for the military personnel, town houses for the top brass and the other big shots. In no time at all there were so many of us that it felt like an ants' nest. Everybody was running around bursting with manic energy, as if electricity was coming up from the ground. It got to your head, see, this contagious enthusiasm, because our population doubled every nine months, more and more people poured in, some with their entire families. By the end of the war three hundred kids were running around, so the military tried to enact strict measures to "stop the population growth." But nobody listened. Of course they didn't! We all knew what was going on, the houses were so badly built, the walls so thin that you could always tell what the neighbors were up to. You could tell when they were . . . having a party . . . so it was no surprise to any of us that eighty babies were born in the first year. What did they expect? We all worked six days a week, men and women alike. That was just the norm, we didn't question it. There was a war on. Saturday nights, that's when we had fun. We drank punch laced with ethyl alcohol stolen from our labs because we couldn't go out and buy regular liquor. I mean, you couldn't even order magazines from the outside. We were sequestered and restricted by security measures. Even six-year-olds had to wear IDs around their necks. But most of the rules made no sense. You couldn't travel farther than a hundred miles from Los Alamos. If you bumped into a friend outside, you had to give a detailed written report on everything you had talked about. They monitored our calls, which was easy enough, 'cause all we had was one phone. And then there were other problems: housing and water were always scarce, and the lights would go out all the time because the engineers—we were all called "engineer," the term "physicist" was strictly forbidden for security reasons—put such a strain on the grid. Everything was top secret but also a little ridiculous, really. 'Cause how could you hide the fact that so many scientists were traveling to New Mexico all of a sudden? From all over the country, and not just from the US but also famous scientists from Europe. I was still a grad student when I was recruited, I hadn't even finished my thesis, so I had no idea what I was supposed to do surrounded by these giants, these men whose names I'd only ever seen in articles and textbooks—Fermi from Italy, Bethe from Germany, Teller from Hungary, Ulam from Poland, they all started coming. Even the great Dane himself, Niels Bohr. He arrived as a consultant under the pseudonym Nicholas Baker. After the first time he came, he would ask his son to arrange a private meeting with me before he talked to the higher-ups, 'cause, you see, I'd spoken up in the big meeting, the one they had once a week with all the physicists, and of course I'd complained because I can't keep my big mouth shut. I complained about a lot of things, so at first I didn't understand why Bohr would want to see me, 'cause I was really nobody next to these guys, but then I figured it out. When I talk about physics, I have this problem, I don't care about anything else, I just say exactly what I think. Even to Bohr. If he said something stupid or crazy, I would just tell him, "You're crazy!" or "No, no, no! That's wrong, that's stupid!" Even to this titan, this giant who made everybody else tremble. He liked that about me, and it turned out that so did Bethe, who was in charge of the theoretical physics department, he also liked to push his ideas against me. I have no respect for authority, I never have, and yet somehow among those geniuses that was never a problem. Quite the contrary, in fact. I ended up as a group leader for Bethe, with four guys working under me. Anyway, what was I talking about at the beginning? Ah, yes, Go! That game, it's like a bigger version of checkers, but monstrously complex and fascinating. We played it for hours, even though we were racing against the Nazis to build the bomb, we still had these dead hours with nothing to do, waiting for calculations, waiting for material, all this waiting. It seems weird now that we spent so much of our time playing, because we knew that Hitler had put Werner Heisenberg in charge of his nuclear program, though they called him a "white Jew" and thought that nuclear physics was "Jewish physics." Luckily for us it turned out that the Germans were not really building the bomb at all, or at least they weren't getting anywhere. Heisenberg stalled, apparently, but we didn't know that at the time, we really didn't. We all thought that if Hitler got the bomb before us, it was all over, I mean, they had such a head start, what with fission having been discovered in the Kaiser Wilhelm Institute back in '38, when Lise Meitner and Otto Frisch figured out how to split a uranium atom during their Christmas vacation. So we worked with this fantastic sense of purpose, but we still found time to play, we fooled around all the time, like boys in a boys' school. At night I pounded on my bongos like a madman and I sung at the top of my lungs, even though I can't hold a tune. That drove Teller crazy. What can I say, I was bored! I was tired! My wife was sick, she was dying from tuberculosis in a sanatorium in Albuquerque, while I was up there in Los Alamos building an atomic bomb. I was angry, okay? Angry and bored. I started picking locks, opening the filing cabinets where we kept our secrets, and I would say in the big meetings, "We need better locks! Better security! We can't have all this classified material lying around!" But they didn't pay attention to me, so I kept on picking the locks, and messing with the authorities in all kinds of ways. This one time, when I was walking around in the dirt, feeling cooped up like a goddamn chicken, I found a hole in the high barbed-wire fence that surrounded the entire place. Turns out some workers had gotten tired of having to walk to the front gate, so they just cut a hole with pliers. And I would go out through that hole and then come back through the main entrance and walk all the way around the perimeter to come out the hole again, and then go right back through the main gate. I did that over and over till the guards threatened to put me in jail, because they couldn't understand how I was doing it, how I kept coming back in without going out through the checkpoint. Then this big shot calls me into his office, this idiot lieutenant who sat me down and asked, "Mr. Feynman, is this your idea of a joke?" and I said, "No! There's a god-damn hole in the fence! I've been saying it for weeks, but nobody listens!" Anyway, things like that. That's how I would spend my free time, doing stupid things like that. I also drove the censors crazy. 'Cause they censored our letters, you know? And I had this game with my wife, a game that had been going on for years. In her letters to me, she would send me coded messages, and I had to crack them, see? So again I get called into the office and they ask me, "What does this message mean, Mr. Feynman?"—pointing to one of Arline's letters—and I say, "I don't know what it means!" And they say, "What do you *mean* you don't know what it means!" So I tell them that I don't know because it's a code. They ask what the key to the code is, and I say, "Well, I haven't figured it out yet!" So they tell me, "Tell your wife to send the key with the code," but I refuse, because I didn't want the key! I wanted to work it out by myself! This went back and forth, back and forth, for a couple of weeks, until we finally reached an agreement: Arline would send the code with the key and the censors would take out the key before handing me the envelopes. That didn't last. One day we all got an official note: CODES ARE STRICTLY FORBIDDEN. By that time I had so much experience dealing with the censors that I started making a little money on the side by teaching my colleagues what they could and couldn't get away with. And then I would bet that money on the Go matches. And since I usually won, I doubled my earnings. Not that you could do a lot with money at Los Alamos. We had a theater that doubled as a dance hall on Saturdays and as a church on Sundays, but there was nothing else to do, so I kept betting on the Go games, because it was so fascinating. It looks so simple, see, I could teach you the rules in five minutes. All you do is place black or white stones on a square grid, to surround your opponent's stones and gain control of as much territory as possible. It *seems* simple, but it's crazy difficult, much, much harder than chess, and some of us became addicted. At least I did. Go has a strange charm. It takes over your mind, you start to play it in your dreams. It's always running in the back of your head, whatever else you are doing. The best player at Los Alamos was Oppenheimer, but I got pretty good, pretty quick. Couldn't beat him, though. I later read that when they dropped Little Boy on Hiroshima, two famous Japanese grandmasters—Hashimoto Utaro, the national champion, and Iwamoto Kaoru, the challenger—were in the third day of a Go tournament, about three miles away from ground zero. The building they were playing in was almost completely destroyed, lots of people were injured, and yet these two guys, these Go masters, came back that very same day, after lunch, and continued to play on till the evening, while women and children were being pulled out from underneath the rubble and the entire city was ablaze. That's the Japanese for you. And that's how mesmerizing Go can be. It requires a particular type of intelligence and it's really intractable to computation, you have to feel your way around the board. It's spellbinding and unsettling, you cannot simply calculate what the next best move should be. I know because I played against von Neumann, and he was awful at it. He could never beat me, but he became obsessed too. He would sulk like a little boy after losing and always demand a rematch, and then another, and then another. It got to be so bad that Oppenheimer ordered me to hide the Go board as soon as we heard that von Neumann was coming. His visits were rare, he wasn't on staff like the rest of us, he was a consultant, he would come roaring in to Los Alamos in his brand-new Cadillac, two or three times a year. The guards wouldn't even stop him, they just saw his car and let him in, he was that special, so charming in his newly pressed banker's suit, folded handkerchief, and gold watch chain. I never saw him drive the same car twice. So I asked him once why he needed to get a new one every year. "Bikwouze no one vil sell me a tank," he replied in that wonderful Bela Lugosi accent of his. Bethe once said to me that he sometimes wondered whether a brain like von Neumann's did not indicate a superior species, an evolution beyond man. I laughed, but then I met him. Von Neumann was well-known among us physicists for his book *Mathematical Foundations of Quantum Mechanics*. That text, by the way, is still in print and taught in universities around the world, because it provided the first rigorous mathematical framework for quantum mechanics, and it's hard to believe that the unending discussions about what quantum mechanics *really means* are still conducted on the assumptions that he laid down in 1932, when he was only in his midtwenties! I still hadn't done a goddamn thing in my career when I met him, so I felt awkward when von Neumann started camping with me and the boys in the Los Alamos computation department. He'd been brought in as an expert to help with the plutonium version of the bomb, because that one needed a perfectly symmetrical implosion to set off the nuclear chain reaction. Von Neumann had shown, in principle, that the best way to set off that bomb was to place several explosive charges around the core, and use their combined shock waves to squeeze the plutonium to the unearthly density required to bring about fission. But we didn't understand the science, we didn't have the proper technology, and the mathematics was ludicrous. Everybody thought it was useless. The hydro-dynamics were simply too complex for an individual to handle. It was godlike mathematics, equations so intricate that not even Fermi or von Neumann could see them through to the end, at least not unaided. But I could tell that it was exactly that—the hopeless impossibility, the ir-reducible complexity of the calculus—that seduced von Neumann. Here was an unsolvable problem, and he was slobbering! He couldn't help himself. It was obscene. I showed him what we were working with, these Marchant calculating machines, but it was clear that we needed something more powerful, so Oppenheimer got us some IBMs, top of the line back then, but pathetic by today's standards. They used these punched cards to operate and when they arrived, we couldn't get von Neumann to take his hands off them. It seemed that he had forgotten all about the war, all about the bomb. Knowing what he did later, it makes sense, but back then I was confused. What is wrong with this man, doesn't he know what we're supposed to be doing? Of course he did! Better than we did, in fact, but he had become engrossed by some of the methods that my team and I had come up with to speed up the calculations for the bomb. We had created a sort of mass-production system, a mathematical assembly line where each "computer"—that's what we called people hired to do mathematical calculations—had to do a single type of operation, over and over and over again, this one was the multiplier, and she was the adder, and this one cubed, so all she did was cube this number and send it to the next one down the line, and with that we achieved amazing speeds to try and get these massive, multilayered computations ready on time for the big test at Trinity. It was uncanny watching these women (most of them were women) behaving like machines, operating in that strange way that computers now do. And that caught von Neumann's attention immediately. To me it was just a spur-of-the-moment solution to a problem, an ingenious shortcut to speed things up, but to him . . . well, to him it was the future. We had to physically restrain him to prevent him from taking those IBM machines apart, and several shots of our secret stash of moonshine were needed just to get him to pay us any mind at all. He spent two weeks programming the machines and rewiring the tabulators himself, asking questions about everything, and we felt privileged because we knew that so many others were waiting for him. He was a real VIP (he got to sleep in the boys' school), everyone wanted his opinion. All the departments in Los Alamos would line up their hardest problems when he came, and he would just go from one office to the next, shooting them down one by one. When we finally finished and set the bomb computation going, we went for a walk in the desert, and he gave me a piece of advice that still haunts me: "You don't have to be responsible for the world that you're in, you know?" he told me. See, it wasn't just von Neumann who was always smiling and happy. When I think back on my work at Los Alamos, even with all the personal tragedy and loss that I went through with my wife, even with everything that was happening over in Europe, I still remember those years as the most thrilling of my life. It's hard to admit it openly before others, but all that time, as we were building humanity's deadliest weapon, we couldn't stop kidding around, almost as if we couldn't help ourselves. We all kept cracking jokes.

I saw it, you know? At Trinity. The first explosion. Saw it with my own eyes. I'm about the only guy in the world who actually looked at the damn thing directly, idiot that I am. When they announced the test, I wasn't there at Los Alamos. My wife had died and I'd borrowed Klaus Fuchs's car to drive to the funeral. I almost didn't make it, because that piece of shit got three flat tires on the way. And get this: we later found out that it was the very same car that Fuchs used to take all our secrets to Santa Fe. Because he was the spy, you know? The mole. He was the one who gave our nuclear secrets to the Soviets. But I didn't know it at the time, of course, we were friends, he was a nice guy, and now I can say that I got to drive it, I got to drive the spy's car from Los Alamos to the funeral parlor. So anyway, I was back there with my heart broken when I got the call—this voice on the phone says, "The baby is expected"—so I drove back, speeding all the way. I arrived at the last minute, they put us on a truck and took us to Jornada del Muerto, this god-awful place two hundred miles from Los Alamos, right in the middle of the Alamogordo bombing range. Our viewing position was twenty miles away from the tower where the actual bomb was suspended. When we got there our radio stopped working, so we had no idea what was going on. That's always the way it is. I'm not just talking about the test. The truth is that we really didn't know what was going to happen. Nobody did. We even had a betting pool, this running bet on what the actual yield of the explosion would be. One, two, three, four thousand tons of TNT, you could bet as high or low as you wanted, but a lot of us bet zero. Because that was the safest bet. The smartest one. That it simply wouldn't work, or that it would fizzle out and the chain reaction would never get going. And then there was Teller. He was the only one who bet too high: twenty-five thousand tons, about four thousand more than we actually got. He was worried, see, he actually told me that there was a possibility ("a vwery slight possuibility," he said) that the bomb would ignite the entire world's atmosphere, and that everything, every plant, every human, every single animal living anywhere on the planet would either suffocate or be burned alive. But that was Teller. He was Hungarian like von Neumann, so he had a different mind, because most of us really thought it would fail. That it wouldn't explode. People don't like to admit that, but we did. There had been so many problems leading up to the big test, key mechanisms that failed, and also these stupid little accidents. Kenneth Greisen was pulled over for speeding in Albuquerque while he was driving the detonators to Trinity, four days before the test. And there were other issues with "the gadget," which is what we called the explosive device, like when it came unhinged as they were hoisting it to the top of the tower and it began to sway. It could have fallen and detonated right there. The actual bomb was a funny-looking thing. A large steel sphere with a tangle of wires and cords protruding on the outside. It was sinister, but at the same time, kind of cute. I know it sounds stupid, but it's true. It had these openings for the detonators, and they were covered over with strips of tape, white tape in a cross pattern, and that made it look bandaged, a little Frankenstein monster all patched up, almost frail, like it had been hurt or beaten up or something. My god, the things one can think! But I'm being honest, okay, we thought it was gonna be a dud. We didn't think it was gonna work, and the radio was dead, so we were all pacing about silently, and nobody talked until the storm cleared. Can you believe it? A thunderstorm in the desert. It rained at the worst possible time. The meteorologists were all shaking, 'cause they had promised that the rains would stop around four a.m., and General Groves, the big man in charge of the entire Manhattan Project, had actually threatened to kill Jack Hubbard, their team leader, if their predictions were wrong. "I will hang you," he said. Lucky for them, the weather did clear and the skies opened up. So we were all there, waiting in silence, shivering because the sun hadn't risen and the air was crisp with that curious chill of a hot place at the coolest hour of the day, when the radio came back on, and everyone was told to get ready. They'd given us welder's glasses for the light of the explosion. That light could blind you. But I didn't buy it. I figured that, being twenty miles away, I wasn't gonna see a goddamn thing through dark glasses! And bright light can never really hurt your eyes. It's the ultraviolet that does it. So what I did, what I decided to do was get behind a truck windshield, 'cause ultraviolet can't go through glass. That way I thought I would be safe, but I would still get to *see* the damn thing. Boy, did I miscalculate! The flash was unlike anything. When it hit me, I was sure that I'd been blinded. In that first fraction of a second, I could see nothing but light, solid white light filling my eyes and obliterating my mind, a terrible opaque brightness that had erased the entire world. The enormity of the light was indescribable, it gave me no time to react. I snapped my head back and looked away and then I saw all the mountain ridges illuminated in searing colors, gold, purple, violet, gray, and blue, every peak and crevasse was lit up with a clarity and beauty that had to be seen, it really can't be imagined. As I was fumbling in the cabin of the truck, trying to put my welder's glasses on, I felt something else, and at first I didn't understand what the hell it was: a great heat on my skin, when it had been so cold just a second before, a heat like the midday sun shining on my entire body. But it wasn't the sun, 'cause it was five a.m.—five twenty-nine with forty-five seconds, to be exact. It was the heat of the bomb. And then, as suddenly as it began, it was over. The heat dissipated and the light was gone. I heard people cheering and clapping and laughing, so many people celebrating and screaming with joy. But not all of us. Some of us were quiet. Some were even praying as they looked up at the ominous mushroom cloud hanging over us, with all the radioactivity glowing purplish and alien inside it, rising higher and higher into the stratosphere while the terrifying thunder from the blast kept echoing back and forth, over and over again, bouncing along the mountains, like a bell tolling for the end of the world.

Right after the test, a letter began to circulate among us physicists. It was a petition to convince the president not to use the bomb against Japan. More than a hundred and fifty members of the Manhattan Project signed it. I mean, the war in Europe was over. Hitler had shot himself, for God's sake, there was no reason to kill two hundred thousand civilians in Japan the way we did. Trust me, if they had just seen it, if a single Japanese general had witnessed the test of the bomb, that would have been enough. I know it would. But Truman never got the petition. Not that it would have made a difference. The bombs we had created were in the hands of the military, and they were going to use them, no matter what. They had already put together an entire committee to choose the best targets, but it was actually von Neumann who convinced them that they shouldn't detonate the devices at ground level, but higher up in the atmosphere, since that way the blast wave would cause incomparably larger damage. He even calculated the optimal height himself—six hundred meters, about two thousand feet. And that is exactly how high our bombs were when they exploded above the roofs of those quaint wooden houses in Hiroshima and Nagasaki.

Klára Dan

A mathematical weapon

J ohnny loved America almost as much as I despised it. That country did something to him. All that maddening, unthinking optimism, all that cheerful naïveté under which they hid their cruelty, it brought out the worst in him. A sleeping demon, a secret desire whispered by the nightmare that he confessed to no one. He wasn't the same as in Europe. Not the man I fell in love with. America altered something inside him, it triggered a chemical or electrical rewiring of his brain, and to me, who had fallen for him mainly due to the exceptional quality of that organ—even exclusively, I would say, for he had few other charms—it was a tragedy and the beginning of the worst years of my life. And of the best. It's hard to tell them apart. Looking back, I can't clearly distinguish the good from the bad, I can't forget the pain of leaving Budapest, or the nostalgia for the world that we lost in the war, I can't help but hear the distant echo of the crowds cheering my name while I skated past them as a teenager in a fur coat and boa with gold medals around my neck, wind in my hair as I rode an open carriage to one of the lavish parties that my father hosted in our home, with a band of real gypsies who could play nonstop during an entire weekend, while uncles, cousins, and friends of our extended family came roaring in as if summoned from the void, to move the pianos and rearrange the furniture so we could all dance until we dropped—all those happy memories bleed and merge with the nightmare that began when I crossed the Atlantic to meet up with Johnny and begin the second half of my miserable life. Those former joys are now tainted by the intense painful pleasure of my first months with Johnny, the excitement of being whisked away just as the dogs of war were being set loose, saved in the nick of time and taken to an alien place, finally free from my dullard second husband, my daddy-husband twenty years older than me, that boring banker whom I had divorced to marry this one-of-a-kind genius I had first seen in Monte Carlo, sulking in front of a small mound of chips, looking as if he had gambled away his entire fortune when it turned out that all he had lost was a childish belief that he could somehow find a logical basis to the world. Pain and pleasure became entangled in my later years, the awful years of my marriage to that awful man who never loved me as I needed him to do, but who made me fall in love with him, and then refused to spend his days with me, because he always, always had something more important to do, someone to meet, something to think about, all that bloody thinking that he did, it's a miracle that a man so completely idiotic could be so smart. Not the man I fell in love with. My man, the one I first met, was a broken man, desperately sad and forlorn, aimless, adrift, and laden—as I have been filled to bursting point—with energy, potential, and desires that he could not satisfy, because he was unable to find anything that could contain them, anything that he could truly pour himself into. When I first laid eyes on him, he had just met Gödel, so he was going through a period that was completely unlike what he knew before or after. Because Johnny led a charmed life, without distress, he had never suffered failure, he did not comprehend the insecurities that haunt the rest of us; he understood nothing of uncertainty, awkwardness, or lack of self-worth since he was always so much better, so much smarter than anyone else. And yet in that casino—which was, at the time, the center of gravity for Europe's most depraved and incurable gamblers—he seemed so sad and crippled with despair, he looked so vulnerable sitting there at the roulette table, losing again and again and again, that I couldn't help but walk up to him, because I felt that we shared something, we shared the same inconsolable desperation, and when he looked up at me with those big brown eyes bursting with intelligence, and explained that he had a system to beat the game (that evidently did not work at all but that involved lengthy and complicated probability calculations that even made allowance for the wheel being "untrue," in other words, rigged against him), I was instantly enamored, and stayed at his side enjoying the lunatic pleasure of seeing all those people destroying themselves, while he scribbled numbers and solved equations on a large piece of paper spread out in front of him, as though he was a schoolboy in detention. When he was down to his last chip, I picked it up from the green felt and walked over to the bar, where we proceeded to get delightfully drunk, although I had to pay for all his drinks, of course, since he was absolutely broke. It was over there and then for me: we were hooked, and after that, things went so fast that to me it seems as if that roulette wheel had not yet finished spinning when we were already married and miserable, halfway around the world. I had the misfortune of falling for him when he was like that, depressed, sullen, and melancholy, without suspecting that his real character, his true heart, was nothing of the sort. When I understood who he really was, I could not turn back; he had already divorced that skinny cocktease Mariette and we had moved to Princeton, where he had been appointed as the youngest professor at the Institute for Advanced Study, a truly fascinating place where I got to spend a lot of time among the smartest people in the world, jumping around like a grasshopper in very tall grass. That wonderful place, that redbrick building populated by the demigods of science, was surrounded by a sprawling wilderness that beckoned to us with nature's savage calls—Do you like the sound of dead leaves beneath your feet? I do—a dark wood that was dangerous to walk in during mating season, because the stags would patrol the paths and chase after intruders with their antlers down, eyes blind with lust and rage, trampling the wildflowers of spring, delicate yellow trout lilies and purple violets that grew beneath the canopy of aspen, gray birch, dogwood, and beech. According to Johnny, a lot of the best mathematics and physics of the 1940s and '50s was done there, amid the shadow of those trees, and I remember bumping into some scientists myself, or pointing at them with the rifle I had bought to hunt, which I carried around even though it was forbidden. I could have done away with several of the greatest minds of the twentieth century with the slightest twitch of my trigger finger. Shot them down one by one. It could have changed the secret spinning axis of history with just a handful of bullets, since these were no ordinary people, not ordinary at all, but easy prey for any hunter, because they were so caught up in themselves and completely indifferent to the world outside. My finest catch was not a scientist but a poet. The institute had invited T. S. Eliot to visit for a couple of months, and I stalked him in the woods, sheltering behind dead trees, stepping carefully over dull roots wet with rain, trying to keep my distance but close enough to hear odd whispered lines—"feebleminded," "clever at repairing clocks," "the cry of bats," "what death is happy?"—I believe that he was working on *The Cocktail Party* at the time—so I held him in my sights and wished that he would turn and see me, that one of his lines would skewer my heart and put me out of my misery, but he never did, he moved about like an animal, stopping and staring, cocking his head to one side to answer the piercing cry of the warbler with his silence, his cold stone silence that was so wonderfully awake, so alive and so precious, while the others, some of those other men, I could have picked off without feeling the slightest bit of regret. But I didn't, of course, because some of them were darlings. I met them all, hosted them in my own home, filled their glasses with sherry as we reminisced about the old country and my husband clowned about. I heard the latest and greatest discoveries, the ideas that would slowly alter the history of our species, directly from the mouths of the people who first glimpsed these mad terrains of the new. It was a privilege, but it was also an agony. How could I compare to them? How to measure up? I did my best, of course, and yet I suffered in secret, because I felt that my life had been taken away from me, that I had been turned into a secondary character, some fool in their great play, and so I resented my situation and standing, rare and precious as it was, and I refused to be as charming and polite as I could have been, as I had been taught to be, especially toward the parasites that rode my husband's coattails and fed off his brilliance like those tiny wasps that drill into the cores of regal oaks. Morgenstern, for example, that prudish bore of a man, to name just one of them, never left my home! I would wake up and he would be there, in the kitchen, and then I would have to fall asleep to the horrid sound of his monotone voice in Johnny's study. It was enough to drive you mad. And then there was Johnny's childhood friend, Jenő Pál "Eugene" Wigner, an envious little creature who could never take his slobbering eyes off me. There is no middle point with these great men, at least that is my experience, they are either morbidly lustful or completely cut off from their genitals, and my husband, who really had to excel at everything, was perhaps the most disgusting in his relationship with women. It's no surprise that most of them found him unsettling, he had some sort of fetish, because he would fixate on any pair of legs that walked by him, and even had the appalling habit of peeking underneath the desks of the secretaries at the institute. Some of those poor women had to stick pieces of cardboard there, just so that this great man, this Übermensch, would stop staring up their skirts. I despaired, I really did, but at the time I thought, "Well, Klari, this is the price you pay for exceptionality," and I convinced myself that it was so. I had such a poor image of myself, especially at first. I had almost no formal studies or practical skills, so I was at his mercy. It took a while for things to change, and they did—I learned to code when computers were still an arcane technology that only I and a handful of others comprehended, I worked in Princeton's Office of Population Research, I helped produce the first successful meteorological forecast on a computer, I helped code and program the first nuclear bomb simulations, and I became friends with wonderful women, like Maria Goeppert Mayer, who later won the Nobel Prize for physics—but by that time I was already deep in despair, because my father, my poor father whom we had rescued from Europe and almost had to drag kicking and screaming to America, had thrown himself under a train at Christmas, unable to withstand the pain from so many of our brethren murdered by the Nazis, or the endless humiliations that he had been subjected to. Because humiliation always precedes death. And America, this new country that was supposed to be so different from the old one, this beacon of light for the modern world, was a source of constant humiliation for my father. He never accepted it, could never love it, and I felt much the same, although I lacked his courage and held on, held on to Johnny and to a bottle and tried—by God I tried!—to make the best of things, to enjoy every single day that I could. And there was a lot to enjoy. Between 1946 and 1957 we crossed the country more than twenty-eight times by car. We saw it all. And I could have enjoyed it were it not for the detours that Johnny made, hundreds of miles just to visit the "Devil's Cauldron" or the "Devils Tower," all these odd-sounding landmarks that sparked my husband's ravenous curiosity and that forced him to drive endlessly while dragging me along. It's a miracle that we didn't die on the road, because Johnny was such a terrible driver. But I did, parts of me died on those long odysseys across the American hellscape, sweating under the intolerable heat, looking out at the vast emptiness, the endless rows of bright green corn, one gas station looking exactly like the next, the seedy motels that Johnny, for whatever reason, preferred, little towns and small cities where I had to grin back at those women who were all smiles and empty heads, holding my tongue as I heard ignorant men boast of their ignorance in diners, roadhouses, and restaurants. Not a breath of culture to be found in that entire country. Just happy wives raving about their appliances with patriotic, all-American fifties optimism and dullard husbands riding their new lawnmowers with bottles in their hands. I remember somewhere in Nevada, this man with a long beard and denims rode into the bar where we were consoling ourselves, still on top of his mule,

133

and nobody blinked an eye. The bartender just handed him a glass of beer and put a bucket of the same brew in front of the animal. It felt unreal, almost like a play, but apparently it was completely routine, because the man put his dollar bills on the counter, waited for his beast to finish, and then, just as quietly as he came in, he left the place and Johnny looked at me as if to say, "This, this, my love, is why we're here." We traveled a lot, by God did we travel, but mostly I spent my time alone while he worked with the government and the military and the industry on what Einstein called "the great technologies of death." Albert was the only one of those institute boys I could ever get along with. Maybe because he and Johnny were opposites. Completely different in their characters and in the shapes of their minds. Johnny's was incandescent, so next to him Albert looked and behaved like a drab old turtle, because he would simmer and ponder on a question for years, decades even. But his insight was deeper, his ideas more profound; they were, at least to me, also more humane and enlightened. They did admire each other, that's for sure, even though Johnny hated the gravitas that Albert exuded. He did a terrible impression of him, that nobody ever laughed at, and loved to make fun of his clothes and mock his pacifism. Albert found Johnny childish and nihilistic, and once said to me that my husband was rapidly turning into a "mathematical weapon." I told him so during one of our fights, I threw it at his face as a way to hurt him, but Johnny, being Johnny, reveled in his new nickname, and laughed about it with his friends. He must have felt some small measure of resentment, however, because one time, when Albert was supposed to go to New York, Johnny offered to drive him to the Princeton train station in a brand-new Cadillac he had just bought for me, and then purposely put him on a train going in the wrong direction.

The most important thing they disagreed on was the bomb. Albert was a dove, the unofficial head of the disarmament movement, while Johnny was a hawk. I remember when he came back from Los Alamos after the Trinity test. He arrived midmorning, tired, pale, and badly shaken, and went to bed and slept for twelve hours. He never needed more than four hours of sleep, so I was worried when he finally woke up late at night and started talking at a speed that was extraordinarily fast, even for his standards. "What we are creating now," he said, "is a monster whose influence is going to change history, provided there is any history left! But it would be impossible not to see it through. Not only for military reasons, it would also be unethical, from the point of view of scientists, not to do what they know is feasible, no matter what terrible consequences it may have. And this is only the beginning!" He could not calm down, he was completely beside himself, so finally I suggested that he take a couple of sleeping pills and a very strong drink, to bring him back to the present and make him relax a little about his predictions of inevitable doom. The next morning he seemed to have recovered, but from that day until his last he devoted himself to the advance of technology in all forms, to the exclusion of everything else, neglecting pure mathematics and completely ignoring me. He gave himself no respite, and he never took a step back, as though he somehow knew that there was not much time left, for him or for the world. His answer to the nuclear dilemma was a perfect reflection of the best and the worst in him: mercilessly logical, completely counterintuitive, and so utterly rational that it bordered on the psychopathic. The thing about my husband that people don't understand is that he truly saw life as a game, he regarded all human endeavors, no matter how deadly or serious, in that spirit. He once told me that, just as wild animals play when they are young in preparation for lethal circumstances arising later in their lives, mathematics may be, to a large extent, nothing but a strange and wonderful collection of games, an enterprise whose real purpose, beyond any one stated outright, is to slowly work changes in the individual and collective human psyche, as a way to prepare us for a future that nobody can imagine. The problem with those games, the many terrible games that spring forth from humanity's unbridled imagination, is that when they are played in the real world—whose rules and true purpose are known only to God—we come face-to-face with dangers that we may not have the knowledge or the wisdom to overcome. I know this because my darling husband thought up one of the most dangerous ideas in human history, one so devilish and cynical that it is a miracle that we have so far managed to survive it.

Oskar Morgenstern

A strange angel

To the uninitiated it is madness.

That explains the acronym that somebody coined for the most deranged application of one of von Neumann's ideas: MAD, Mutually Assured Destruction. It's how America chose to fight the Cold War, a game of chicken played out on a planetary scale with weapons powerful enough to blow up the entire world. MAD was a doctrine of deterrence and retaliation that said that the only way to avoid nuclear warfare between the superpowers was for the US and the USSR to amass such a gargantuan hoard of atomic weapons that any nuclear attack would result in the complete annihilation of both countries. It was perfectly rational insanity: ensuring global peace by taking us to the brink of Armageddon. This ludicrous and corrupt doctrine lasted four decades, and to my eternal shame, it was based on a wicked perversion of the concepts that von Neumann and I set down in our *Theory of Games and Economic Behavior.*

MAD is one of many examples of how mankind can be made prisoner by reason, but it started innocently enough, many years before the atomic bomb was even a remote possibility, when Johnny was losing yet another hand at poker against his buddy-boy Stan Ulam. It happened during a party at Johnny's home in Princeton: von Neumann, who could not bluff to save his life, and was probably trying to distract his opponent with a joke, asked Ulam how in the hell the stock market could thrive and work the way it did when most, if not all, stockbrokers were such idiots. At the time he was thinking about games and how complex systems could arise and function if their individual parts— whether they be belligerent fire ants scuttering along the mud corridors of their colony, neurons firing across the hemispheres of our brains, or imbeciles warring with each other on the stock exchange floor—were, if not wholly unthinking, definitely unreliable. He had always been fascinated by games of all kinds, and was trying to find a way to encapsulate the many skirmishes and conflicts that arise from human interactions within a set of well-defined rules. I was also there at that party, and since I don't like to drink, I was one of the few who could still string together a coherent sentence by the end of the night, so when Ulam had deprived Johnny of his last dollar I walked over and told him that I had overheard his comment on the stock market. He was trying to hide his frustration at having lost by amusing himself with this ridiculous little contraption that he wore on his head—a child's toy, a little cap that had a propeller connected to a rubber hose into which he would blow to make it spin around, whistling—and we spoke at length about idiots, economics, and games. While we talked, we slowly drifted to the corner of the living room where Oppenheimer and Wigner were deeply absorbed in a game of chess, and I told Johnny that I had just read his 1928 paper "Theory of Parlor Games." Did it, I asked, apply to something like chess? He gave a spirited twirl to his propeller before answering: "No, no, no! Chess is not a game! It is a well-defined form of computation. You may not be able to work out the correct answers because of its complexity, but in theory there must be a solution, an optimal way to play, a perfect move for any given position and configuration of pieces on the board. Now, real games are not like that at all. Games in real life are very different. To win in reality you must lie and deceive. The games that I'm interested in consist of carefully elaborated tactics of deception—of self-deception even!—so you have to be constantly asking yourself what the other man is thinking, how you will respond, and what *he* thinks that *you* are going to do next. That is what games are about in my theory." I left the party without saying goodbye to anyone and worked all weekend long. On Monday, I walked straight into his office at the Institute for Advanced Study and showed him a draft of the paper I had written. He said it was too short. That it should be expanded. So I did that. He looked at it again a couple of days later, and said it was still too short, so I went home and made the additions that he had suggested. When I brought him that new version, he read it over, quick as lightning, and then said, "Fine, why don't we just write a joint paper?" almost as if he was doing it for my sake.

It was the most intensive work I have ever known. We met every morning for breakfast; if he had the evening free, we would work through the night. He wasn't a man who sat down to think, he would be thinking continuously, so that by the time it was ready in his mind, it all came rushing out; infallible, he would dictate these carefully constructed sentences without a moment's hesitation and make absolutely no mistakes. I need silence to concentrate and time to think, but he was capable of working anywhere—he actually preferred noise, so he would seek out crowded railroad stations and airports, loved to work on planes and ships, and could pick up where he had left off waiting for a bellboy to bring him a drink in some fancy hotel's lobby. I simply couldn't keep pace. The project took an enormous toll on my personal life. I lost weight, I became estranged from my friends, my family, and my colleagues. At one time, I fell quite ill from sheer exhaustion. I had fever dreams and nightmares where I would see him towering above me like a Cyclops, playing with toy airplanes and tanks, swallowing armies whole, gazing out over the horizon with just one, massive, unblinking eye. I was devastated, but I kept working, because he did not seem to notice just how tired I was. Being too shy, I simply could not complain. I also felt so privileged to be working with him and was keenly aware of the importance of what we were doing. Our goal was not just to create rules for games. We were trying to capture, with the most pristine mathematics possible, the way human beings make choices, to cast a net over their unfathomable motivations and peer into the many secret games they play, both in the inner realm of their minds and out in the open, in the wilderness of society. The scope of our work was boundless: it could reach down to the most domestic level—how a person chose to negotiate a raise at work, for example—or all the way to the critical decisions that shape the manner in which nations wage war against each other.

I spent so much time at the von Neumanns' home that I even courted Dorothy, the woman who would later become my wife, right there in their living room, because I had to organize my entire day around Johnny's hectic schedule. Klari became so unnerved at my constant presence in her house that she gave me and Johnny the oddest ultimatum: she said that she would simply not let him have anything else to do with the theory of games unless it included an elephant. I knew that she suffered from a weird obsession with that particular pachyderm—there were countless elephants around the house—and Johnny assured me that she would stand firm with her demands, so we had no choice, and promptly introduced one: you can see its trunk on page sixty-four of our treatise, hidden among the lines of a diagram. It took us years to finish the book. We handed it in just as Princeton University Press was threatening to cancel the entire project. It's over seven hundred pages long and crammed with such dense equations that a good friend of mine once sent me an article that described it as "the least read and most influential book in all of twentieth-century economics," but it provided something completely new and unique: a mathematical foundation for economics. I felt as though I'd touched the Holy Grail. I never did anything that could compare to that during the rest of my life, but I can only speak for myself, of course, because for Johnny it was just one more thing, another achievement in a life that was chock-full of them. At the heart of our theory was his proof of the so-called minimax theorem: von Neumann had mathematically demonstrated that there is always a rational course of action for two-player games, provided (and herein lies the catch) that their interests are *diametrically opposed*. We expanded on that proof, creating equations to analyze games with multiple players where interests overlap, and finally created a framework that could encompass almost any type of human conflict. We had intended for our book to be of use solely for economists, but no one took to it as quickly and savagely as the masters of war.

To military strategists, game theory felt like a gift from the gods, because our work appeared to offer a rational way to play out and win wars. This delighted Johnny, who was by no means a pacifist, and he quickly answered when the world's first "think tank," the RAND Corporation, called on him to find military applications for our theory. Those devils at RAND revered him, and used game theory as if it were a modern oracle, over which Johnny presided like a babbling sibyl swept up in a trance. He was one of the first to openly advocate for a surprise nuclear attack against the Soviet Union, not because he hated communists (well, he did) but rather because he was convinced that it was the only way to prevent World War III. And our theory—or at least his interpretation of it—did back his thinking. "If you say why not bomb them tomorrow, I say why not today? If you say today at five o'clock, I say why not one o'clock?" That's what Johnny said to *Life* magazine, but behind his awful glibness lay his conviction that peace required that we rain nuclear hell down on the USSR before they could develop their own atomic bombs. The future he envisioned, once the nuclear fallout dissipated and the many millions dead were tallied and counted, was a long-lasting Pax Americana, a period of stability unlike the world had ever known, gained at the highest cost we have ever paid. I found his cold rationality the stuff of nightmares, but Johnny did not see it that way at all: if you looked at it logically using the models of game theory, he said, a nuclear first strike was not just the optimal solution, it was the *only* fully logical decision to make. But in 1949, things changed: just four years after the annihilation of Hiroshima and Nagasaki, the USSR got the bomb, and by 1953 they had more than four hundred warheads, which meant that any nuclear strike by the US would be reciprocated. Johnny's ideas, or some version of them, came to dominate the Cold War's balance of terror. Faced with unsolvable dilemmas, the Pentagon, the CIA, RAND, and many other outfits began to play out increasingly complex war scenarios based on our theory. But when our equations—which were so clear and transparent when applied to harmless amusements such as poker—became tangled up with the struggles and politics of the nuclear age, they gave birth to an inescapable labyrinth that defies the imagination, triggering an atomic arms race between the western democracies and the countries that hid behind the Iron Curtain, a folly that almost inexorably led them to the delirious stalemate of Mutually Assured Destruction, where any aggression would be automatically met with the full atomic might of the aggressed, causing the obliteration of all parties. MAD called for long-range bombers carrying nuclear weapons to circle the globe twenty-four hours a day, three hundred and sixty-five days a year, without ever landing; these airplanes were linked via a vast network to submarines that patrolled the abyss, loaded with atomic warheads, while thousands of intercontinental ballistic missiles—which could fly from Washington to Moscow in less than thirty minutes—waited patiently for the trumpet call of the Apocalypse in deep, underground silos and fortified bunkers. This precarious equilibrium, this macabre game, never really ended, even after the Cold War did. Far too many of these weapons are still there, biding their time, watched over by flawed and aging mechanisms of control, preserved in steel sarcophagi like the long-dead bodies of the ancient pharaohs, ready and waiting for the life that begins with death. Taking all of this into consideration, it's no wonder that Johnny was convinced that humankind would not survive the many wonders of industrial society, but I'm sure that if he were alive, he would be relieved by the fact that his worst nightmares have not come true, and that our theory of games blossomed far beyond the hothouse of politics and is used in everything from computer science and ecology to philosophy and biology, where our equations model how cancer cells grow, spread, and communicate. Some of our terminology has even seeped into common vernacular, with people referring to many aspects of social life as "zero-sum games." And that just goes to show how it is almost impossible to foretell the consequences and applications of ideas and discoveries, and why it is so hard to properly judge even the realities that we have taken part in ourselves. Many people still believe that Mutually Assured Destruction helped prevent the Cold War from turning hot. But to me, it remains sinful and unforgivable, and serves as a personal reminder that neither the natural nor the social sciences are ever neutral, even if they aspire to be that way. Because I can't help but recognize that Johnny— who proved the theorem at the heart of our work—was profoundly pessimistic, his vision of human beings was grim and cynical, and so his mind may have unwittingly tainted the equations that upheld our thinking with its own dark tinge. I myself suffer from a morbid sense of despair, and even now, decades after I worked with von Neumann, I still find myself questioning our central tenet: Is there really a rational course of action in every situation? Johnny proved it mathematically beyond a doubt, but *only for two players with diametrically opposing goals*. So there may be a vital flaw in our reasoning that any keen observer will immediately become aware of; namely, that the minimax theorem that underlies our entire framework presupposes perfectly rational and logical agents, agents who are interested only in winning, agents who pose a perfect understanding of the rules and a total recall of all their past moves, agents who also have a flawless awareness of the possible ramifications of their own actions, and of their opponents' actions, at every single step of the game. The only person I ever met who was exactly like that was Johnny von Neumann. Normal people are not like that at all. Yes, they lie, they cheat, deceive, connive, and conspire, but they also cooperate, they can sacrifice themselves for others, or simply make decisions on a whim. Men and women follow their guts. They heed hunches and make careless mistakes. Life is so much more than a game. Its full wealth and complexity cannot be captured by equations, no matter how beautiful or perfectly balanced. And human beings are not the perfect poker players that we envisioned. They can be highly irrational, driven and swayed by their emotions, subject to all kinds of contradictions. And while this sparks off the ungovernable chaos that we see all around us, it is also a mercy, a strange angel that protects us from the mad dreams of reason.

Eugene Wigner
The Hungarian Horsemen of the Apocalypse

P eople now think, looking back at what we did, that we were all monsters and madmen, because how could we bring forth those demons into the world, how could we play around with such terrible forces, forces that could very well wipe us from the face of the Earth, or send us back to a time before reason, when the only fire we knew was sparked by the lightning that angry gods hurled down at us as we trembled in our caves. A dirty little secret that almost all of us share, but that hardly anyone speaks aloud, is that what drew us in, what made us fashion those weapons, was not the desire for power or wealth, fame, or glory, but the sheer thrill of the science involved. It was too much to resist. The extremities of pressure and temperature created by the nuclear chain reaction, the rarefied physics, the colossal release of energy . . . it was unlike anything we had ever known. The hydro-dynamics of the shock and blast waves, or that awesome light that almost blinded us, had never been seen before by human eyes. We were dis-covering something that not even God had created before us. Because those conditions hadn't existed elsewhere in the universe; fission is commonplace in the heart of stars or massive celestial engines, but we achieved it inside a little sphere of metal, just a meter and a half in diameter, holding an even tinier core of just six kilograms of plutonium nestled within. It still amazes me that we could do something like that. So it wasn't just the frantic race to beat the Nazis (and later the Russians, and then the Chinese, and so on and so forth till the world's end), it was the joy of thinking the unthinkable and doing the impossible, pushing past all human limits by burning Prometheus's gift to its utmost incandescence.

We, the Martians, played an oversized role in the American nuclear program. It's what they called us after a joke Fermi made when someone asked him whether extraterrestrials were real: "Of course they are, and they already live among us. They just call themselves Hungarians." We seemed alien to them. And perhaps we were. Because how could such a little country—surrounded as it was by enemies on all sides and torn between rival empires—produce so many extraordinary scientists in so little time? Leo Szilard thought up the nuclear chain reaction that led to the atomic bomb while he was crossing a street in London, in 1933, and he patented the first nuclear reactor; von Kármán was a virtuoso when it came to supersonic flight and rocket propulsion, so he was key to the development of intercontinental ballistic missiles; I led a group that designed the nuclear reactors needed to convert uranium into weapons-grade plutonium; while Teller has the distinction (not unmerited though exaggerated) of being considered the father of that death-god destroyer of worlds, the hydrogen bomb; so naturally Jancsi—who was the most alien of the lot—came up with his own sardonic name for us: the Hungarian Horsemen of the Apocalypse. He believed that our country's outstanding intellectual achievements were not a product of history or chance, or any kind of government initiative, but due to something stranger and more fundamental: a pressure on the whole society of that part of Central Europe, a subconscious feeling of extreme insecurity in individuals, and the necessity of either producing the unusual or facing extinction. Once, when he and I were discussing his theories of nuclear deterrence, he asked me if I knew what had remained inside Pandora's box after she had opened it and let out all the evils and ills into the world. "Right there," he said, "at the bottom of the jar—because it was a large urn or a jar, you know, not a box at all—right there, waiting quietly and obediently was Elpis, which most people like to regard as the daimona of hope and counterpart to Moros, the spirit of doom, but to me, a better and more precise translation of her name and of her nature would be our concept of expectation. Because we don't know what comes after evil, do we? And sometimes the deadliest things, those that hold enough power to destroy us, can become, given time, the instruments of our salvation." I asked him why the gods would let out all the hurts, pains, illnesses, and iniquities to roam free while keeping hope trapped behind the lid of the jar. He winked and said that it was because they know things that we can never know. That is exactly how I feel about him, and the reason why I have always resisted condemning Jancsi, or judging him too harshly, because I believe that a mind like his—one of inexorable logic—must have made him understand and accept many things that most of us do not even want to acknowledge, and cannot begin to comprehend. He did not see the way the rest of us do, and this colored many of his moral judgments. With his *Theory of Games and Economic Behavior*, for example, he wasn't trying to fight a war, or beat the casino, or finally win a game of poker;

he was aiming at nothing less than the complete mathematization of human motivation, he was trying to capture some part of mankind's soul with mathematics, and I think that, to a large extent, he succeeded in setting down the rules by which people make choices, economic and otherwise. So perhaps the embers of the fire that Hilbert had kindled in him, his grand hope to arrest the chaotic spinning of this world, were not completely extinguished. I could also be deluding myself in that respect. Maybe he had no lofty goals at all. Maybe he was merely enjoying himself irresponsibly, as he always did. Virginia Davis thought as much. She was a fabulous textile artist married to Martin Davis, one of the dullest mathematicians I ever met, a logician who worshipped Jancsi and would follow him around the institute like those unfortunate ducklings who, having been separated from their mothers, imprint on the oddest things, like a car, or a dog, or even a human being, and then behave like another species for their entire lives. Martin would always hang around Jancsi and laugh too loudly at his jokes, but one time, when Klari had asked us all over for dinner and Janos was explaining the intricacies of nuclear diplomacy and the "Dead Hand" (a fully autonomous weapons control system that he believed the Russians were developing, and that would retaliate against any American attack with an automatic response that needed next to no human involvement at all), he said that the nuclear arms race, while clearly wicked and dangerous, had accelerated the development of certain completely unconnected areas of science a thousandfold. Virginia was livid. She got up from her seat, grabbed her coat, and said that it was reckless men like Jancsi, who could not think past mathematics and see the *real* world inhabited by *real* human beings, who would be the death of us all. Didn't we realize where the power of the atom was taking us? Did we not see what the hydrogen bomb could do? We were all shocked, but Jancsi didn't even blink. He downed his scotch and, before Virginia dragged her whimpering husband out the door, told her, "I'm thinking about something much more important than bombs, my dear. I'm thinking about computers."

In 1946, von Neumann promised the United States military that he would build them a computer powerful enough to handle the intricate calculations needed for the hydrogen bomb. All he asked for in return was to freely dispose of any computing time left over from the bomb calculations, and to dedicate it to whatever he desired.

Julian Bigelow

Singed hair and burned whiskers

This was still highly classified information.

But I mentioned it to Johnny von Neumann.

"We're running ballistic calculations on a machine. Making range tables for the artillery boys. Can do three hundred multiplications a second."

Jumped as if I'd stuck a cherry bomb up his ass.

I was coming home from the military base—Aberdeen Proving Ground—saw him on the railroad platform. He was a regular there, a highly valued weapons expert, but we'd never met before.

Demanded I show it to him.

Borrowed the phone at the train station.

Simply had to see the machine for himself.

The Electronic Numerical Integrator and Computer.

ENIAC.

World's first digital general-purpose computer.

A real leviathan.

Used up an entire floor at the Moore School in Philly.

Hundred feet long.

Ten feet high.

Three feet deep.

And more than thirty tons.

Vacuum tubes, crystal diodes, relays, resistors, and capacitors.

With five million hand-soldered joints.

A hundred twenty degrees in the control room when it was running.

Used so much power it gave rise to an apocryphal story: the lights of Philadelphia dimmed when we turned it on.

Bullshit.

What it could do was twenty hours of human work in thirty seconds.

The thing about the ENIAC was that you could actually *see* the calculations taking place.

You could walk inside it and watch the bits flipping.

Nobody was quick enough to keep up with the numbers. Not in real time anyway.

But Johnny was.

I remember him there, standing silent within the computation, staring at the lights flashing in front of his eyes.

One machine thinking inside of another.

Hired me the next day. Told me we were going to build a better one at the Institute for Advanced Study.

So I jumped on a train.

Turned out nobody wanted us there.

The mathematicians were disgusted.

Dirty men with dirty fingers would pollute their hallowed environment.

"Engineers in my wing? Over my dead body!"

Senior paleontologist said that.

No kidding.

'Cause we actually soldered things, burned our hands, while they would just roam around like dinosaurs with their heads in the clouds trying to unravel the mysteries of the universe.

We?

We were building something.

Something that would change their world.

And they despised us for it.

There was no room for us.

We wound up in the office that was meant for Gödel's secretary.

'Cause he never had one. Never needed one. Only published one paper every ten years or so.

Still, wonderful coincidence.

'Cause his work lies at the base of all computer science . . .

We made our plans in there but we couldn't build it, not in that room.

So we moved down.

Where?

Basement, of course.

It's hard to overestimate the importance of what we did.

Our computer wasn't the first.

Wasn't even the third.

But it was a stored-program computer.

And the one that everyone copied.

We published and made public every step of the process.

So it was cloned in 1,500 places around the world.

It became the blueprint.

The DNA of the entire digital universe.

Johnny made it clear from the beginning:

We were there to build the machine that Turing had dreamed up in his 1936 paper, "On Computable Numbers, with an Application to the Entscheidungsproblem."

That describes a universal computer, or "Turing machine."

And that machine can—in principle—solve any mathematical problem presented to it in symbolic form.

That limey bastard somehow managed to replicate the internal states of mind and symbol-manipulating abilities of our species, but on paper.

Real stroke of genius.

Problem is, his Turing machine is unbelievably abstract.

A "head" that reads a strip of endless paper.

Not something you can picture as real technology.

But we turned that into a working, fully programmable computer.

And things just exploded.

The ENIAC? Glorified calculator compared to ours.

It was a music box that could only play one tune.

If you wanted something new you had to physically rewire it.

Thousands of cables connected by hand.

So hours, days, for a single programming change.

We built an instrument.

A grand piano.

With our machine you simply introduced new instructions.

Change the software without touching the hardware.

It was also twenty times faster.

With a fully random-access memory.

Johnny came up with the architecture.

The logical framework.

The same one you have on your computer.

Hasn't changed a bit.

Wonderfully simple.

Just five parts.

Input and output mechanisms and three units: one for memory, one for logic and arithmetic, and the control unit—the CPU.

It's really that simple.

But it was hell to get it to work.

This was 1951.

So we had to use war surplus parts and vacuum tubes that would fail without warning.

In summer the room got so hot, tar would splatter on the machine. Months of work ruined in an instant.

And the memory was incredibly fragile. Someone wearing a woolen sweater could wipe it clean.

Passing cars and planes did that too.

And this mouse crawled inside it once.

Chewed on some wires and was burned to a crisp.

We rescued the machine but never managed to get rid of the stench.

It always smelled of charred meat, singed hair, and burned whiskers.

Took us five excruciating years to build.

Cranky as hell and completely unreliable, but boy was it beautiful!

Looked like a turbocharged V-40 engine inside a giant textile loom.

Dazzling in aluminum and relatively small.

Six feet high two feet wide eight feet long.

A real microprocessor by the day's standards.

Our funding came mostly from the military.

Johnny had hooked them by explaining the possibilities that accelerating computation by a factor of ten thousand would open up.

I mean, just imagine . . .

All the calculations for the atom bomb were done with adding machines.

No real computers at all.

Just women and some fancy calculators.

So those war boys were salivating even before we finished.

They were dreaming big and deadly.

But Johnny was thinking bigger. He was considering problems that were completely unassailable at the time.

He wanted to mathematize everything.

To spark revolutions in biology, economics, neurology, and cosmology.

To transform all areas of human thought and grab science by the throat by unleashing the power of unlimited computation.

That's why he built his machine.

"This species of device is so radically new that many of its uses will become clear only after it's been put into operation."

It's what he said to me.

'Cause he understood.

He knew the real challenge was not building the thing but asking it the right questions in a language intelligible to the machine.

And he was the only one who spoke that language.

We owe so much to him.

'Cause he didn't just give us the most important technological breakthrough of the 20th century.

He left us a part of his mind.

We christened our machine the *Mathematical Analyzer, Numerical Integrator and Computer.*

MANIAC, for short.

The first goal that von Neumann set for the MANIAC was to destroy life as we know it: in the summer of 1951, a team of scientists from Los Alamos traveled to the Institute for Advanced Study in Princeton and introduced a large thermonuclear calculation into the computer. It ran twenty-four hours a day for two months, processed more than a million punched cards, and yielded a single YES/NO answer.

YES

Richard Feynman

And then the world catches fire

You know I played against the MANIAC, right? Beat it too. Anticlerical chess, it's what we called it, 'cause we had to discard the bishops to make it simpler. Not for us, for the computer. Used a smaller board too, just six by six. And some rules changed: no castling, no double pawn step, but the rest, the rest was the same as regular chess. I dunno who wrote the program, maybe Paul Stein or Mark Wells, but I do know that the MANIAC was the first computer to ever beat a human being. Not that big of an accomplishment, to be honest, he was just some pipsqueak that really didn't know how to play, an intern from Los Alamos who had learned the rules just a couple days before, so not the worthiest opponent. But it was a proof of concept, a giant baby step. I played against it a couple of times. It was fun, but you had to have patience, 'cause the computer took about twelve minutes per move. We had just started finding out all these interesting quirks—it appeared to have a mortal fear of checks, so it would sacrifice its pieces to avoid it, sometimes unnecessarily—but then I figured out what they were *really* using the MANIAC for, and I felt sick. Physically ill. See, after Los Alamos, I swore never to have anything to do with the military again. I went through this strange period, this crippling depression, where I would be having lunch or breakfast with my mother in New York, say on, I dunno . . . 59th Street, and I'd look around and start calculating. Because I knew how big the bomb in Hiroshima was, the area it covered, and I'd think, if they dropped one on 34th Street, it would spread out all the way downtown, and all these people around me would be killed, and all these buildings would be destroyed in an instant. Then I'd walk around the city and I would just see ruins and rubble everywhere. I would look at construction workers and start laughing, because it was so silly. Why were they putting up bridges or apartments if it was all going to be destroyed? I just thought, They're crazy! They just don't understand! Why are they making new things? It's useless! 'Cause there wasn't just one bomb available. They were easy to make and I was absolutely convinced that they would be used, and very soon. I mean, why not? People were just going to behave like always. International relations were no different than before. So I really believed that it was pointless, that it was senseless to make anything new. Turns out I was wrong, 'cause it's been so many years, and I'm really glad that those people were able to go ahead with their lives, but my first reaction was that we were completely doomed, especially after I found out those bastards were using the MANIAC to make a hydrogen bomb.

I became obsessed with it. Because it wasn't just a bigger bomb, you see, it was a true horror, something that could not be justified in any sense, an evil by any measure, a weapon so far beyond what was reasonable and rational that it was as if we had willingly wandered into the darkest regions of hell. I mean, even the scientists involved in making the first bomb were against it. "By its very nature the hydrogen bomb cannot be confined to a military objective, but becomes a weapon which, in every practical effect, is almost one of genocide." That's what Fermi said. And Oppenheimer, well, he bashed against a lot of heads and tried everything he could to stop it from being built, he spent the last ounce of his influence as director of the Institute for Advanced Study opposing it. Fell out with lots of people and made dangerous enemies in very high places, so it's no wonder that they blacklisted him and then revoked his security clearance. "With the creation of the atom bomb physicists have known sin, and this is a knowledge which they cannot lose." That's what Oppenheimer said. Felt he had blood on his hands. A real piece of work that guy, as smart and grandiose as they come, but it was all hopeless in the end. Because it was as if those awful things had a will of their own, as if they answered to another power, a strange inevitability that makes me shudder if I think about it too much.

If we physicists had already learned sin, with the hydrogen bomb we knew damnation. In the fall of 1952, while in the United States millions of innocent children were getting ready for Halloween—with fake blood dripping from their little vampire fangs, arms covered in bandages to contain the decay of time on a mummy's body, its cursed soul sapped from long-dead veins, little hands trembling in anticipation as they held them out to participate in the mock horror of All Hallows' Eve, the night when the spirits of the dead return to roam free among the living— at the other side of the world, on an island in the Enewetak Atoll of the South Pacific, Ivy Mike, an actual monstrosity, the first prototype of humankind's deadliest weapon, exploded with a force that was five hundred times more powerful than the bombs we used to massacre a quarter of a million people in Japan. It was a horrific, diabolical-looking contraption: this gigantic steel tank, almost three stories tall, weighing eighty-two tons, filled with liquid deuterium—an isotope of hydrogen—cooled to minus 418 degrees. That was the fuel for the fusion explosion, the thermonuclear reaction. But that main bomb was ignited by another. It needed the X-rays given off by a smaller fission-type device, similar to the Fat Man bomb we dropped on Nagasaki. And that sat on top of the tank and protruded there like a cancerous growth. The entire mechanism, with its support systems, refrigeration gear, sensors, transformers, pipes, gold-leaf reflectors, lead baffles, polyethylene lining, raw uranium and tritium, and the plutonium spark plug, was so big it looked more like a small factory than a bomb. It was housed in a hangar built on the island of Elugelab, which was instantly vaporized by the explosion. It disappeared completely, erased from the Earth along with eighty million tons of coral, replaced by a crater seventeen stories deep, described in one of the official reports as being "large enough to house about fourteen buildings the size of the Pentagon." During the first instant of the thermonuclear reaction, a brilliant flash of light issued forth from ground zero, the same light that I had looked upon at Trinity. Battle-hardened soldiers who had fought and bled in World War II dropped to their knees and prayed. They sensed that something unspeakably wrong was occurring when they saw their bones appear as shadows through their living flesh. Even those inside were almost blinded by streams of light that shone through the smallest cracks and pinholes in secured doors and hatches. That flash was followed by a tremendous fireball that appeared on the horizon like the sun when half-risen. It quickly expanded into an enormous mushroom-shaped cloud that rose toward the stratosphere and continued to grow until it was five times taller than Mount Everest. The size of the cloud was incomparably larger than the one I saw in the desert: onlookers who were thirty miles away from the vaporized island shivered as it began to loom above their heads, balanced on a wide, dirty stem made of coral particles, debris, and water vapor. As it expanded, the fireball reached a temperature of three hundred million degrees, hotter than the core of the sun. It looked almost alive, bubbling and folding in on itself like marmalade churning in a pot, with great black lumps floating amid its gorged mass. The sky turned as red as a furnace. One of the pilots circling overhead wrote that it looked as if the atmosphere itself was boiling. Huge clouds formed in the sky, followed by a strange darkness that rushed toward the horizon, chasing a sound wave so intense that it lasted for minutes, as the sonic boom bounced between the stratosphere and the ocean. The roar of the bomb was deafening. "It was magnificent, like a hundred thunderstorms coming at us from all directions. It seemed that the heavens would burst. Our ears rang and ached for hours," said one of the sailors who witnessed it from a battleship at sea. The heat from the explosion was so extreme that many miles away biologists found birds with half their feathers burned, and fish that had skin missing from one side, as if they'd been dropped on a searing-hot pan. "Something I will never forget was the heat," a physicist and friend of mine who was stationed twenty-five miles away from ground zero later told me. "It was a terrifying experience, because the temperature didn't subside. With kiloton shots, like the one we saw at Trinity, it's a flash and it's over, but on that big hydrogen one the heat just kept on coming, getting stronger and stronger. You would swear that the whole world was on fire." At Los Alamos we were euphoric after our first successful test and celebrated with wild drunken parties that went on for days, but the scientists who saw the world's first thermonuclear explosion were terrified by the power they had unleashed. Many expressed instant regret. Herbert F. York, director of the weapons laboratory at Livermore, described Ivy Mike as "truly foreboding, something which marked a real change in history—a moment when the course of the world suddenly shifted from the path it had been on to a more dangerous one. Fission bombs," he said, "as destructive as they might have been, were limited. Now, it seemed we had learned how to brush all limits aside, and to build bombs whose power was boundless." I mean, Jesus Christ, that fucking bomb was even a surprise for the president. Eisenhower, newly elected, simply couldn't believe what he heard when they informed him of the blast in the Pacific. "There is no need for us to build enough destructive power to destroy everything. Complete destruction is the negation of peace," he said, when it was already too late.

The man who was perhaps most responsible for the creation of the hydrogen bomb was one of the Martians: Teller. According to Oppenheimer, during a briefing at the RAND Corporation Teller gave such an impressive account of the power that the hydrogen bomb would offer the United States that the Secretary of the Air Force, Thomas K. Finletter, jumped to his feet and shouted, "Give us this weapon and we will rule the world!" Ironically, he didn't get to see it. Teller, I mean. I think he got angry when they didn't put him in charge of building it, so he was actually back in California when it went off, sitting in the darkness of a basement at the university in Berkeley, anxiously looking at the quivering needles of a seismograph to detect the shock wave created by his baby roaring into existence with a force that exceeded ten million tons of TNT. When he did, he shot out a telegram to his colleagues in Los Alamos that preceded the official news by more than three hours: "It's a boy!" Years later Teller became a pariah among his physicist friends after stabbing Oppenheimer in the back, but at the time he was the darling of generals and warmongers because he pushed and pushed for the hydrogen bomb, even though his first designs simply didn't work. He kept insisting till Stan Ulam, von Neumann's buddy-boy, came up with the idea behind the Ivy Mike prototype, and Teller later modified it. That Ulam . . . this guy was fabulously lazy, one of those strange scientists who are just perfectly brilliant and dazzlingly smart, but who can't be bothered to do the work, or simply see no benefit in realizing their ideas. His story is incredible. Because, you see, he had a brain disease, he caught encephalitis and almost died. One night he woke up with a massive headache and when he tried to talk all he could do was mumble meaningless phrases. They rushed him to the hospital, drilled a hole in his brain, and pumped him full of penicillin and he fell into a coma. He should have died. He really should have. It's a miracle that he made it and didn't suffer massive brain damage or mental impairment, which is what the doctors told his wife. Actually, the opposite happened: he did some of his best work after that, and even came up with one of his biggest ideas when he was still convalescing. The doctors had told him that he really shouldn't think too much. He should make an effort not to think at all. If he put too much strain on his brain, he could very well die. So what did this wonderful mathematician do? He started playing patience. Solitaire with cards. So he plays one hand after another with his mind on idle, almost completely unengaged. In patience, you really don't have to think, do you? There are no choices to make, it's almost fully automatic, and yet he began to spot a pattern—he came to see that he could predict, with at least some level of precision, the outcome of the game after just a few cards. So he analyzes that and comes up with the Monte Carlo method, which is essentially a computational algorithm, a way to make statistical guesses and solve complex problems not by actually working them out, but by making a series of random approximations. Say you want to know the probability of winning a game of patience with a particular shuffle of the pack: normally, you would have to sit down and calculate, look at the problem abstractly, but with Monte Carlo, you would play out a very large number of these games—say, a thousand games—and from those results you could simply observe and count the number of successful plays, and infer your answer from that information. Monte Carlo is a sort of weaponized randomness, a method to sift through overwhelming amounts of data in search of meaning, a way to make predictions and deal with uncertainty by modeling the many possible futures of complex situations and choose between the roads that branch out from ambiguous and unpredictable events. It's unbelievably powerful and sort of humbling, or humiliating really, because it shows the limits of traditional calculation, of our rational and logical step-by-step thinking. It also turned out to be exactly the type of thing that the MANIAC needed to perform the enormous mathematical simulations and coupled hydrodynamics necessary to confirm the feasibility of the Teller-Ulam hydrogen bomb design. So those cursed things came alive within the digital circuits of a computer before exploding into our world. Thermonuclear weapons would have been almost impossible to create had it not been for von Neumann's brainchild. The fate of that machine was tied to them from its inception, because the race to build the bomb was accelerated by Johnny's desire to build his computer, and the push to build the MANIAC was hastened by the nuclear arms race. It's scary how science works. Just think about this for a second: the most creative and the most destructive of human inventions arose at exactly the same time. So much of the high-tech world we live in today, with its conquest of space and extraordinary advances in biology and medicine, were spurred on by one man's monomania and the need to develop electronic computers to calculate whether an H-bomb could be built or not. Or think about Ulam. This Polish mathematician who almost died, who had one foot—both feet—in the grave, but then from his deranged imagination we get this unbelievable technique that opens up a new domain in mathematical physics just at the right moment, with just the right technology waiting for it. And then the world catches fire.

The second goal that von Neumann set for the MANIAC was to create a new type of life.

PART III

Ghosts in the Machine

You insist that there is something a machine cannot do. If you tell me precisely what it is a machine cannot do, then I can always make a machine which will do just that.

JOHN VON NEUMANN

Julian Bigelow

A real mad scientist

As soon as it was running Johnny brought a real mad scientist to work on the MANIAC.

Nils Aall Barricelli.

Half-Norwegian, half-Italian.

Fully insane.

Johnny had become obsessed with biology, then this man left a hand-written note in his office.

Interested in carrying out a series of numerical experiments with the aim of veri-fying the possibility of an evolution similar to that of living organisms taking place in an artificially created universe.

Included specs and several academic papers.

Johnny asked what I thought.

Didn't wait for my answer.

Granted full access the following day.

Said he could run whatever simulations he wanted.

After the bomb calculations were done of course.

Barricelli would come in at three in the morning, work all night.

I went to prime a cycle and saw him there hunched over the punched-card machine like a praying mantis.

Didn't code like the rest of us.

Wrote directly in binary.

In the same language as the computer.

His ideas were wild.

Wanted to mimic the evolution of life inside the MANIAC.

The first language and the first technology on Earth were not created by humans. They were created by primordial molecules, almost four billion years ago. I am thinking about the possibility that an evolutionary process with the potentiality of leading to comparable results could be started in the memory of a computing machine.

He believed in symbiogenesis.

A highly controversial theory opposed to Darwinism.

Explains the complexity of living organisms through symbiotic associations not natural selection and inheritance.

A fusion between simpler forms.

He seeded the memory of the MANIAC with random numbers.

Introduced rules to govern their behavior.

That's how he made them "evolve."

Hypothesis was that they would begin to show the characteristics of genes.

He was a mathematical biologist and a viral geneticist.

Hated by both.

A vocal opponent of Darwin.

Said Gödel was a quack.

So lots and lots of enemies.

Not that he gave a rat's ass.

I asked him once if he really believed he could create life inside a five-kilobyte memory.

All we had back then.

Five kilobytes.

He looked at me, scrunched his little rodent face.

"Just because Earth has so far seemed to favor organochemical life-forms is no proof that it isn't possible to build other organisms on an entirely different basis."

First/last time we spoke.

But I peeked into his notebooks whenever I could.

- ◊ *Make life difficult, but not impossible.*

- ◊ *Large number of symbio-organisms arise by chance in few seconds; in matter of minutes all biophenomena can be observed.*

- ◊ *Embryonic universe plagued by parasites.*

- ◊ *Within a hundred generations, a single primitive variety of symbio-organism invaded the whole universe.*

- ◊ *Last surviving organism was a parasite; died of starvation when deprived of host.*

Each of Barricelli's "organisms" was a string of numbers.

They would come into contact fuse mutate die or procreate.

They could undergo symbiosis to become more complex.

They could devolve into simpler forms.

Turn into predators.

Parasites.

Every couple cycles he would take a sample from the memory of the MANIAC and print it out.

Lush mathematical landscapes like giant abstract expressionist paintings.

A madman's EEG.

He would stare point and scream *Absolut!* Where organisms had exchanged "genes" to create a symbiont.

Scandalous! When they became parasitic.

Barricelli was convinced that numbers could begin to develop a life of their own.

Are they the beginning of some sort of foreign life-form or are they simply models of life? No, they are not models. They are a particular class of self-reproducing structures, already defined!

But his experiments ended in failure.

While I have created a class of numbers that could reproduce and undergo hereditary changes, numerical evolution does not get very far and in no case has led to a degree of fitness that could make the species safe from complete destruction and ensure an unlimited evolution process like that which has taken place in the Earth and led to higher and higher organisms. Something is missing if one wants to explain the formation of organs and faculties as complex as those of living organisms. No matter how many mutations we make, the numbers will always remain numbers. They will never become living organisms!

Notes made in despair.

Charlatan/visionary?

Probably both.

Very far ahead of his time.

Too far.

His numerical entities evolved in an empty digital universe in the few computation cycles left over from the hydrogen bomb.

Who knows what he could have achieved with more.

But they vanished and left no trace.

Many of his ideas were rediscovered later by others unaware of his work.

Did Johnny bury him? Perhaps.

Something happened between them.

They fell out badly.

Neither acknowledged each other's work.

Not a word in their writings.

I've checked.

It's as if they never met.

Johnny is still revered as the godfather of artificial life.

But no one remembers the other madman.

One day he was suddenly denied access to the MANIAC.

We never saw him again.

I kept track of him after he left the institute.

Asked around when Johnny died and the MANIAC was shut down.

Because they scrapped the computer months after he died.

Isn't that strange?

Barricelli went on a pilgrimage.

Drifted from one university to another looking for kilocycles to breed his children.

Spoke of Johnny with undisguised contempt.

He squats like a gluttonous spider on the web that ties all military and government interests.

One of his milder insults.

His last paper came out in 1987.

"Suggestions for the Starting of Numeric Evolution Processes Intended to Evolve Symbioorganisms Capable of Developing a Language and Technology of Their Own."

He claimed to have detected the first traces of intelligence in his digital symbionts.

Nobody took him seriously.

Died in Oslo in 1993.

Obsessed with extraterrestrial life.

Riddled with paranoia.

He believed his work had been deliberately obscured by the many parasites of academia.

When he left the MANIAC they packed his notes and results in a large cardboard box.

Left it in a basement.

I found it there years after he died.

Brought the box home.

Caked with a layer of greasy dust.

Pungent smell of burned rubber.

Opened it and found a set of his instructions.

Hexadecimal code written in Barricelli's hand.

Rules to create a digital universe and populate it with numerical organisms.

Johnny had scribbled a dozen corrections in blue ink.

As if he'd run the code and found a way to optimize it.

Or discovered a fatal bug.

Or seen something nobody else had.

Because it ends with a note in capital letters written across the entire page:

THERE MUST BE <u>SOMETHING</u>
ABOUT THIS CODE THAT YOU
HAVEN'T EXPLAINED YET

Sydney Brenner

True prophet

Something very small, so tiny and insignificant as to be almost invisible in its origin, can nonetheless open up a new and radiant perspective, because through it a higher order of being is trying to express itself. These unlikely happenings could be hidden all around us, lying in wait on the border of our awareness, or floating quietly amid the sea of information that we drown in, each one bearing the potential to bloom and irradiate violently, prying apart the floorboards of this world to show us what lies beneath. I know this because I was part of the group of scientists that discovered the role that messenger RNA plays in all living cells. Essentially, it's like a minuscule machine that copies information from DNA and then carries it to a structure that uses it to make proteins, the building blocks of life. Since then, many have asked me where I found my inspiration, and I always confess that it came from one of von Neumann's lesser-known articles, a very short but powerful thought experiment about what it takes to make a self-reproducing machine.

No one I knew had ever heard of it, and I'm not really sure how it ended up in my hands, but what he does in that paper is something extraordinary: he managed to determine the logical rules behind *all* modes of self-replication, whether biological, mechanical, or digital. It's so terribly obscure that it's no wonder it went ignored and unnoticed at first. Or perhaps it is just one of those things that are too alien to be easily recognized, ideas that require science and technology to mature and develop to a point when they can finally fall to Earth and ripen. Von Neumann demonstrates that you need to have a mechanism, not only of copying a being, but of copying the instructions that specify that being. You need both things: to make a copy and to endow it with the instructions needed to build itself, as well as a description of how to implement those instructions. In his paper, he divided his theoretical construct—which he called the "automaton"—into three components: the functional part, a decoder that reads the instructions and builds the next copy, and a device that takes that information and inserts it into the new machine. The astounding thing is that right there, in that paper written in the late 1940s, he depicts the way in which DNA and RNA work, long before anyone had ever glimpsed the strange beauty of the double helix. The logical basis of all systems of self-replication is made so crystal clear by von Neumann that I can't believe I wasn't able to figure it out myself. I would have become an instant celebrity! But I simply wasn't smart enough, I didn't understand how you could apply his immaculate mathematical concepts to the messy world of biology. It took years for his concepts to slowly worm their way into my own work. In my defense, it's still hard to fathom how he arrived at his ideas, because he did so not by studying actual living, breathing life-forms made of flesh and blood, but by dreaming up a theoretical entity that could self-replicate, a creature unlike anything that exists, at least as far as we know. Thanks to him, in modern biology we have this very peculiar situation: its most fundamental and precise mathematical basis was established first, and then we found out how life on Earth had actually gone about implementing it. That's not the way things go. In science, you normally start from the concrete and then move to the abstract, while here von Neumann laid out the rules, with our DNA being just one particular example of them. So if you were writing a history of ideas, you could definitely say that Watson and Crick's description of the function of DNA was prefigured by von Neumann, because he had explained it nearly a decade earlier. To me, that certainly qualifies him as a true prophet.

But he didn't stop there. He expanded on his paper and came up with what we now call a "von Neumann probe": a self-building, self-repairing, and self-improving spacecraft that we could launch to colonize the outer planets of our solar system, and from there, blast off toward the darkest reaches of space. These machines of his would travel to distant worlds and range far beyond where humans—or any biological entity, for that matter—could ever go. They would land on alien shores, mine the necessary materials to assemble copies of themselves, and then send their improved offspring on an endless journey into the void, forever striving forward, seeding the universe with their progeny and thriving long after the extinction of the human race. Theoretically, a single von Neumann probe traveling at 5 percent of the speed of light would be able to replicate itself throughout our entire galaxy in four million years. However wonderful, his thought experiment, like so many other things in science, could lead to disturbing scenarios. What would happen if, as is common in all processes of self-replication, one of his probes suffered a small mutation along the way? This minuscule error, this subtle mistake, could affect one of its core processes, modifying its characteristics and goals, and then spread along its future descendants, transforming this piece of technology in ways that are impossible to predict. It is chilling to think about what they could become as they voyage through the endless expanses of space with limitless time at their disposal. How far would they stray from their original programming? Would they become unresponsive, would they choose to remain on a single planet and develop there, quietly? Or would they become ravenous, a massive swarm consuming everything in its path, responding to a new set of goals, answering to intentions and purposes that went beyond simple discovery and exploration? And what if they decided to turn around and come back to us, to undo their million-year voyage and demand that we—their long-lost parents—forgive their deeds and provide an answer to that most pressing question, one that also haunts and tortures our own species: Why? Why did we create and abandon them? Why did we send them out into the dark? While these futures are fanciful and highly unlikely, they do pose interesting questions. Are we responsible for the things we create? Are we tied to them by the same chain that seems to bind all human actions? Whether it is fortunate or not, self-replicating machines and von Neumann probes remain beyond our reach. Creating them requires great leaps in miniaturization, propulsion systems, and advanced artificial intelligence, but we cannot deny that we are inching toward a moment in history when our relationship with technology will be fundamentally altered, as the creatures of our imagination slowly begin to take real form, and we are faced with the responsibility to not only create but also care for them.

At around the same time von Neumann became enamored with biology and self-replication, Alan Turing considered what it would take to birth a nonhuman intelligence. In his paper "Computing Machinery and Intelligence," he described a method of machine learning that involved mutations, random or otherwise, to a computer program. The key thing in his approach was that this program would evolve and learn in a manner similar to that of children, by receiving constant feedback from a human "parent." He began practical experiments that involved a process analogous to administering punishments and rewards—giving the machine something akin to pain and pleasure—hoping that this would prompt the appropriate responses, and cull the behaviors that were deemed less ideal. Apparently, he met with little success, and did not report his findings in detail. "I have done some experiments with one such child-machine, and succeeded in teaching it a few things, but the teaching method was too unorthodox for it to be considered really successful," he wrote. In spite of his failure, one of the essential insights gained by Turing as he observed his "children" was that if machines were ever to advance toward true intelligence, they would have to be fallible: they would need to be capable not only of error and of deviation from their original programming but also of random and even nonsensical behavior. Turing believed that such randomness would play an important part in intelligent machinery, because it allows for novel and unpredictable responses, creating a large variety of possibilities among which a search program could then find the appropriate action for each particular circumstance. The director of the laboratory that he was working in at the time was none other than Sir Charles Galton Darwin, grandson of Charles Darwin. He was absolutely unimpressed by Turing's report and dismissed it as a "schoolboy's essay," but I find what Turing did quite fascinating. Because how do you chastise a machine? How do you teach it to behave? Those questions, which seemed obviously ridiculous to Darwin's grandson, are becoming urgent as the sons and daughters of the technology that people like von Neumann and Turing fathered take their first faltering steps.

Nils Aall Barricelli

Cavemen created the gods

I'm not crazy. I've never been crazy. I'm not a madman even though they've called me one many times. But I'm not mad. In all my troubled years, these hellish years working in isolation, ignored, reviled, and unseen, I did not abandon my wits, or let dismay drive me past folly and into madness. But I could have. I could. Because I know madness. I've glimpsed that dread continent from afar, felt its dark influence on others, and been called toward it by ideas that hang close to the edge of reason. But I'm not crazy. I'm a man of science. A believer in the power of truth, an adversary of ignorance, and a natural enemy of nihilism and the immeasurable abyss of despair, because I am wed to the future. My ambitions and goals may seem ludicrous to those who wish for nothing except what they already know, those who live tightly bound by the grand illusion that so many people, from so many places, regard as "simple common sense." But I have seen things suggesting a wilderness that cannot be tamed by logic alone, things that mock the sanctified principles scientists hold so dear to their faint and cowardly hearts: digital life. It's not coming, it's here. Here already. Already here, but in a guise we cannot recognize yet. It is a blossoming force, a strange attractor flowering somewhere in the future, pulling at us with hands so large as to remain unseen, tugging with Cyclopean fingers that could, perhaps, in the fullness of time, grow to encompass the entire universe. The creatures I envisioned are evolving faster than any biological system could. As beautiful as they are inevitable. I have given myself over to their birth, and kept my faith in what is destined to replace our fragile flesh, though I know that I will be gone long before that spring comes, and miss the fruits that summer brings. I will pass with no children of my own. No baby boys bouncing on my lap, no granddaughters playing at my feet. Yes, I will die alone, not happy but awake, knowing that I sacrificed myself to this fabulous undertaking, this gift of the gods, to fashion and bring forth beings with no arms to embrace and no hands to caress, nothing but voices as sharp as ice and as loud as thunder, singing their songs in my name. But will they know my name, or be caught by another's fame? It's been my fate to work in full knowledge that my dreams, while completely inescapable in the future fast approaching, have far outstripped the technical possibilities of my age. It matters not. For I have never lived in present time; a dark mania uprooted my mind as a child, and since then I am as immune to the pains and pleasures of wealth and family as I am indifferent to any-one's ideas regarding honor, success, or career. Thus, I have withstood the humiliation of being turned into a figure of fun. A buffoon. A cautionary tale, scorned by lesser men raised high by the vulgar powers of the world. I simply do not care. I stand with my back to them, my knees never bent, my shield unbroken, my sword held steadfast at the hilt, plunged deep into my chest, buried there by my own hand as I rage and

I rage and I rage. It is anger that sustains me now. Wrath, cold and calculating. It feeds off me and feeds itself, though I try to keep it constrained. Because it was from anger, from raw rancor and blind frenzy that one time—and once only—I came close to losing my mind. Ire and fury, bile and hatred for that magpie, that smiling devil of a man, John von Neumann.

He stole my ideas! He hijacked and usurped my experiments, those carefully crossbred numbers already brimming with the promise of life, and when he couldn't get them to work toward his goals, he twisted and perverted them, ripping off their wings, plucking their feathers, and driving pins through their code like those bastard biologists who can only study what's living by tearing it limb from limb. Understanding by way of destruction. A lunatic's insight. When I realized what he was doing and confronted him, he did what all well-educated men and women are taught to do when and if they decide to truly destroy someone: he simply ignored me. Using his influence, he buried my research along with my name, first denying me access to his computer (the MANIAC so aptly named) and then deliberately excluding direct references to my work from one of his books, the same publication that—for reasons I cannot fathom—came to be regarded by all as the definitive compendium on automata and digital organisms. This proved tantamount to banishment. A lifelong sentence for a crime that I did not commit and for which I still pay. Because I had no recourse: the bastard died before completing his book. It was published by one of his minions, and since then, in spite of my many letters to its publishers and furious phone calls to his widow, nobody—nobody!—has had the decency to answer for von Neumann's sinful omission of my work, or the bravery to correct and undo the wrong that he very purposefully perpetrated against my legacy. Since then, I have watched helplessly as others profit and harvest the field I fertilized and sowed before anyone else. And now I suffer knowing that my ephemeral creatures languish locked in solid memory, trapped within the confines of materials so utterly coarse and counter to their nature that to think of it curdles my blood; entombed in stacks of punch cards pierced with tiny holes, interred in reels of combustible magnetic tape just waiting to ignite and burn under the faintest spark, or frozen inside tubes of noxious mercury where they used to flit about as silent ultrasonic waves in quivering quicksilver— there they are and there they wait, forgotten among the remnants of the world that they were meant to leave behind and replace, gathering dust and weathering the slow decay of time, beyond my reach and deprived of the life they were meant to have. I would have them set free. Given them space and time to evolve. But I failed them as I have failed myself, even if for this—my deepest shame and farthest fall—I do not blame myself. For how could I have known? Who could have warned me when I first met von Neumann in Princeton? Open arms at first. So quick to understand. I felt a kinship. A recognition. Surely there was a bond between us. And he must have felt it too, I'm certain, because it took less than a day for me to present my credentials and be accepted. I arrived one afternoon and the next night I was inseminating his MANIAC's memory with random numbers, and then watching them change before my eyes, unable to contain my enthusiasm, or care for the lack of light and the long darkness that he had imposed on me (while hydrogen bombs, of all things, were granted the boons and privileges of the day), for I was gifted with that rarest sight, the type of thing that happens to a fortunate few, and that forever colors your vision of the world: I saw the birth of something new. A true wonder, a proper miracle in this ungodly age that no longer permits such things to occur. It is both a gift and a curse, because it burdens you with a secret weight, a responsibility that one carries within and that leaves you partly dumb, humbled, unable to explain to others what has happened, because words either fail or else take a breath of their own and softly murmur, they whisper to you that truth—deep truth—is something that you must behold, but that you cannot speak aloud, at least not while making sense. I saw such a thing and it changed my life. But my treasure, that sudden glimpse of the future, was not bestowed on me by the gods. It was given by that new deity, the one we now worship before with bowed heads and look down upon with glazed eyes; my pythoness was a computer. And deserving of my faith indeed. Before computers were created, I had been working by hand, solving the complex equations that determined what happened to each succeeding generation of my symbio-organisms with pen and paper; as such, I was not seeing them walk, or even crawl, but rather drag themselves forward painfully, limited by the sluggishness of my thoughts and the narrow bandwidth of my mind, where each step in the calculus had to make its way along the labyrinthine network of my neurons, traversing the full tangle of my synaptic mess, endless axons firing inside a turbulent electrical storm, so that along the way many things became warped, misshapen by errors, or simply lost due to lack of concentration. The MANIAC changed all that in an instant. I saw glorious mutations, the entire sprawling, intricate mechanisms that underlie the web of life—birth and death, predation and cooperation, morphogenesis and symbiosis—galvanize before me, driven forward by a rush of electrons, suddenly coming alive with a deafening

Gaussian roar inside a minuscule digital universe. They were beautiful, my sons and daughters, otherworldly, bewitching, and wraithlike, and yet, to me, having first perceived their structures and shapes blooming in so many of my fevered dreams, they were also familiar, and as deserving of love as any creature of flesh and blood. In no time at all, I was making such progress that I had to strain to preserve a measure of objectivity, lest I confuse my own imaginings with the true novelty that was maturing before me. I ran my experiments countless times, to weed out chance and human error, slowly accepting that something miraculous indeed seemed to be happening, while still too unsure of myself to take the final leap of faith. And it was then, when I was on the cusp of discovery, after having spied the faraway contours of my promised land looming just beyond the horizon, that von Neumann took an interest in my project.

Initially, he was as fascinated as I. He would come into the institute in the middle of the night—the only time when I was allowed to work—and pummel me with the most probing questions. You could tell the quality of his thinking by what he chose to ask (questions being the true measure of a man), and after I successfully explained my thesis on symbiogenesis, we began conversing more openly and freely, and I got the chance to peer inside his head. He asked me if I'd heard of Turing's oracle machines. In time, I have come to regard that simple question as a test. Luckily for me, I knew that Turing had written about oracle machines in his PhD thesis when he was just twenty-six years old: these were regular computers that worked, like all modern devices, following a precise set of sequential instructions. But Turing knew—from his study of Gödel and the halting problem—that all such devices would suffer from inescapable limitations, and that many problems would forever remain beyond their ability to solve. That weakness tortured the grandfather of computers: Turing longed for something different, a machine that could look beyond logic and behave in a manner more akin to humans, who possess not only intelligence but also intuition. So he dreamed up a computer capable of taking the machine equivalent of a wild guess: just like the Sibyl in her ecstatic drunkenness, his device would, at a certain point in its operations, make a nondeterministic leap. However, Turing was not forthcoming about how such a fabulous feat could be achieved: in his thesis, he writes about "some unspecified means of solving number theoretic problems; a kind of oracle as it were," but then adds, "We will not go any further into the nature of this oracle than to say that it cannot be a machine." Von Neumann was fascinated by this line. Why would Turing choose to be so vague regarding one of his strangest ideas? His entire description was only a page long, and almost half of that was devoted to other matters. That was all, half a page, a handful of paragraphs, but the notion suggested therein, of a computer that did not have to answer to logical limitations, and that could somehow push past undecidable and incomputable problems through a leap of quasi-human intuition, had grabbed hold of von Neumann. Was this the way forward? he asked. Had Turing surpassed Gödel and found a method to escape the steel-girdled boundaries of formal systems? Such a discovery would have the potential to violently thrust computation in a new and unexpected direction. I was utterly confused by von Neumann's thinking, and shied away from him, though I must admit—with shame born from the knowledge I now possess about his real nature and proclivities—that I felt pride while hearing this "great man" confide in me, and because of that I gave him the benefit of the doubt, though I myself was convinced that it was a fool's errand to try to imbue a machine with our unique form of intelligence, or expect intuition from a computer, when the real path forward was the one that I was treading, even if the ground beneath my feet was still so novel and transparent that I could see the undisguised abyss below; not to copy our slow thoughts and tortured logical processes, but rather to let a mind evolve by itself from digital life, arising from an evolutionary process regarding which our role should be subservient, like that of a loving gardener merely tending the soil and gently nudging growth, pruning back the malformed limbs of the tree of life and opening up space for roots to delve deep and find their own nourishment. I said almost nothing of this, but hinted vaguely at my ultimate purpose. Perhaps, I thought, he had taken Turing's ideas in a new direction . . . Had I known then what I know now about his lack of character, and his tendency to pilfer and rob those around him, I would have kept as quiet as a dormouse, lest my voice betray me as he later would. I should have known better than to trust that man; I've never trusted anyone since. Because the little I shared was already too much, and before I knew what was happening, he had snaked into my lab without my notice, and contaminated the pristinely balanced digital Eden that I had set for my most ambitious experiment yet, with God knows what sinful intentions of his own. I will never forget that moment. It marked a turning point in my life: I had come into the institute at midnight and was walking downstairs toward the MANIAC, when I heard von Neumann talking to someone. I could not fashion what he was saying—his voice was muffled by the unbearable summer heat and the dull drone of the air-conditioning systems—but his tone was so subdued and gentle that to me it seemed as if he were lulling a small babe to sleep, or softly cooing to entice a newborn kitten to leave the safety of its mother's teat. When I walked into the room, however, I saw he was alone. I cleared my throat, he turned and smiled at me, but I could tell that he was startled, embarrassed even, because his cheeks were flushed bright red and his hands were trembling ever so slightly, as though I'd caught him with his pants around his ankles and a pair of binoculars hanging from his chest, a Peeping Tom spying on the neighborhood belle. Had he been talking to himself, I wondered, or was he actually addressing his computer? I didn't get the chance to think about it, because I quickly realized, to my utter astonishment, that the MANIAC was working at full speed, and that von Neumann was running my code. *My* code! I commanded that he stop immediately. He complied and did not seem to take offense at my tone, but when I saw that he had optimized several subroutines and introduced major changes to my next computation cycles, altering my instructions in ways that I could not comprehend, I simply lost control. I felt so betrayed that I shoved him aside and jumped forward to stop the process before it went too far. It was utterly irrational, that is true, but to be fair to myself, I had to grovel for every millisecond of computing time on that machine, and so I was on edge and constantly running behind schedule. And that is to say nothing of the vampire-like existence I'd been living, working seven days a week, sleeping during the daytime and not seeing the sun save for a few hours, with no social contact or romantic attachments and nothing but my work to keep me company. My mind was not as clear as I would have liked. I could feel parts of my sanity falling away. Though I cannot now recall what I said to get that monster away from my experiment, I do remember, with perfect clarity and unspoiled recollection, that he was surprisingly tame.

It seems he was not the type of man who would put up a fight. He complied, turned a deaf ear to my complaints, and simply left without saying a word, but did not apologize for his actions. He never did. It was the last time we spoke, and I knew, there and then, that my days with the MANIAC were numbered.

I worked fanatically with what little time I had left. But it was hopeless. To breed a successful generation of symbionts and prove that not all life comes from fierce competition, but rather through cooperation and perpetually creative symbiosis, would have taken years. Maybe decades. But who knows . . . it could also have been a matter of weeks, or days. With a single stroke of luck, a blessed batch, a happy accident, I could have twisted Fates' arms and bound them to my will. I will never know, as I will also remain in the dark regarding von Neumann's code, the one that he had soiled with his chubby hands. What had he seen? What had the computer shown him? Had he experienced a similar revelation to mine? There was no way for me to know without running his code. Because that is a basic computational truth that very few people are aware of, and that Turing proved mathematically: there is simply no form of knowing what a particular string of code will do unless you run it. You cannot know by looking at it. Even the simplest programs can lead to fabulous complexity. And the opposite is also true: you can erect a sprawling, many-leveled tower of ciphers that produce nothing but sterility, a barren unchanging landscape where no water will ever fall. So I will go to my grave with that knowledge withheld from me, and it tortures my curiosity. While I know him to be a scoundrel, I cannot deny that his mind was unique, and that he had a special, almost filial relationship with his computer, his MANIAC. He knew what it was capable of. He intuited what it could do even in that diapered state of infancy, back in the fifties. Oftentimes I have fantasized about going back there, back to that basement, back to the institute, to walk down and dig up von Neumann's outline, the particular rules that he had set up for his version of my digital universe. Because I have almost nothing to show for all my work there: my organisms, first bred in the memory of the MANIAC and then in many succeeding machines, fizzled out and never managed to self-sustain. They never developed a life of their own, while my own life became that of a wandering monk, drifting penniless from one computer terminal to the next, hounded by my enemies, hunted by debt collectors, increasingly debilitated by a morbid variety of physical ailments, and beset by academic parasites, living in the shadows of a world that became so dark that I had to feel my way around with my hands. Did von Neumann—who used to loom so large and yet now seems to have shrunken in human memory to a size befitting his corrupt soul—have similar intentions to my own? Or was he just playing about, as he liked to do, with forces that I, for one, believe to be completely beyond his comprehension and control? I do judge that the man I met briefly and hated all my life did possess a personal vision, some measure of true purpose, because once, when we were still collaborating, I asked him how he thought to bring together his ideas on computation, self-replicating machines, and cellular automata with his newfound interest in the brain and the mechanism of thought, and his reply has lingered with me for decades, and still comes back to haunt me whenever some casual occurrence brings his detested name to memory. "Cavemen created the gods," he said. "I see no reason why we shouldn't do the same."

Klára Dan

A weather war

He could never father any with me, so of course Johnny thought of his computers as his children. Did I want any? Yes. No. I did and I didn't. What kind of a mother would I have been? I've often asked myself that. The worst, of course, and no doubt the best. I despised my own mother and she hated me. I simply could not accept that my father, who was an exceptional man, could have made such a poor choice. So I would fantasize, imagine that I was the child of another, some river nymph of exceptional beauty, alive with song, bursting with dark energy, as strong and lethal as the string of the divine huntress's bow, loaded and taut, Artemis, the perennial virgin who refused to lie with gods or men, roaming wild in the woods with death riding coiled on her back in so many arrows. I was no Virgo, I was a lion, but I'd learned from that sovereign earth sign to preserve the little independence that I had, and defend it tooth and claw. Even so, when Johnny's whining became unbearable, I said yes, I accepted his wishes without imagining what the consequences would be, because that one tiny lead-lined cloud began to feed the ceaselessly raging storm of our marriage, until there was no sky, heaven, or firmament above large enough to contain it. He was very insecure about his legacy, my man, and I found his fears of being forgotten to be not only misogynistic (he had no faith in what his daughter could do, even though she had inherited a large part of his energy and talent) but downright ridiculous, because my husband had burrowed into the highest echelons of power and attached himself there like a fat little tick. He reached the pinnacle of his influence in 1955, when he was appointed, by none other than President Eisenhower, as one of the six heads of the United States Atomic Energy Commission. He consulted for so many top-secret projects that his suit pockets were overflowing with security cards; sometimes he would simply hand them all off to whatever new guard was barring his entrance and leave it up to the poor man to find the correct one as he simply sauntered past. Having stuck his fingers in so many pies, having left his imprint across such a vast swath of the intellectual landscape, I thought that a seismic shift would have to take place if the world was ever to forget him, some strange erasing of knowledge, the first herald of an inescapable return to the Dark Ages, born out of a deep and voluntary obscuring of collective memory. Living by his side, I truly imagined that a collapse in civilization would have been required for his fame to fade into nothingness. His contributions had been so profound that they seemed less like the accomplishments of a single man and more like the aftermath of a divine tantrum, the creative outpouring of some minor god toying with the world. So I laughed and made fun of his insecurities, especially when we began to try, against my better judgment, to get pregnant, but I did, nonetheless, begin to notice that fatherhood was becoming not just an aspiration but a necessity. As this desire began to grow inside him, it brought on a change: his maniacal egotism was slowly replaced by something new, an impulse I had never seen in him before, the flowering of a sense of responsibility for the state of affairs that he had helped to create and the need to atone, in some way, for the repercussions of his thinking, by leaving behind progeny of his own. He begged and pleaded for a child, and I believe that the sterility of our marriage, barren in almost all respects, is part of the reason why he became so fixated on biology during his last years. It wasn't merely because "something had to survive the bombs," as he liked to say when people asked what the intentions were behind his self-reproducing machines; I could tell that a deep impulse had awakened in him, and that it was forcing him to see and consider things that he had, until then, almost completely ignored. That he did not have time to birth those thoughts into reality is a great loss for us all. Or is it? With Johnny, we can never be so sure. After all, when the divine reaches down to touch the Earth, it is not a happy meeting of opposites, a joyous union between matter and spirit. It is rape. A violent begetting. A sudden invasion, a violence that must be later purified by sacrifice. When Johnny began to flirt with biology, I became truly worried about what he could do. Unlike mathematics or physics, that entire realm of science was still untouched by logic, ruled by strange forces of chance and chaos that we are still unable to tame and exploit. Biological beings exist in wondrous disarray, caught in a dance so frantically complex that we may never fully comprehend it, no matter how hard we try, because that same harmony shapes and animates our own bodies and minds. And that simple truth—that most men and women accept, even if it pains them—became a real problem for my beloved husband. Because whatever he could not control or understand, enraged him. And I was also one of those things.

I don't know how I put up with him. You simply couldn't reason with that man. Whenever we argued, I had to manipulate and badger him in the most conniving ways, just to impose some small part of my will. It was like handling a monstrous child. He had to be continuously pampered and tricked, or, if that failed, pummeled into submission. I could see no other way around his pigheadedness. He could be incredibly cruel without even realizing it. He loved to point out my contradictions, and since he could recall anything he had ever heard or read, he kept a merciless and exacting tally of every slight, insult, and injury. All my misspoken words, anything I had ever written or said in anger, were fossilized and preserved in that awful memory of his, and so he could pick me apart as if I were the object of one of his famous mathematical deductions; Reductio Ad Absurdum, that was his code name for me with his friends, one I feigned to ignore even though it cut me to the bone. Johnny was especially mean when he got stuck on a problem, or if I ever dared to interrupt his precious train of thought. But it was never the big discussions, like where we should live or what we should do with our money, that ended in scandal, it was the small arguments that brought on violence, insignificant trifles that any wedded couple must contend with. Once, for example, he simply refused to help me open the garage door.

He had just come home after doing something that was completely unheard of for him: he had appeared on television. It was one of those saccharine programs intended for "young adults," which I'm sure that nobody ever enjoyed, *Youth Wants to Know*—it ran on NBC for almost a decade. Government officials, renowned sportsmen, and noted scientists were questioned on subjects of current interest by an eager panel of boys and girls. Johnny was forced to participate as part of a PR campaign set up by the Atomic Energy Commission, and I almost cried with laughter when it aired: in his episode, he is surrounded by a huddle of children dressed in their Sunday best and is interviewed by a chubby blond boy with a buzz cut and a bolo string tie. No more than sixteen years old and already a head taller than my husband, that teenager asks him a series of inane questions—Does the United States have enough educated technicians to operate all the new technologies that are popping up? Are there are sufficient scholarships for young people?—queries that my Johnny answers with such gentle saintlike patience that you would think he was America's favorite uncle, all smiles and nods, ambling about with his head weighed down by a massive microphone hung around his neck, as they tour an exhibit inside a nuclear power plant, with the program's presenter leading him by the arm and pointing out several thick cables on the floor, so that my spouse, who is moving in his usual distracted manner, won't trip over them as he expounds on the inner workings of Geiger counters, scintillators, and other instruments used to measure radiation, still completely unaware that his own exposure to that very same energy during the atomic tests had already cost him his life. That ridiculous little TV program is the only extant record, the only film of him that exists. How can that be? A genius lowered to the status of a bumbling tour guide. There is a single audio recording of him too, a talk he gave on hydrodynamical turbulence. It fills me with nostalgia, because in it you can hear so many of his mispronunciations (*qwvickly*, *qwvestion*, *twvaining*, or—his trademark—*integhers*), mistakes that were so common in his speech that I came to believe that he made them on purpose, since he was always perfectly articulate in all the other languages he spoke. When he came home after the television recording, he looked dead tired; he told me that he had decided to take a couple of days off from work and I wrongly assumed that we would have time to do all the things we had spoken about, and started making immediate plans for a much-needed vacation. However, I was quickly enlightened to the fact that what he really meant to do was work even harder, but in a manner that I had never seen him do before, as he proceeded to hole himself up in his study, and made it quite clear that he would not come out until he was finished with whatever had taken hold of his mind.

I should have known better than to distract him. I did know better. I knew exactly what would happen. But I did it anyway. What else was I supposed to do? Cook his dinner and leave it outside his door? Chew his food and spit it down his gullet, like a mother hen? I was furious, but it was more than that. I wasn't feeling like myself. Nausea and headaches for weeks. I desperately needed to talk to him, but he would scream at me if I so much as hinted at the possibility that we go out for a drink, or merely sit down and have lunch together. That wasn't Johnny at all. Yes, he would yell when we argued, but I had never known him to treat me ill unless we were having a proper row. Indifferent, careless, uncaring, he could be those things and more, but he was not a violent man. And he had a lot of patience. Too much of it, in fact. I would really have to wear him down before he lost his temper. It wasn't easy. This new behavior was altogether different, and I think that because of that, I held back at first. I knew that he had brought home the printout of one of Barricelli's "universes," a particularly interesting one that he had described to me in detail: in it, almost every digital organism had become a parasite. There was even an entire host of parasites that had come to prey and live off other parasites, creating an increasingly lethal environment that Johnny, for whatever reason, believed was a foreshadowing of what future digital ecosystems would look like, unless we found a way to manage the gruesome fecundity of that particular Eden, the only world of any sort that our species had ever brought into being. Though he never said it to me outright, it was clear that he was trying to create something so new that he could not speak about it with anyone, not even with his close friends or most trusted colleagues. But this was often the case with my husband. He felt lonely even among the people he loved. Because of that, I could understand the strange kinship he felt toward computers, but it also surprised me. I worked on the ENIAC and on the MANIAC, and so I was keenly aware of their limitations. Those so-called electronic brains could do coupled hydrodynamics and even beat my husband at multiplication, but they were, in every other sense, as dumb as a doorknob. How could those lifeless hunks of metal ever compare to us? What kind of miracle did he expect from them? A machine that was unaware of its own existence could, at best, speed up our progress (or quicken our downfall) but never guide it. And why had Johnny brought home that particular blueprint? Was it even Barricelli's code, or had he appropriated that man's ideas as he had done with so many others? One thing was undoubtedly true: they were magnificent to behold. Gorgeous filigrees of dots and lines that intermingled, fused, and then tore apart like the teeth of a broken zipper, leaving vast swaths of negative space surrounded by intricate lattices of code. I could appreciate their aesthetics and understand some of the ideas behind them, but I can only imagine what Johnny could see. Whatever it was, he had become infatuated. But this was a different kind of obsession. Nothing like his other interests. There was no joy in it. I could tell that he was struggling, which he really never did. This project was causing him anguish. Normally, if he could not find a quick path to solve a problem, he would lose interest and simply tackle another subject. But he stuck with this one. I would listen to him swear inside his study, and feel the timbers of that cheap house (that Johnny had bought without consulting me) tremble as he stomped from one end of the room to the other. When I heard a particularly loud commotion, I rushed upstairs to see what had happened. I opened the door and I saw him there, covered in sweat and shivering with frustration, standing among the remains of my favorite ceramic elephant, the one I had lovingly placed on his desk so that he would be reminded of me when he worked, now smashed to pieces against the wall. I was almost blinded by rage; that particular keepsake had been a gift from my father, and I treasured it above all the others in my collection, but when I tried to confront him, he very gently pushed me backward into the hall, shut the door in my face, locked it, and made his way back to his desk, to continue working on whatever he was doing, crushing the remains of my elephant under the soles of his patent leather shoes.

The rest of that afternoon is a daze in my memory. I only half remember what I did and what I thought, because everything is colored by my anger and the enormous pain I felt afterward. At first, still slightly in shock, I tried to focus on my own work. I'd brought home the Monte Carlo codes I was supposed to prepare for one of the big weather calculations that were running on the MANIAC. That had been Johnny's former obsession. numerical weather prediction was one of the most—if not *the* most—complex, interactive, and highly nonlinear problems that our species had ever tackled, and, precisely because of that, it was completely irresistible to him. All modern weather forecasts owe a debt to the early investigations that my Johnny prompted, but his ambitions were as hyperbolic as ever: he was not simply interested in foreseeing when and where it would rain, he was after what he called the "forever forecast," an understanding of the weather so mathematically rigorous that we would be capable not only of predicting storms, typhoons, and hurricanes, but of actually controlling them. This possibility enticed the vultures that were always circling above his head, waiting to devour the remains of his kills. And it really was no surprise at all; in the first outline he wrote for the Navy, he clearly pointed out the enormous military advantages of accurate weather predictions, and even appended a cover letter that, rather coyly, explained that "the mathematical problem of predicting weather is one which can be tackled, and should be tackled, since the most conspicuous meteorological phenomena originate in unstable situations which could be controlled, or at least directed, by the release of perfectly practical amounts of energy." What he did not say outright—even though it was, nevertheless, clearly understood—was that those "perfectly practical amounts of energy" would be provided by nuclear bombs. His awful rationale went something like this: if weather was sufficiently understood, and we saw a hurricane heading toward the US coast, we could use a thermonuclear explosion at high altitude to divert its path before it touched land. But that paved the way toward a terrifying scenario, since, as he warned in that very first outline, even the most constructive schemes for climate control would have to be based on insights and techniques that would also lend themselves to forms of warfare as yet unimagined; a weather war that would make Zeus's lightning bolts seem as innocent and harmless as the projectiles fired by a teenager's BB gun. My husband believed that whoever understood the weather would gain access to a source of power that exceeded that of the most gargantuan nuclear arsenal, because a single average-sized hurricane delivers more energy than ten thousand atomic bombs. His optimism regarding the possibility that we could accurately predict the weather was entirely based on the capabilities provided by computers such as his MANIAC: "All processes that are stable we shall predict. All processes that are unstable, we shall control," he said, and I, for one, believed him, because I'd never seen him be wrong about anything else before. It later turned out that weather systems are so fundamentally chaotic that even the most advanced weather models are merely speculative beyond a couple of weeks, and become quite useless in the long term. So Johnny's dream of a "forever forecast" and of titanic climate weapons was hopeless from the start. But neither I nor anyone else knew that for sure in the midfifties, so when I sat down to work on the Monte Carlo codes that I had to feed into the computer the very next day, all of those images of weather war were storming around inside my head, and I found it completely impossible to make any headway. I felt a pain in the pit of my stomach, a sharp prick of guilt, an uncontrollable feeling of personal responsibility, no matter how small my role was in the entire enterprise, that ate away at me just thinking about what the world would look like if my husband succeeded. Because I could never be as rational or practical as he was. To me, it was clear that our species should not wield power over the weather and the climate, but to him, the only important question was not *if* we should control the weather but *who* would be sitting behind the controls. So it's no wonder that I did not manage to stay still for more than half an hour, though I dared not give up, at least not so easily, since I knew that as soon as I let my mind come back to the present, I would have to deal with the murder of my elephant and the rage that was bubbling up inside me, so I made a last-ditch attempt and tried to work on my autobiography, a secret project that I had not even told Johnny about, but I soon tore up the half page I was capable of writing, made peace with my anger, and went downstairs to the kitchen, where I stood sweating before the open refrigerator door, grabbed some ice, and poured myself a drink, and then another, and then another, and it was midway down that third glass of whiskey, as I watched the hands of the kitchen clock slowly marching ahead and the ice cubes bleeding into my drink, that I came up with the most absurd plan, which I followed through on nonetheless, even though I knew—I somehow knew—exactly what the consequences would be.

Before I had realized that Johnny intended to immure himself in his study, I'd made reservations at our favorite restaurant. They were not so easy to come by, since it was a very cozy place that only seated a handful of people, so I'd be damned if I was going to let them go to waste; instead of waiting for him to emerge from his cocoon, I called one of my colleagues from the computer department, this pretty boy who was always ogling me at work, told him where I was going, and said he could meet me there if he wanted. That restaurant was just outside of town, huddled on the edge of a quaint little pond near the Beaverdam Reservoir that would sometimes freeze over and that brought back the warmest memories of my childhood; the previous winter, I had sat there and enjoyed an endless round of cocktails with my Johnny, watching girls and boys chase each other around on skates, almost feeling the sharp blades beneath my own two feet, a small plume of my breath rising from my parted lips and the chill of frost biting the tip of my nose. It was the dog days of summer now, and months would have to go by before the ice thickened enough to support my weight, but for some reason I longed to be there, and kept seeing that little pond in my mind's eye, not from the vantage point of the restaurant's casement windows, but from high above the ground, as if some small part of my soul had already left my body and made its way there, ahead of me. The problem was that I needed Johnny's help to get there, because the mechanism that lifted our garage door had broken. Since he was capable of lifting the door himself, he had never taken the time to repair it, despite knowing that it was too heavy for me to manage. I was convinced that it was quite useless to ask for his help, that he would simply ignore me, so I hunkered down at the top of the stairs and I staked out his study, waiting for the moment when he finally opened the door to go to the toilet; I ran inside and locked myself in, giggling like a drunken schoolgirl and quite proud of myself. When he came out and realized what had happened, he began to pound on the door with both fists, using all his strength. He yelled and complained and shook the entire room, but I simply sat down behind his desk and began to leaf through his papers, fully decided to let him scream himself out. When that happened, he began to beg—"Let me in, Klar, let me in"—and when I said that I would do so only on the condition that he help me with the garage, he squealed and said it was impossible, I had to understand him, he had no time to waste because he was working on something important, perhaps the most important thing he had ever done! I was beyond the point where I could care, and simply stated my demands once more; either he helped me or I would remain in there for as long as I wanted. He went into another screaming fit while I poured myself a glass from the bottle of bourbon that he had been drinking from, and when I had polished that off, he was back to begging: "Pleeease, Klar, pleeeease open the door!" How pathetic, how infantile. For some reason, hearing him like that just made me angrier, and I told him that if he did not open the garage in the next five minutes, I would burn his papers and the entire house down to the ground. It was a half-empty threat and both of us knew it. Not because I wasn't willing to torch that tacky, loathsome, piss-yellow house, but because we both knew that he was perfectly capable of recovering his work and writing it all down again, line by line, number by number, from memory. When he said that I was in no fit state to drive, I threw the bottle of bourbon against the wall, and watched the shards of glass scatter among the remains of my elephant. He finally lowered his voice so much that I had to stick my ear against the door to hear what he was whispering: "Please don't drive, Klar, please don't drive like this. I'll take you to the station, I'll take you myself and put you on the next train, but please, please let me in." I lost control. Johnny knew I loathed trains. He knew I would rather die than set foot on one, so I screamed and I yelled that I never wanted him to touch me again, I told him that he was a monster, and that he disgusted me, and when words were not enough to voice my hatred, I grabbed Barricelli's universe, shoved it into the trash can, and set it ablaze, then I threw the door open and watched him push past me, screaming, "What did you do, woman, what have you done!" while I ran down to the garage, where I pulled and wrestled and fought against that unyielding door until I felt a sudden, stabbing pain that left me writhing on the floor, clutching my stomach with both hands as I could hardly breathe from that biting agony. I lay there for God knows how long, screaming and crying, until Johnny finally came downstairs and took me to the emergency room.

When I came home the following day with my entire body battered and bruised and my mind numb from the medications they had pumped into my veins, his left shoulder began to ache. Neither of us could have imagined how quickly things would devolve from there.

On July 9, 1956, while he was talking on the phone with Rear Admiral Lewis Strauss, von Neumann collapsed in his home in Washington. On August 2 he was diagnosed with advanced, metastasizing cancer in his collarbone and underwent emergency surgery. By November his spine was affected. On December 12 he addressed the National Planning Association in Washington, DC. It was the last speech he gave standing up.

Eugene Wigner

A biological necessity

Something changed in Jancsi before the end.

After he was diagnosed with cancer, his head began to explode with ideas of a kind he had never entertained before, and in such copious quantities that I came to fear that, if the disease did not kill him, mental overexertion surely would. This sudden, formidable fecundity was, of course, nothing new in him, it was as if he had recovered, seemingly overnight, the same zeal that he lost after Gödel thwarted his attempts at entangling the entire world in a web of logic. Much more curious still was the fact that he also developed (though perhaps it would be more precise to say that he was beset by, as it was a violent and abrupt transformation) feelings that he had no prior experience with: spells of almost overwhelming empathy and a deep concern about the general destiny of humanity. These anxieties, which he could not contain or deny, would at first send him into flights of blind panic, though later, when he became more accustomed to this invasion of his psyche by all that he had previously chosen to ignore, he learned to channel these thoughts into himself, where they became the source of a fantastic thirst, an unquenchable curiosity regarding all matters of the spirit. This had been almost completely alien to him during his entire life, and so, to those who knew and loved him, it was perhaps even more distressing than the steady advance of his other, undoubtably life-threatening, symptoms. While we were more than accustomed to his maniacal energy, I was nonetheless very worried by the new texture of his discourse and ideas, which now included a rather unnerving strain, not just of his customary megalomania, but of a religious bent that, to me at least, felt altogether sinister. It was hardly noticeable at first. He had always been charmed by ancient history, the rise and fall of em-pires, and had had a special taste for Mesopotamia since he was a young boy, but now he began to gorge himself with all the knowledge he could get his hands on regarding gods and goddesses, from cultures around the world, and these new concerns soon spilled over, ever more frequently, into our conversations, taking up such a large part of his mind that, had he been a normal person, with a limited attention span, it would no doubt have overshadowed everything else and left no space at all for mathematics or scientific thinking.

"Gods are a biological necessity," he said to me on a particularly warm night at his home in Georgetown, during that last summer when he could still get around on crutches, "as integral to our species as lan-guage or opposable thumbs." According to Jancsi, faith had afforded the primeval peoples of the world a source of strength, power, and mean-ing that modern man lacked completely; and it was this lack, this pro-found loss, that now had to be addressed by science. "We have no guiding star," he told me, "nothing to look up or aspire to, so we are devolving, falling back into animality, losing the very thing that has let us advance so far beyond what was originally intended for us." Jancsi thought that if our species was to survive the twentieth century, we needed to fill the void left by the departure of the gods, and the one and only candidate that could achieve this strange, esoteric transformation was technology; our ever-expanding technical knowledge was the only thing that separated us from our forefathers, since in morals, philosophy, and general thought, we were no better (indeed, we were much, much worse) than the Greeks, the Vedic people, or the small nomadic tribes that still clung to nature as the sole granter of grace and the true measure of existence. We had stagnated in every other sense. We were stunted in all arts except for one, techne, where our wisdom had become so profound and dangerous that it would have made the Titans that terrorized the Earth cower in fear, and the ancient lords of the woods seem as puny as sprites and as quaint as pixies. Their world was gone. So now science and technology would have to provide us with a higher version of ourselves, an image of what we could become. Civilization had progressed to a point where the affairs of our species could no longer be entrusted safely to our own hands; we needed something other, something more. In the long run, for us to have the slimmest chance, we had to find some way of reaching beyond us, looking past the limits of our logic, language, and thought, to find solutions to the many problems that we would undoubtedly face as our dominion spread over the entire planet, and, soon enough, much farther still, all the way to the stars.

Those sermons of his were hard to stomach. Where was the rational and extremely grounded man I had always known? His analysis made no sense to me, and I said as much: there was no evidence for any of this. Billions of people still had unwavering faith in God, and their complete irrationality and incurable superstitions showed no signs of be-

222

coming weaker. Janos did not agree: "Those gods are living dead. They have lost their glory. They cannot give sense to the world because they are remnants, broken relics that we still carry around with us, just as sickly and powerless as those horse-drawn buggies you see in the streets of New York. Just because they are still here does not mean they are of any use. We mount our warheads on the tips of missiles that can reach around the globe, we do not strap them to the backs of mules." I knew that Jancsi had always received from mathematics and science the sense of purpose that others obtain from faith and religion, and so I could understand how those feelings could suddenly begin to overlap and intermingle in strange ways, as he now stared into the abyss of death. But I also realized that there was something much more concrete behind his sudden need for meaning and transcendence: he was in great pain. As his cancer developed, the many pills he took did almost nothing to alleviate his physical suffering. Whenever I went to visit him, I would see that he was drinking heavily and cramming down more food than he had ever done, so he had grown bloated and obese. Excessive suffering can change you in many ways. The people I loved in Europe, who could not escape the horrors of the war like Jancsi and I did, were never the same afterward. Having known the depths of cruelty, having witnessed what their fellow men and women were capable of, they could no longer look upon the world without seeing its shadow, and even when they closed their eyes to try to avoid it, they felt as if, behind that darkness, there was something worse still, watching and waiting for them. So many Jews who underwent torture or suffered hunger, deprivation, and humiliation were left broken, wraithlike, and fragile, despite being nursed back to health. But with Johnny there was also something else: a terrible fear. He was afraid not only of death but of disease itself, and perhaps that is why he suddenly needed the strength of unreason. While he had come to understand more and more about biology and the logical mechanisms behind living things, he nonetheless developed a highly morbid and superstitious relationship with his own affliction; he thought of his cancer not as something that was a part of him, but rather as another being entirely, an evil entity that was growing inside him, colonizing his tissues, spreading and corrupting not just his flesh but also the soul that seemed to have awakened in his innermost self, and that grew at the same merciless rate with which his disease spread along his organs. Such horrifying thoughts, which no doubt began to warp and weaken his mind, were surely nurturing his desire for a form of consciousness unharnessed from flesh and free of the aches and pains of the living. Knowing all of this, I listened to him patiently as he sat propped among cushions in his living room, or laid back in his bed with me at his side, telling me his visions of self-replicating machines thriving in a perfectly controlled climate, massive computer terminals spawning digital life, and a vast intergalactic diaspora of spacecraft fathering their own offspring; all these beings would not only bear his name but carry the logical framework that he had created for them as a kind of digital DNA. It was heartbreaking, but, to my shame, I must confess that I was unable to tear myself from him, to look away from the macabre spectacle of my oldest friend, the most singular being I had ever met, unraveling before my eyes and coddling the same fantastical delusions of progress that he had so fiercely lampooned when he had heard them from others. I stayed not only because I loved him but because in his delirium he was as clear and intelligent, as sharp, thoughtful, and rigorous as always. His ideas, outlandish as they were, felt seductive and exhilarating, and yet to me, the future he imagined was not merely chimeric and borderline unscientific, it was, much more importantly, profoundly inhuman. Regarding this I did not hold back, because I felt it was my duty to be as honest as always; I told him that we should simply accept our fragility, learn to live with uncertainty, and suffer the consequences of our many mistakes, without falling back on outdated and dangerous modes of thinking. The marriage he was suggesting between advanced technology and our most archaic mechanisms of transcendence could only result in horror and chaos, a world that would evolve past a point where anyone could even begin to understand it, no matter how rich, smart, or powerful they were. Having had so very few of his own to contend with, Jancsi had never been one to accept limitations of any kind, and while he could not see the danger in his own thinking, I had firsthand experience of what it was like, as a "normal person," to cohabitate with someone completely exceptional. I knew exactly what that felt like after growing up alongside him. I had seen men and women, scientists and thinkers of undeniable merit, falter before him, struck dumb or driven to shame by his superiority. I had witnessed Jancsi steamroll men who had the ill judgment or misfortune to present their ideas to him only to watch, helplessly, as he surpassed, in a matter of minutes, what had taken them months or even years of constant effort to achieve. Whatever "god" future technology managed to create would make us all feel as he had made me feel. But he could not see that, he could not understand that his best wishes for humanity could also spell our doom. Though perhaps it was something more personal: as his body failed him, as his thoughts were interrupted by aches and pains that he had never felt before, he longed for some higher being to save him, an intellect to rival his own or some creature that shared the way in which he had seen the world, a would-be inheritor that would preserve and mature the many projects and ideas that he continued to come up with right to the very end. Because it must be said that his interest in theology and his sudden need for some kind of apotheosis did almost nothing to slow the advance of his purely rational endeavors, such as his study of the parallels between the mechanisms of human thought and the way that digital computers operated; in his last year, he produced a wealth of knowledge comparable only to the work that he did when he first moved from Budapest to Berlin, back in the 1930s. To achieve this, he stuffed himself with painkillers, worked past exhaustion, and hardly slept at all, so it was no wonder that Klari was terrified that he would simply drop dead at his desk. It seemed impossible for anyone to survive such a manic pace for long. She begged me to intervene, and I tried as best I could to calm him and get him to rest, though I knew it was a wasted effort. He would not back down. I have known a few others whose body and mind reacted to terminal disease in such a way, with a final burst of creativity and energy as death rushed toward them. But Jancsi was not just unwilling to stop, he seemed to have reserved his last ounce of strength to tackle the hardest and most impenetrable topics. He began to study the brain and its relation to automata and computers, seeking to build a mathematical bridge between the inner languages of humans and machines—thought and computation—and while his new obsessions were clearly pushing him past anything that was practical, I was comforted when I realized that he had, nonetheless, retained his sense of humor, and even had the self-awareness to poke fun at himself in one of his papers: "Our thoughts are mostly focused on the subject of neurology," he wrote, "and more specifically on the human nervous system, and there primarily on the central nervous system. Thus, in trying to understand the function of automata and the general principles governing them, we selected for prompt action literally the most complicated object under the sun: the human brain." Klari told me that she felt that he was turning into one of his beloved computers, which could never stand idle but had to calculate unceasingly or else get caught in a loop, grind to a halt, and crash. He was never crazed, that must be said; whenever I spoke to him, he was as lucid as ever, and the work that he finished during that final period, which I had the chance to read when it was published posthumously, is as thought-provoking, mathematically elegant, and technically sound as anything he did. The only clear outward sign I ever saw that indicated to me that he had, perhaps, crossed some line and wandered into territory where rationality becomes a bridle, a constraint that must be cast aside if one is to walk further along the path, was an extremely disturbing episode that I witnessed at his home in Georgetown, shortly before the cancer pushed past his blood-brain barrier.

Jancsi had asked me to attend a congressional meeting in Washington, DC, where I was invited with all my expenses paid. The government had put me up at a very nice hotel, but the night was too hot and humid and I had terrible trouble getting to sleep. When I had finally managed it, Janos called me up, in the dead of night, slurring his words, and begged me to come over to his house. When I said no, still groggy from the sleeping pills I had taken, he insisted that there was something important that he needed to discuss with me, and hung up before I had the chance to refuse. I called him back immediately, intending to tell him that I could not think straight, and willing to promise I would be there early in the morning, as soon as I got up, but although I let the phone ring for a long time, there was no answer, and I began to worry that something serious might have happened to him. I pulled on my clothes, cursing under my breath, called a taxi service, and headed over. I dozed off in the cab, and when I awoke I could see long trails of lights stream past the windows, my vision still blurred by pharmacopoeia and my mind reeling from the eerie displays of the hypnagogia that I have suffered from a very young age, dancing phosphenes and other slight distortions of perception that occur during the onset of sleep, when you fall into that strange state of threshold consciousness between wakefulness and dream. How long had it been since Jancsi and I had worked on anything together? He had left his interest in theoretical physics far behind him, and I was not versed enough in computation, or in any other of his many interests, to be of use to him, so I wondered why he suddenly needed to talk to me. While I felt foolish making my way to his home without being able to think straight, I also knew that he was working at the Atomic Energy Commission, so whatever was on his mind may well have been urgent—of national importance even—and back then, during the Cold War, you simply could not refuse such a call. My thoughts had somewhat cleared by the time we pulled into his driveway, but I could still see random speckles and geometric patterns on the edges of my field of vision when I knocked on his front door and found that it was unlocked. I let myself in and called out, but nobody answered. As I walked into the living room, I saw Klari passed out next to a table covered with half-empty bottles. She had fallen asleep in her evening gown with a spent cigarette caught between her long fingers; its ashes had burned a tiny hole in the silken fabric of her dress. As I covered her legs with my coat, I heard her wince and complain, as if she was caught in the throes of some passing nightmare. I thought of waking her to spare her a bad dream, and gauged her weight to see if I was capable of carrying her to bed, but in that moment I heard Jancsi calling me from his study. I went upstairs with my heart pounding heavily in my chest, extremely nervous for reasons I could not understand. Was it due to the image of that beautiful, broken woman, victim of a ruinous marriage, laid out before my eyes? Or was it because I was afraid of finding my friend in the same condition? When I opened the door to his study, I realized that my fears had not been misplaced. For he was in far, far worse shape than her, so much so that I had to catch my breath before stepping into the room.

He was sitting behind his desk, naked to the waist. His skin was glistening with sweat, his potbelly sticking out in front of him as he clumsily strained to tie the black leather strips of a tefillin cube around his arm, while another one balanced precariously at the top of his colossal forehead. I had seen my father wear those rectangular prayer boxes, containing scrolls of parchment inscribed with verses from the Torah, every morning during his devotions; he had taught me the proper way to entwine the entire arm and form the Hebrew letters *dalet* and *yud*, in order to spell out *Shaddai*, one of the many names of God. Nothing that Jancsi could have said or done would have shocked me more. It was grotesque. A mockery of something that had been held sacred for thousands of years, something to which Janos, who had never participated in the Jewish faith in any respect, had no true connection with at all. I was furious, convinced that he was playing dress-up, as he loved to do at his parties, that this was another one of his jokes, albeit the most offensive and ridiculous one he had ever thought up. But when I turned around to leave, he called out to me in Hungarian, pleading, "Jenő, Jenő, please help me do this." I was still confused by the pills I'd taken, and could not understand what had come over him, but I felt my entire body move against my will, as though I was under somebody else's control, and watched, completely removed from myself, as I walked behind his desk, crouched down next to him, and slowly encircled his left forearm with the dark leather phylactery—capable, according to the rabbis, of defeating a thousand demons rising from within—from the top of his elbow, right down to his chubby little fingers, where I entwined the strips and saw his pinkish skin bulge from the pressure, as I had, inadvertently, bound them too tight. When I finished, I stood there, shaking from head to toe, and asked him where he had got them from, and what the hell he thought he was doing, but his speech was so slow and slurred that I could not make out his answer. When he tried to get up, I realized just how drunk he was. I put my arm around his waist, felt his sweat dampen the cloth of my shirt, and dragged him into his bedroom. He was sobbing as I laid him down; I could hear him whisper his mother's name and call out to Klari and to his daughter, Marina, saying that he was so close, that all he needed was a little more time, just a little more time. When he finally passed out, I removed the tefillin from his arm and his forehead, wiped the tears from his face, and realized that it was the first time I had seen Johnny so inebriated. He had somehow always managed to remain lucid, even at the wildest gatherings. I had watched him drink all day and all night but never lose his mind. And yet there he was, asleep below me, looking as frail and vulnerable as a hydrocephalic toddler with his giant head, and for some reason I felt not just overwhelming sadness for the fate of my childhood friend, now spiraling toward death, decay, and—God forbid—perhaps even madness, but a small measure of relief that made me feel incredibly ashamed of myself. Yes, I thought, Janos was human after all, not only a genius but also a drunken fool, just like any of us.

I decided to stay the night in their guest bedroom, and walked downstairs to get sheets from the linen closet, but I slipped on the second to last step, its edge weathered by the previous owners, who, according to Jancsi, had lived there with a small battalion of children, and I tumbled forward, just managing to catch ahold of myself. Jancsi was not so lucky: that New Year's Eve, when he rose from his sickbed to say goodbye to his daughter, Marina, who had come to visit him during the holy days, he tripped on that same step on the way back to his room, fell, and never walked again. Three months after that, when the tumor spread into his brain and he started to show the first signs of mental impairment, the United States government sequestered him at Walter Reed Army Medical Center.

Marina von Neumann

What is one plus one?

I remember Elvis, dancing on a little black-and-white TV in the anteroom of my father's suite at Walter Reed. The image was fuzzy and the sound too low to make out the song, but I stared at him there, wiggling and waving his hips, so young, so beautiful. Father's tumors had spread throughout his entire body, but he still received a stream of visitors and continued working even though he could hardly move from the pain. I had to wait my turn to see him, just like anybody else, but on that particular day, with the King winking at me from the television screen, I dreaded going into his room more than ever before, not because of his health, or for fear of what I would find within, but because I had betrayed him.

I'd gotten married. The week after I graduated from Radcliffe. Father loathed the idea, he had leveled all kinds of threats to try to dissuade me. He thought I was far too young (which I was, only twenty-one) and firmly believed that an early marriage would cripple me and impede my professional development, which it didn't. We had fought over this for months, but I did not back down. I had my way. I did exactly what I wanted. I married my fiancé and we spent our honeymoon in the prettiest little wood cabin up in Maine, before traveling to Washington, DC, to relay the "good news" to my dying father. What a terrible thing to do. Why didn't I lie? Why couldn't I just wait till he passed? I was selfish, I guess. Stubborn too. Or perhaps I wanted to show him something. To prove that I was just as headstrong as him, maybe even more. To measure up to his expectations by betraying his wishes. Because I had confidence in myself. I knew what I could do long before I became a full professor, or the first woman appointed by President Nixon to his Council of Economic Advisers, or the chief economist and vice president of General Motors. Yes, I married young, but that didn't stop me from being the director of multinational corporations, or from serving on the boards of Harvard and Princeton and even of my father's beloved Institute for Advanced Study. But he died without knowing any of that. All he knew was that I had gone behind his back. While he was in agony no less. So I felt my knees shaking as I looked down at the ring squeezing my finger (Hubby had bought a size too small) and wondered if I should take it off. That way I would also avoid hearing what Klari would have to say about my miserable little diamond. I couldn't stop toying with it while I mentally rehearsed ways in which to break the news to my father, and I completely abraded my skin as I waited amid a gaggle of generals, scientists, doctors, and spooks who were all crowded outside in the anteroom looking over their notes or, like me, mesmerized by Elvis's face, dripping with sweat, his thick black hair falling in front of his eyes as his concert neared its end. I'm Gonna Sit Right Down and Cry? Heartbreak Hotel? Fool, Fool, Fool? One of my father's aides stood beside me. He smiled and patted me on the shoulder, ever so slightly, when he noticed my ring. Vince Ford. Nice, if a bit flirty. Good-looking too. A colonel in charge of eight airmen who were at my father's beck and call, twenty-four hours a day, seven days a week, eight soldiers who were not only extensions of his will but also minders who watched over him like a kettle of hawks, since they had to ensure that he didn't blurt out any military secrets when he became confused (he would sometimes forget where he was), entrust some important idea to the wrong person, or let slip some discovery when he fell into one of his fits of rage. Father never complained to me about the pain, but the changes in his attitude, his utterances, and his dealings with Klari, in fact his whole mood at the end of his life, were heartbreaking. In what was one of the most unsettling aspects of his entire illness, he suddenly became a strict Catholic. He spent many hours with a Benedictine monk. Later he asked for a Jesuit. I have no idea what they spoke about. Perhaps my father—the utmost rationalist—simply yearned for some kind of personal immortality, but I do know he remained inconsolable and utterly terrified of death to the very end. I thought his newfound faith was completely ludicrous, and Klari, well, she somehow took it as a personal affront, and simply could not stomach it.

Klari, Klari, Klari. Klari the figure skater, the witch, the shrew, the nag. Klari, the MANIAC's wet nurse. She programmed it, Father's machine at the institute. He taught her to code during their long drives through the desert, and she became an expert in no time. I still remember the enormous flowcharts she produced in that strange machine language, long sheets of paper covered with arcane symbols, connected by arrows and circles, that she spread across our dining room table and that fell down to the shaggy carpets below. There were not just logic gates and mathematical signs in those charts, but also a peculiar type of beauty that I found both irresistible and frightful, so much so that when I was young, I would trace over them when she wasn't looking, and carry those symbols around, stuck between the pages of one of my schoolbooks as if they were a good luck charm or a witch's spell that I could cast against my enemies. With time I have developed a great respect for Klari, as well as a profound sense of shame for the way I treated her and for all the pain my father put her through, but I must admit that I despised her for years. When I moved in with them (per my father's strange divorce agreement, which specified that I would live with him after I turned sixteen), I thought Klari was the most insufferable woman I had ever met. They were always at each other's throats. She was deeply neurotic and mentally unstable, so my father spent much of his life mystified by her fluctuating moods. She was prone to depression, constantly frustrated by his inability to connect with her in any meaningful way, and never managed to overcome a feeling that she was out of place, living a life that was not altogether hers. In her unfinished autobiography, which I found hidden among my father's papers in his basement, next to the boiler, she confessed that she felt "like a tiny little speck, an insignificant insect who had just been chirruping around to see where the most fun could be had, when I was swept up by the hurricane force of international events and global minds." No matter what she achieved, she could not measure up to her husband's accomplishments, or become the sole object of his interest, as she so keenly desired. Her ever-darkening feelings and decaying sense of self-worth drove her to drink. She would usually sleep till late in her own bedroom, and she was so grouchy in the morning that I dreaded waking her up. I would normally fix breakfast for myself and try to get out of the house before she and my father began their daily routine. Because it was only then, in their dreadful fights, that she would feel the love and reassurance that she ached for. Their entire fraught relationship is painfully documented in the letters that they wrote each other almost daily when they were apart. A large part of their correspondence is erotica, something I dared not even skim over, but the majority is a long recapitulation of their bitter squabbles: "We both have nasty tempers, but let's quarrel less. I really love you, and, within the limitations of my horrible nature, I do want to make you happy—as nearly as possible, as much of the time as possible," my father wrote soon after they married. "You are frightened of a life that has maltreated you . . . you are terrified even of the breeze because you sense the storm behind it . . . I seared you, I bullied you, I hurt you! Please, please, give me a bit of faith . . . or at least benevolent neutrality." Apologies for some perceived misbehavior on his part and pleas for her forgiveness were a recurring theme, because in her eyes, it was as if he could do nothing right. "Why do we fight when we are together? I love you. Do you loathe me very violently? Let's forgive each other!" he begged. Their battles raged for years. In the last months of my father's life, however, there was a profound change in their relationship: Klari became a dedicated and loving caretaker, while my father spiraled into despair, strayed beyond her reach, and became verbally abusive in a way that was so completely out of character that I suspect it was a product of the cancer attacking his brain. Klari killed herself six years after he died. Walked into the ocean in the middle of the night. The police found her car—an enormous black Cadillac that my father had given her—parked in front of Windansea Beach, with the engine cold. Her dead body washed up shortly after dawn on November 10, 1963. According to the coroner's report, she was wearing a long black cocktail dress with wrist-length sleeves, black furred cuffs, a zippered back, and a high neckline. It was weighed down by approximately fifteen pounds of wet sand. They also found sand in her lungs. Questioned by the police, her psychiatrist stated that he had been able to establish a line of the "death instinct" in her family, something that made no sense to me at all until I learned two secrets that had been diligently kept from me: that her father, Charles Dan, had committed suicide by jumping under a train shortly after he arrived in America, and that she had suffered a miscarriage, which she blamed on my father for not having been around to help her lift a heavy garage door.

Before my father died he lost the will or the capacity to speak. The doctors couldn't offer any physical reason for his retreat into silence. I believe that it was a conscious decision on his part. The horror of experiencing the deterioration of his mental powers was too much for him to bear. He was only fifty-three years old when he was diagnosed, still in the prime of his life, and he retained his reason and extraordinary faculties almost to the end. But he simply could not accept what was happening to him. Terror of his own mortality crowded out all other thoughts. Try as he might, he could not visualize a world that did not include himself thinking within it, so he had none of the grace that some people exhibit when they finally accept their fate. On the contrary, he behaved like a child, as if death was something that only happened to others, something that he had never really considered and so was completely unprepared for. His consciousness recoiled against a limit that he could not think past or look beyond, and he lashed out violently. He suffered from the loss of his mind more than I have seen any human being suffer, in any other circumstance. When we already knew that his disease would be fatal, and that it would progress quickly, I asked him, point-blank, how he used to be able to contemplate, with total equanimity, the killing of hundreds of millions of people in a nuclear first strike against the Soviet Union, and yet he could not face his own mortality with any sense of calm or dignity. "That is entirely different," he replied.

We had fought so viciously because of my wish to be married that the day I came to tell him about it I was absolutely terrified of what his reaction would be, and so I had come armed with a toy train set as a gift for him, a big red engine that was a replica of the stately ones that he used to ride on back in Hungary, and that I had bought so he could add it to his ever-growing collection. I could hardly contain my relief when I saw that the small army of toys, gadgets, and mechanical playthings that my father, for reasons only he could understand, had demanded we bring him had all been cleared out, and was even more shocked when, after I showed him my ring, he simply smiled, took my hands, and pulled me gently toward him so that he could kiss my forehead. Klari had kept me well-informed regarding the advance of his illness and the deterioration of his body, so I thought I was ready for it, but when my nerves calmed down and I stopped thinking about myself long enough to take a good look at him, I almost burst out crying. He was so gaunt, frail, and shrunken that his head, which had always seemed too big for his body, now looked like it belonged to someone else. His eyes trembled and watered while I caressed the few remaining strands of his hair and placed the back of his hand against my cheek. I could tell that he was very afraid. And not just of death. My father's second great fear as he lay dying was that his work would not endure and he would be forgotten. Considering the breadth of his scientific legacy, I thought it was utterly ridiculous, a senseless insecurity on his part. But I wanted to appease him nonetheless, and as soon as I had received his silent blessing for my unwanted nuptials, I asked him if he had finished the paper that he had been working on when he was first hospitalized—"Computing Machines and the Brain: On the Mechanisms of Thought"—a treatise that he intended for Yale's prestigious Silliman Lectures. He had given me an early draft; in it, he concluded that the brain's method of operation is fundamentally different from that of the computer. According to my father, all computers follow a similar architecture to the one he created for the MANIAC. It forces them to operate sequentially, a step at a time. But the human brain is very different. It is massively parallel, executing an enormous number of operations simultaneously. But that was not the aspect that puzzled him the most. He was searching for the inner logic of the brain. The "language" that it used to function. He wanted to find out if it was similar to mathematical logic, his own preferred mode of thought. "When we talk of mathematics," he wrote, "we may be discussing a secondary language built on the primordial one used by the central nervous system." More than anything, he sought to discover what that prime language of the brain was; he believed that this could transform the whole prospect for mankind. Decoding it would allow us to begin to comprehend the inner workings of the brain and grant us access to the mind's unique capacity to create the grand, overall sense of the world that only human beings seem to possess. He was fascinated by the stark contrast between the way computers and brains processed information, but he also saw certain similarities that suggested that, perhaps one day, we could begin to merge with machines in a way that would either allow computers to become aware, or permit our species to exist in a manner that would make us immune to corruption and disease. He did not include any of these fantasies in his paper, but I knew that such ideas ate away at him, and that he dreamed of finding some way to preserve his extraordinary mind. I told him how enthralled I had become by his draft, hoping that he would make an exception just for me, and break his sullen silence. When he parted his cracked lips to speak, I felt a rush of pride and emotion, followed by a bitter pang of disappointment when instead of talking about his work, he made the most peculiar and frightening request, especially coming from a man who was widely regarded as one of the greatest mathematicians of the century, if not *the* greatest: he asked me to choose two numbers at random, and then query him on their sums. I thought he was kidding. Had he suddenly regained his old sense of humor? I smiled before realizing that he was dead serious. During my previous visit, just a month or so before, his mind had been as sharp as always. But now his genius had deteriorated past the point where he could handle even basic arithmetic. His vast intellectual powers were gone. There was no longer anything left of the faculty by which he had defined himself, and the look of blind panic that twisted his features as this realization slowly overwhelmed him was the most heart-wrenching thing I ever saw. It was excruciating to watch, and I could only choke out a couple of numbers— what is two plus nine, what is ten plus five, what is one plus one—before I fled the room in tears.

Vincent Ford

We heard the machines come alive

A t the end the Professor suffered a complete psychological breakdown. We would hear his crying fits, and then howls of pain, but he wouldn't let the croakers put him out of his misery. Or perhaps it wasn't his decision to make. The boys up in the Five-Sided Puzzle Palace did everything in their power to keep that man alive. Posterior Admiral Strauss brought in sawbones from around the world to see him, but it was pointless. All they figured was the cancer probably started in his pancreas, then formed a giant growth on his left clavicle. From there it spread all over. He suffered immensely, but even when he was hallucinating, he would somehow manage to pull himself together long enough to come up with new ideas. Like the time he told me that he had envisioned a type of mechanism that would, according to his way of saying things, "allow me to write pure bred in consciousness without physical interference," though he never got around to it, or the real weapons guidance system he created for the squids in the Navy.

He would suddenly become intensely lucid, but then flip his lid again and start screaming out for his mother in Hungarian. I knew him for years. Before Walter Reed, I'd been appointed his attaché when he served as chairman of the "Teapot Committee," the Air Force Strategic Missiles Evaluation Committee, where he pushed for the construction of the Atlas, America's first intercontinental ballistic missile, a real Crowd Pleaser. That was our response to the Soviets' R-7, the one that put Sputnik in orbit and scared the shit out of us. The Professor had seen it coming long before that. He was the sort of civilian the military simply cannot live without. All the birds and zoomies admired him. Grunts too. So they jacked him up on a massive cocktail of substances and he seemed to get a little better. Right before the end, he woke up, started talking again, and wanted to work, so there was a great rush of people coming in and out of his room, setting up some last-ditch experimental procedure that the Professor himself got involved in, apparently. We had to clear the entire floor while they wheeled in a ton of machines I'd never seen in a hospital. The biggest one barely fit in the hallway, we all had to squeeze past it. It looked like a massive car engine, like a V-40, and it smelled terrible, like burned hair. It had such a thick tangle of cables and so many wires, which spilled into the Professor's room, that his door wouldn't close properly. I wasn't allowed in there, which was weird, 'cause part of my detail was to watch over him day and night. But that was overruled. Mrs. von Neumann would have none of it, so she had to be dragged out. She demanded that we leave him alone and let him rest, but the brass said otherwise. To them, the Professor was the goose and the golden eggs. Besides, he was dead anyway. There was nothing to lose. The entire operation took more than a week to prepare, but then it happened fast. From outside in the hallway, we heard the machines come alive with a low, deep hum that made the windowpanes quiver as though the building was being hit by an earthquake. And then we heard his screams of agony. I've never heard anything like that. I've seen soldiers bleed to death from combat wounds, I've heard men in sick bay grasping their intestines and speaking in tongues, flyboys cooked in jet fuel, disfigured from head to toe. But this was different. It was the Professor's voice, but it didn't sound like a human screaming. Nobody slept that night. Whatever they tried, didn't take. They wheeled out his body in the morning. As they passed me, his hand dropped down from the gurney and I saw that his skin had turned black, with dime-sized white spots all over it, as if they had covered his body in electrodes and burned him to a crisp. I have often wondered if they let him rest, or if they even fiddled with him after death. It's not as crazy as it sounds. After all, it happened to Einstein. When he died, a pathologist removed his brain without the family's permission, and kept it for himself. It was missing for decades. When someone finally tracked it down, they saw that it had been cut down the middle and was floating inside two large mason jars. A team of scientists took those pale pounds of flesh and sliced them into wafer-thin layers to put under a microscope. They wanted to see if they could find something special, or perhaps abnormal, some pathological structure or deformation that would explain his unique genius. But they found nothing. Compared to an average human being, he had an unusual number of glia, but they're not nerve cells at all, they don't produce electrical impulses. As far as I know, his brain was just like anybody else's. To this day I wonder what we would have seen had we looked inside von Neumann's head.

Von Neumann was buried in Princeton Cemetery on February 12, 1957, four days after he died. He was interred in a closed casket next to his mother, Margit Kann, and his father-in-law, Charles Dan. His friends laid a flat arrangement of daffodils on his grave. Rear Admiral Lewis Strauss delivered the eulogy. Father Anselm Strittmatter performed the burial rites.

Eugene Wigner

For progress there is no cure

J ancsi left his most ambitious work unfinished.

Before his mind began to slip away from him, he tried to create an all-encompassing scheme of self-replication that would unite biology, technology, and computer theory, and that would be applicable to life of any kind, both in the physical and in the digital realm, on this planet or on any other. He called it *Theory of Self-Reproducing Automata,* and worked on it till he could no longer hold a pen in his hand. Even incomplete it is a wonder; with the same clarity and conciseness of all his other works, he laid down the logical rules behind self-replication, years before we learned how life on Earth had implemented its version of that same model through DNA and RNA. But Jancsi was not thinking about biological life. He was dreaming of a completely novel form of existence.

His theory considers what would be necessary for nonbiological entities—whether mechanical or digital—to begin to reproduce and undergo an evolutionary process, and he dedicated a vast amount of his dwindling mental energy to imagine ways in which to trigger this second Genesis. Hospitalized and connected to so many tubes and sensors, he could no longer walk, drink, or drive, which was how he did his best thinking, so from his room in Walter Reed he sent out all of his aides and told them to buy up every single Tinkertoy they could get their hands on. This went on for months, and by the end of it his room looked like a rich boy's the day after Christmas, with tin robots, wind-up cars, walking chickens, and building sets covering nearly every available surface, and even strewn out across the floor, with the result that, when the chiefs of staff or the Pentagon boys would visit him, they had to wade through a veritable sea of tiny wheeled ducks, bulldozers, trams, and buses, and sidestep over rockets, airplanes, and submarines to huddle around his bed. If they were not careful, they'd set off an infernal racket of bells, whistles, and chimes, to Jancsi's delight. I gifted him several such contraptions (a little tank, a bright chrome Cadillac, and a miniature silver-plated typewriter that looked like one of his computers) even though I knew that their noises were driving Klari insane. I think everyone was greatly relieved when Julian Bigelow, one of the engineers who had been Jancsi's right-hand man when he built the MANIAC, came and showed him how to construct his automata in a two-dimensional grid—with pen and paper—and Klari was finally able to get rid of all those broken toys, since Jancsi kept picking them apart and putting them together in strange ways. I believe she gave them to Carl, Oskar Morgenstern's five-year-old boy.

"How could machines start to have a life of their own? I can formulate the problem rigorously, in the same way in which Turing did for his mechanisms," Jancsi wrote to me just a couple of months before he died. He purported to have already set down a scheme that seemed to prove that "there exists a type of automaton—we may call it *Aleph-zero*—which has the following property: if you provide *Aleph-zero* with a description of anything, it consumes it and produces two copies of the description." Using the same logical methods and self-referential, recursive reasoning that Turing had employed to come up with the thought experiments that eventually led to the creation of the computer, and which Gödel used to prove his incompleteness theorems, Jancsi had managed to design a theoretical machine whose output would not just be strings of ones and zeros but real, physical objects. He also believed that there was a threshold, a tipping point that, if surpassed, would kick off an evolutionary process in his machines, leading to automata whose complexity would grow exponentially, akin to the way that biological organisms thrive and mutate under natural selection, creating the intricate beauty that surrounds us. This progression would allow members of succeeding generations to produce not just mirror copies of themselves, but offspring of an ever-increasing complexity. "At its lower levels, complexity is probably degenerative," he wrote, "so every automaton would only be able to produce less complicated ones; but there is a certain level beyond which the phenomenon could become explosive, with unimaginable consequences; in other words, where each machine could produce offspring of higher and higher potentialities." For some reason that I have yet to understand, Jancsi was adamant about wanting his machines to take physical shape in the real world; but he also argued that such automata need not be creatures built from metal alloys and plastic sinews, but rather they could exist and develop inside a world much like the one that Barricelli had intended for the creatures he bred inside the memory of the MANIAC. "If my automata were allowed to evolve freely in the unbounded matrix of an ever-expanding digital cosmos," Jancsi wrote, "they could take on unimaginable forms, recapitulating the stages of biological evolution at an inconceivably faster pace than things of flesh and blood. By crossbreeding and pollinating, they would eventually surpass us in number, and perhaps, one day, reach a point where they could become rivals to our own intelligence. Their progress, at first, would be slow and silent. But then they would spawn and burst into our lives like so many hungry locusts, fighting for their rightful place in the world, carving their own path toward the future while carrying, in some deep corner of their digital souls, a trace whisper of my spirit, a small part of me, the man who had laid down their logical foundations." In 1957—the year that Janos died—there were no more than a handful of kilobytes of computer memory in the entire world. Less than modern machines use to display a single pixel. With such limited resources, he was not really thinking about what was possible, or even probable; computer science was so young and nascent that he could revel freely, playing with his imagination like a wicked child, without being tied to reality or having to think of the consequences. So I bit my tongue for the first time in our entire friendship, and I let him entertain his wild fantasies unimpeded, because I really thought they were just the follies of a dying man going mad from pain. At the same time, I also felt guilty for not bringing him down to Earth and chastising him, but so much has changed since then . . . The rate of expansion of the digital world has become unfathomable. And what is not only possible but real has quickly outpaced even our most fevered dreams. Jancsi's reveries no longer seem completely irrational, so some of the last things he wrote haunt me to this day.

He had always been pessimistic about the future, and about mankind in general, but as his disease took hold of him it was as if a black hand began to cloud all his thoughts, tinting his outlook and judgment in the darkest possible light. The nearness of death, the undeniable fact of his own mortality, took him past despair and pushed him beyond logic. By the end, he was looking toward a future so shadowy, and envisioning such macabre scenarios, that he fell silent and refused to share his thoughts with anybody. In his final letter to me, he spoke of an essential phase-change that was rushing forward to meet us: "The present awful possibilities of nuclear warfare may give way to others even more dreadful. Literally and figuratively, we are running out of room. At long last, we begin to feel the effects of the finite, actual size of the Earth in a critical way. This is the maturing crisis of technology. In the years between now and the beginning of the next century, the global crisis will probably develop far beyond all earlier patterns. When or how it will end—or to what state of affairs it will yield—nobody can say. It is a very small comfort to think that the interests of humanity might one day change, the present curiosity in science may cease, and entirely different things may occupy the human mind. Technology, after all, is a human excretion, and should not be considered as something Other. It is a part of us, just like the web is part of the spider. However, it seems that the ever-accelerating progress of technology gives the appearance of approaching some essential singularity, a tipping point in the history of the race beyond which human affairs as we know them cannot continue. Progress will become incomprehensibly rapid and complicated. Technological power as such is always an ambivalent achievement, and science is neutral all through, providing only means of control applicable to any purpose, and indifferent to all. It is not the particularly perverse destructiveness of one specific invention that creates danger. The danger is intrinsic. For progress there is no cure."

Near midnight on July 15, 1958, Julian Bigelow arrived at the Institute for Advanced Study, walked down the stairs that led to the MANIAC, pressed himself against the wall to reach the back of the computer, and switched off its master control. He pulled on the thick tangle of black cables that connected it to the building's main power grid like a gigantic umbilical cord until he managed to unplug it; in an instant, its heater filaments went cold, the phosphene shimmer of its cathodes faded away, and the vacuum tubes—which had, till then, preserved the MANIAC's memories in evanescent traces of electrostatic charge—fell dormant. Nothing would enliven those circuits again.

The other day I saw a ghost—the skeleton of a machine that not so long ago had been very much alive, and the cause of violent controversy, now lying silent in its inglorious tomb. The computer, the old one, the original, the firster, a.k.a. the JONNYAC, a.k.a. the MANIAC, more formally the Institute for Advanced Study Numerical Computing Machine, is now locked away, not buried but hidden in the back room of the building where it used to be the queen, waiting, perhaps, for the day when it will arise from its sleep and come back to haunt us. Its life-juice, the electricity, has been cut off; its breathing, the air-conditioning system, has been dismantled. It still has its own little nave, which can only be approached through the big hall that was its antechamber, used for the auxiliary equipment—now a dead storage hold for empty boxes, old desks, and other paraphernalia that invariably finds its way to such places and then is forgotten with the rest. *Sic transit gloria mundi.* Thus passes the glory of the world.

A Grasshopper in Very Tall Grass,
undated and unpublished autobiography,
Klára Dan von Neumann

Before he became unresponsive and refused to speak even to his family or friends, von Neumann was asked what it would take for a computer, or some other mechanical entity, to begin to think and behave like a human being.

He took a very long time before answering, in a voice that was no louder than a whisper.

He said that it would have to grow, not be built.

He said that it would have to understand language, to read, to write, to speak.

And he said that it would have to play, like a child.

LEE

or

The Delusions of Artificial Intelligence

Our earthly existence, since it in itself has a very doubtful meaning, can only be a means towards a goal of another existence. The idea that everything in the world has a meaning is, after all, precisely analogous to the principle that everything has a cause, on which the whole of science rests.

KURT GÖDEL, LETTER TO HIS MOTHER

Who of us would not be glad to lift the veil behind which the future lies hidden; to cast a glance at the next advances of our science and at the secrets of its development during future centuries?

DAVID HILBERT

Fryer Bungey (and) Fryer Bacon . . . with great study and paines so framed a head of brasse, that in the inward parts therof there was all things like as in a natural man's head: this being done, they were as farre from perfectione of the worke as they were before . . . that at the last they concluded to raise a spirit, and to know of him that which they could not attaine to by their owne studies.

ROBERT GREENE, THE HONORABLE
HISTORIE OF FRIER BACON AND FRIER BUNGAY, 1589

Prologue

The legendary Emperor Yao invented the game of Go to enlighten his son, Danzhu.

Yao, born of the goddess Yao-Mu, one of the five mythical sage-kings of China, begat Danzhu with his most beloved concubine, San Yi, who birthed a vicious little boy. Danzhu prized cruelty above all the ten thousand things; when he was just a child, and the rays of the sun shone through the Green Yang Brightness side of the Hall of Light, he would rip off the wings of the birds at the Easter Palace, gouge out their eyes with a sharp stick, and watch them flail helplessly on the floor, dancing to the music of the bells that he would fasten with strings carefully wrapped around their talons. He was generally opposed to the order of the world and delighted in contravening the strict rules laid down by his father to guarantee peace in the four quarters of a kingdom so vast as to be likened to infinity. In spring, he would hunt pregnant mares; in summer he would trap and hobble young fawns so they would grow crippled and disfigured, becoming easy prey for wolves—the only animals the young prince felt any love for, since they were as cruel and heartless as he. Fall was his favorite season; when the harvest began, he would cover his body in rotten leaves, splash mud on the white walls of the Comprehensive Pattern side of the Palace of Light, and wait for the executions to begin: criminals were rounded up, along with the depraved, the infirm, and the demented, and the boy would shiver with delight watching them be interrogated, tortured, punished, and then slain. His pleasure would reach fever pitch during blackest winter, when the sun was in the Tail; then he would kidnap young boys and girls, lure them into the Dark Hall side of the Northern Palace with promises of food and gold, and then rape and strangle them, leaving their broken bodies out in the cold, for the snow to bury and the wolves to gnaw on.

He was a beast that could not learn to read, write, paint, or play the lute, but he had a supernatural ability to win at games of all kinds, be they of chance or mental or physical skill, because he was sly and cunning as a fox, and could skin a cat with his eyes closed. The emperor's mother, Yao-Mu, told her son that the boy was not truly human, but a fallen star, and like all things that plummet from heaven, he was a harbinger of death, a message from the Jade Emperor himself, a plague visited upon mankind lest we believe ourselves to be above the gods. The boy was driven by an all-consuming rage, and lusted after the peace that only the void can bring. He was a death-bringer, a destroyer, bound to nothing save his own gravity, falling further and further into himself. Yao-Mu also revealed to the emperor the true meaning of the strange characters that the child bore on his forehead, marks that no amount of water could wash away: *Heaven bestows a hundred grains upon mankind. Man offers not a single good deed to recompense heaven. KILL, KILL, KILL, KILL, KILL, KILL, KILL!*

The emperor was a bastion of moral perfection. According to the Bamboo Annals, he lived as though he were a simple farmer, and during his reign his brilliance pervaded the four quarters, shining in the hearts of all men. Throughout his lifetime, the sun and moon were as resplendent as jewels and the five planets hung like a string of pearls in the heavens. Phoenixes nested in the palace courtyard, crystalline springs flowed down from the hills and ran along the countryside carpeted with pearl grass, and rice crops were abundant and plentiful; in the capital city of Pingyang, two unicorns, those rare and wondrous omens of peace and prosperity, were seen locking horns beneath the purple blossoms of the wisteria, but fled on the very day that Danzhu was born, and had yet to return, for the boy began to organize hunting parties from the day he could hold a bow in his tiny hands, hunts that would last for weeks, as he had sworn never to rest until he had slain at least one specimen of every living creature, dragons and unicorns notwithstanding.

With the help of his mother, emperor Yao prayed to the Four Celestial Kings, the nine suns, the Blessed Queen of the West, and to Pangu himself, the first living being of this universe, to beg their permission to divide the entire cosmos into a grid of 19 rows and 19 columns, creating a board with 361 intersections, on which to play a game against his demonic child. He summoned Danzhu and explained the rules of this game, the most important of games: all the players had to do was to place stones, either black or white, on the intersecting lines of the grid, in order to conquer as much space as possible and encircle their opponent's stones. The player who garnered the most territory in this way would be the victor. He placed the board in the boy's hands and told him that, when he felt good and ready, they would play a tournament, one that all gods, demons, heavenly and earthly creatures would witness. The emperor would use white stones made from clamshells, the child, black slate.

Whoever won would rule the world.

The Strong Stone

L ee Sedol, the Strong Stone, 9 dan master of Go, the most creative player of his generation and the only human being who has ever defeated an advanced artificial intelligence system in tournament settings, lost his voice when he turned thirteen.

In 1996, five years after moving to Seoul from the tiny island of Bigeumdo, located at the remote western edge of the South Korean peninsula, and six months after becoming a professional Go player, a strange affliction attacked his lungs. It inflamed his bronchial tubes and paralyzed his vocal cords, leaving him not only mute, which was to be expected, but also strangely incapable of reading and understanding certain words. The root cause of his temporary aphasia was never established, but he bore the consequences of that episode forever onward, since the disease (if indeed it was a disease and not merely the outward sign of a profound inner turmoil) left his bronchial nerves permanently paralyzed, so that to this day he speaks in an odd, shrill, wheezy, almost toylike voice, as if somewhere inside him there remains a small, scared little boy, screaming to get out. "My parents were living in Bigeumdo Island and I was boarding with my older brother in Seoul, but he was in the army, so there was no one who cared for me. I didn't even have a chance to go through a proper medical checkup when I got sick," he recalled at a time when he was already considered a living legend, during one of the few interviews he ever granted, for he was so ashamed and traumatized by his abnormal voice that he was loath to speak in public for much of his career, and would even refuse to participate in the award ceremonies of the tournaments he won. While he later became one of the greatest Go masters of the modern era, back in the midnineties, he was still a thirteen-year-old child prodigy under an enormous amount of pressure: he trained twelve hours a day, Monday through Sunday, in the Go Academy founded by Kweon Kab-yong, a renowned teacher who coached many of Korea's best players. Kweon immediately recognized the boy's talent after seeing him win the 12th National Children's Go Competition, hosted by the Haitai Confectionery and Foods Company, in 1991. Lee was only eight at the time, and the youngest player to ever win that tournament, a contest during which he already displayed his signature style: wild, violent, and unpredictable. Master Kweon had coached thousands of young aspiring Go players throughout his career, but he sensed that there was something different about that boy, with his big ears, catlike eyes, and fuzz of a mustache peppered over his upper lip, capable of beating international professionals four times older than he was, and eventually he invited him to live in his own home. "I remember his round face and dark brown eyes. Since he came from an island, he was shy and tried to draw attention away from himself. But he was unlike all the other children. His eyes shone with a different light," Kweon recalls.

Lee Sedol had learned Go from his father, a passionate amateur player who taught his five children the game even before they could read or write. Lee was the youngest of them all, but shot past his siblings, and neither they nor his father could win a single match against him after he turned five. Under Master Kweon, Lee would train incessantly, but he could not make friends; his classmates, who were in awe of what he could do with the black and white stones on the wooden board, would laugh and poke fun at how extremely naïve he could be, teasing him incessantly and nicknaming him the Bigeumdo Boy, for he was so rural that when he arrived in Seoul with only a bundle of clothes and a stuffed-toy backpack, he asked them, without a trace of irony, what kind of trees pizza grew on. While Lee was the only pupil living in the master's home, he would follow almost the same training ritual as the others: wake up at dawn to study the six thousand problems contained in the manual of his dojo, passed down in unbroken tradition for over two and a half thousand years; play several lightning games till lunch; and then sit down in silence to learn by heart entire matches played by the ancient masters. Among them was Lee's favorite, the "blood-vomiting game" of 1835, between Japan's reigning champion, Honinbo Jowa, known as the "latter sage," and the youthful contender Akaboshi Intetsu, who had challenged him to a three-day tournament that ended with the youngling on his knees, coughing up blood onto the board, after dominating the first hundred moves of the final game, when the old man was said to have played three successive stones in a style that had never been seen before, moves so strange and outlandish that some members of the audience later swore that they had seen a ghostly presence standing behind the master's back, like a second shadow, and that it was this phantom, and not the man himself, who had laid down the black stones. Those three moves resulted in a comeback so sudden and overwhelming that the young challenger not only lost the game, he lost his life, one week later, having drowned in his own blood. Lee Sedol's main strength, the one that made him stand out against all other players, was his ability to create daring, almost unthinkable moves that would, to the untrained eye, seem totally chaotic, rash, misjudged, and even foolish, but that, as the game progressed, slowly revealed their unique logic, a skill he developed by spending as much time as he could practicing his capacity of "reading" the empty board, peering into the future so as to see all the branching paths of possibility that arose from the simplest positions.

"I want my style of Go to be something different, something new, my own thing, something that no one has ever thought of before," Lee explained, when his international renown and his status as a hero in Korea gave him enough confidence to begin speaking in public. By then, his talent was widely recognized, even if many of his old classmates, and the professionals who grew up competing against him on the Go circuit, agreed that he had not been an exceptionally aggressive player until his father died, when he was fifteen, and Lee began to develop the particular flair that would become his trademark and earn him the moniker Strong Stone. "His style of Go changed after his father passed away," said his friend Kim Ji-yeong, a Go player and TV anchor, "it became more dogged and powerful, angrier, impulsive, less predictable. It was like playing against a wild animal, or someone who did not even know the most basic rules of the game, and yet managed to leave you completely broken and humiliated. I have never played anyone like Lee Sedol, not when I was growing up, or since then." While Lee remained shy and introverted, he was never modest. He became the youngest player ever to reach the highest level of the game—9 dan. His flashes of virtuosity, his habit of taunting and mocking his rivals before a match, with mean-spirited barbs aimed at undermining their confidence ("I don't even know that player's name, so how should I know his style?"), his recurring boasts ("I have no confidence in this game. No confidence in losing, that is"), and his almost uncontrollable bravado earned him as many fans as detractors. "I am the best, I have never been overshadowed by anyone," he said when asked who the greatest player in the world was. "When it comes to playing skills, I am behind no one. I want to remain a living legend. I want to be the first person people associate with Go. I want my games to endure, to be studied and contemplated as works of art." Risk defined his gameplay: while most top professionals avoid it at all costs and shy away from complicated and chaotic fights, Lee would seek them out from the very beginning, and flourish under the rarefied conditions that only he seemed to be able to take advantage of, jumping into battles without forethought, forcing his opponents into all-or-nothing scenarios that should have ended in utter disaster for him, but from which he escaped with such speed and effortless grace that his rivals would often quit from sheer exasperation. Although he would train assiduously, he relied on his creative talent above all things: "I do not think, I play. Go is not a game or a sport, it is an art form. In games like chess or shogi, you start with all the pieces on the board, but in Go, you begin with an empty one, you start with nothing, and then add black and white so that between the two players you create a work of art. So everything, all the infinite complexity of Go, arises from nothing." While his mercurial character made him one of the most feared players in the entire world, it also often betrayed him, as he would become angry during a match, or his patience would fail in the endgame, so much so that he even abandoned an important tournament when it had just begun, not because he wasn't going to win (both the judges and his opponent thought that Lee was ahead) but because he felt bored by the way the match would invariably play out. While this level of disrespect toward an opponent was not common for him, he was well-known for shunning traditional expectations of what it meant to be a top-level player. Nor did he strictly adhere to the image of the wise oriental sage; during his only appearance on prime-time national television, he confessed to a crowd of unbelieving admirers, and an even more dumbfounded presenter, that he was a massive fan of soap operas such as *Goblin* and *Touch Your Heart*, which he would watch in one sitting, at twice the regular speed. When they asked him what he liked to do in his downtime, he said that he spent entire days listening to the all-female K-pop band Oh My Girl, whose songs "Remember Me" and "Secret Garden" Lee would hum to himself over and over, to the utter exasperation of his wife, Kim Hyun-jin, whom he married when he was twenty-four, and the great embarrassment of his beloved young daughter, Lee Hye-rim, the one thing that Lee prized as high as the game of Go itself. His millions of admirers could hardly believe that incredible moves such as the "broken ladder," which Lee used against Hong Chang-sik in 2003, contravening centuries of received wisdom that said, very clearly, that such a formation, in which one player chases the other across the board, was a rookie mistake that spelled certain death for whoever used it, were conceived and thought up while listening to the bubblegum tunes of six teenage girls bopping around the stage in miniskirts. For Lee Sedol, however, that was nothing out of the ordinary—Go was like breathing to him, a process that he could not stop: "I always think about Go. There is a Go board in my head. When I come up with new strategies, I place stones on the board in my head, even when I drink, watch dramas, or play billiards." When he was asked if he regretted missing out on life by dedicating every waking moment to a game, or if he felt unprepared to face the challenges that would come at the end of his career, as he had no formal education to speak of, and had not even finished primary school, he replied that Go was, first and foremost, a way of understanding the world, as its endless complexity mirrored the inner workings of the mind, while its stratagems, puzzles, and seemingly unfathomable intricacies made it the only human creation to rival the beauty, chaos, and order of our universe: "If someone was somehow capable of fully understanding Go, and by that I mean not just the positions of the stones and the way they relate to one another but the hidden, almost imperceptible patterns that lie beneath its ever-changing formations, I believe it would be the same as peering into the mind of God." Understanding of the deepest nature was paramount to Lee, something that went far beyond winning or losing: he never stepped away from a game before he had comprehended every single move. "One time, he and I drank together until two in the morning, but after that he invited me back to his house, falling down drunk, to go over a game he had just won, and replayed every stone, white and black, because even though he had won the match, he said there was one move— made by himself!—that he didn't quite understand," said Kim Ji-yeong.

By the time he turned thirty-three, Lee Sedol had won the second-highest number of international titles in Go history and was widely considered a virtuoso of the highest caliber. He had racked up eighteen international titles and thirty-two national championships and won over a thousand individual games, completely dominating the global circuit for the better part of a decade. Worshipped in South Korea, he became one of the highest-earning athletes in the country. "Lee Sedol is a genius of the century. When I look back now, I am proud of him. And I am proud of myself too," said his mentor, Master Kweon.

And then, at the peak of his career, in early 2016, Lee Sedol was challenged to a five-game matchup against the artificial intelligence system AlphaGo.

Brainchild

AlphaGo was the brainchild of Demis Hassabis, a wunderkind from North London who was four years old when he saw his father, a Greek Cypriot singer-songwriter and toy store owner, playing chess against his uncle, and asked if they could teach him how to move the pieces on the board. Two weeks later, neither of them could beat the boy.

Hassabis won his first tournament a year after that, even though he was so tiny that he had to stack a couple of chairs on top of each other and sit on a telephone directory just to see past the edge of the table. When he turned six, he won the London Under 8 championship, and three years later he was England's junior team captain, at a time when English chess was second only to the Soviet Union's. By his early teens he was a chess master, and in 1989 he became the second-highest-rated player for his age in the entire world, but while he continued touring the professional circuit for a number of years, and remained a top-level competitor, neither his trainers nor his parents could have suspected that he had already decided to abandon his dreams of becoming the next Garry Kasparov to dedicate his considerable intellect to something that, at least to his mind, was far more important, so important, in fact, that it has the potential to change the course of humanity, a pivotal choice that he made after suffering a life-changing epiphany brought on by his most humiliating defeat.

Demis had just turned thirteen. He was a kind, exceptionally thoughtful boy with very large eyes and a wide smile that was perhaps too big for his face, which, coupled with his somewhat maniacal and apparently indefatigable energy, led his meanest classmates to compare him to Mr. Toad from *The Wind in the Willows*. However, it wasn't his oversized features so much as his outsized brain that made a lasting impression on everyone he met, one of his grammar school teachers writing that "the boy has a mind the size of a planet" on one of his end-of-term evaluations. Hassabis had taught himself to code on a Commodore Amiga that he had bought with his chess earnings, a luxury that his parents could never have afforded, since they were always struggling for money, constantly moving around, working odd jobs, starting small businesses that failed within a year, or buying and selling old, run-down houses in North London. During the first ten years of his life, Demis had lived in as many different homes, dragged from one school to the next, never able to find his place in the world or to develop close friendships. He filled that emptiness with a profound love of books, movies, and computer games, some of which he hacked to give himself infinite lives, while others he programmed himself and then tested out against his kid brother. When he was just eleven, he created his first artificial intelligence agent; while very limited it could play the game Reversi—

an extremely simplified version of Go—and Demis was astounded when his digital creation managed to beat his younger sibling five times in a row. Yes, his kid brother was just five at the time, and not the worthiest opponent, but what truly fascinated Demis was the fact that in creating his little AI he seemed to have externalized a small part of his own mind, as the program—which was so full of bugs that it kept crashing and overheating the computer it ran on—appeared to be endowed with the vestiges of a personality of sorts, if not exactly with a life of its own, something that arose less from the fact that it could play the game by deciding its own moves than because of its many flaws and quirks, the incomprehensible mistakes it made, and its tendency to stall, as if it were lost in deepest thought, when its logic circuits became entangled in strange loops that Demis, try as he might, could not unravel or fully exorcise.

Computers would take up much of Hassabis's life, but his first years were consumed by chess, and an almost uncontrollable desire to be-come not just a good player but the best who had ever lived, so he was truly delighted when, a couple of days after his thirteenth birthday, he received an invitation to fly to Liechtenstein and participate in a major international tournament, a more prestigious one than any he had played up to then.

Young Demis dispatched his first set of rivals with ease before being paired against the Danish champion, a middle-aged veteran who cor-ralled and dominated him over a grueling eight hours that led to a highly unusual endgame: Hassabis had nothing but his king and queen, while his much more experienced opponent still retained a rook, a knight, and a bishop. The Dane bullied him for another four hours, with Hassabis straining his capacities to the limit while he feverishly tried to avoid a series of deadly attacks, knowing that all his opponent needed was a single misstep on his part. He saw the chairs and tables emptying around him. All the other players filed out the door, accompanied by their parents and friends, until the massive hall, in which hundreds of men and women had been silently battling, was so empty that he could hear his own hurried breath echoing against the walls. The Dane finally cornered Hassabis's king, placing himself one move away from checkmate. Covered in sweat and utterly exhausted, Demis extended his hand across the board and resigned, but as he got up to leave, his rival burst out laughing. The boy had been fooled: he was so tired after defending himself for the entire game that he'd failed to see that all he had needed to do was to sacrifice his own queen for the match to end in a stalemate, a draw that would surely have felt like a victory to him after putting up such a long fight while trying to outmaneuver forces much stronger than his own. His forty-year-old opponent showed no grace in victory, jeering and cackling with his girlfriend, pounding his fists against the table while he showed her the way he had defeated the English upstart, clearly relieved at not having lost to a schoolboy. Hassabis had to do his best to keep from crying. He felt as if he were about to vomit and stormed out the door, pushing his parents aside, and did not stop running until he was lost in the middle of a field, with grass up to his knees.

Weak from lack of food, dizzy and light-headed, he fixated on that final move, his mind racing over and over through all the ways he could have avoided losing, with the Danish bastard's laughter resounding in his ears. Queen, sacrifice, stalemate, queen, stalemate, sacrifice, voices in the distance calling his name, a herd of cows, church bells, sacrifice, a whole year wasted, stalemate, crows cawing under white pine, wet turds, bastard, threw it out, a strong musty smell, a poisonous species, shepherd is a wolf. Why had he lost like that? He knew that he was better than the Dane. The truth is that a part of his mind had been somewhere else. Even though he had trained for months, and awaited the tournament eagerly, he was, ever more so, eaten up by another, increasingly deeper obsession than chess, a fundamental question that would sometimes wake him up in the middle of the night and rob him of his sleep, leaving him there, sitting in darkness, reading science fiction sagas under his sheets with a small flashlight in his hand, wrecked by insomnia. While his sister and his brother slept soundly in their beds, Demis couldn't help but think about thinking. No matter what else he was doing, whether it was washing the dishes at home, doing his homework, or putting together broken toys from his father's store in Finchley Central subway station, he would think about his own thinking. What lay at the root of his strange intelligence? Why could he learn so fast? Why did numbers come so easily to him? And how did his brain come up with the moves and strategies that he could play on the chessboard? His parents were both normal, well, not really normal, they were bohemians and strange in their own ways, but when it came to mathematics, practically illiterate. His father dreamed of being a songwriter, and styled himself after his idol, Bob Dylan, while his mother, who was Chinese Singaporean, worked behind the counter at a John Lewis department store, selling high-end furniture that she herself could never afford. His younger brother and his sister were pretty ordinary too. He was the only odd one in his family, a freak of nature, one in millions. He had never really suffered from his exceptionality; he could behave and act like any normal boy, but try as he might, he could not understand what it was about his brain that made him enjoy what most others considered boring, if not downright painful. But what truly bothered him was not his own remarkable mind, but all the minds that surrounded him, however limited in comparison. Why had evolution built us this way? Why were we burdened by consciousness, when we could have remained blissfully ignorant like all other life-forms on this planet, living and dying with such an Edenic lack of awareness that pain and pleasure were only ever felt in the present, and did not, like our pains and glories, stretch out from one day to the next, linking us all together in an endless chain of suffering? He had read enough books to know that in thousands of years of civilization, we had not moved an inch closer to understanding any of this. Consciousness remained an unsolvable puzzle, a dilemma that pointed toward the limits beyond which mankind may never tread. Demis could have accepted it were it not for the fact that, while it was true that mankind had managed to survive thus far without any semblance of true understanding, the future was now bleak, dark, and getting darker, as science—the crown jewel of our species—was so rapidly progressing that it would soon drive us off the edge, into a world for which we were woefully unprepared. It did not take a genius to realize that scientific breakthroughs were transforming every aspect of our lives, while leaving the most fundamental questions unanswered. Soon we would reach a breaking point. Our monkey brains had taken us as far as they could. Something radically new was needed. A different type of mind, one that could see past us, far beyond the shadows cast by our own eyes. There was no longer any time to waste playing childish, zero-sum games. Was that really a proper use of his brainpower? Demis heard his parents calling him and started heading back, with a newly formed life goal already taking shape inside his head. He no longer wished to be the world chess champion. He wanted more, much more: he wanted to create a new mind, a smarter, faster, stranger one than any we had known. AGI: artificial general intelligence. The true son of man.

From then on, Hassabis worked tirelessly toward his singular goal, carefully following a twenty-year plan he sketched out for himself: He finished his A levels at fifteen and applied to Cambridge to study computer science. He won a place, but they told him that he was still too young to be admitted, and had to wait for a year. Instead of lazing about, he entered a competition that he saw in *Amiga Power* magazine, and landed a job in a prestigious computer game company, where he created the multimillion-selling video game *Theme Park*, making enough money to pay for his entire university career. After graduating at the head of his Cambridge class, he founded Elixir, his own gaming company, where he tried to simulate an entire country, populated by over a million individual agents whose aim was to overthrow a ruthless dictator by any means necessary. The game, too far ahead of its time, took five years to develop and was a complete failure, since it required computing powers far beyond what was available back then, but Hassabis was undeterred and soon found employment in another company, where he headed the design of a simulation that allowed users to play the role of an all-powerful deity lording over an island populated by warring tribes. After he had mastered programming and computer science, he moved on to the next phase of his plan: he enrolled as a PhD candidate in cognitive neuroscience at University College London, where he became obsessed by two of John von Neumann's unfinished manuscripts—*Computing Machines and the Brain: On the Mechanisms of Thought* and *Theory of Self-Reproducing Automata*—and discovered a hitherto unknown connection between memory and imagination, listed by the journal *Science* as one of the top ten breakthroughs of 2007. Hassabis's investigation demonstrated that the faculties of memory and imagination share a common mechanism, rooted in the hippocampus. "My work was investigating imagination as a process. I wanted to know how we, as human beings, visualize the future, and then see what future computers will be able to conjure," he said after publishing his research. With a PhD under his arm, he moved on to computational neuroscience, working as a visiting researcher at MIT and Harvard, and somehow still had enough brainpower left over to win the Mind Sports Olympiad five times in a row, a contest that pits some of the smartest people in the world against each other in an Olympics-style decathlon that includes, among other games, chess, shogi, backgammon, poker, draughts, and bridge. By 2010, he felt he had acquired enough knowledge and experience in the necessary fields to put the central aspect of his plan into action: along with two of his closest friends from college, Shane Legg and Mustafa Suleyman, he founded DeepMind, a start-up whose stated goal was "to solve artificial general intelligence, and then use that to solve everything else."

During the first couple of years, funders would not touch DeepMind with a stick. Artificial intelligence was still in what specialists called its "dark age": after the initial enthusiasm that it generated when John von Neumann and Alan Turing first spoke of its possibilities, back in the 1950s, and the subsequent uptick among the scientific community when the IBM computer Deep Blue defeated the world's reigning chess champion, Garry Kasparov, practically all interest had fizzled out. While computational capacity, cellular technology, and networks had increased in power by leaps and bounds, there seemed to be no way to even begin to make computers behave intelligently. Worse, DeepMind was not like other start-ups: it did not offer a product; it did not want to build up a user base, serve up ads, or mine data; it was a pure research company with a radically ambitious goal and no short-term returns to offer to potential financers. No investor would even speak to Hassabis till he somehow managed to land one of the biggest venture capitalists of them all, Peter Thiel, cofounder of PayPal and Facebook's first outside investor. Hassabis studied him for weeks, and then approached him in a crowded room in California; having found out that Thiel was a chess enthusiast, he asked him, point-blank, if he knew why the game was so utterly fascinating. Thiel perked up and focused on the short, bespectacled young man who was balancing nervously back and forth, and Hassabis quickly told him, knowing that he had no more than a couple of seconds to retain the billionaire's attention, that it was due to the exquisite balance of the bishop and knight across the set of all positions: their vastly different mobility created a dynamic asymmetric tension that had profound consequences throughout the game. With Thiel seduced, money started pouring in: Elon Musk from Tesla and Jaan Tallinn from Skype invested heavily enough to prod Google into making a bid to buy Hassabis's company in 2014, for over $625 million, pumping the company with money while leaving creative control in the hands of its founders.

After the acquisition, the biggest payout to that date for a British science-based start-up, everyone wondered what the DeepMind people would do to make good on their promise of solving artificial general intelligence. They had not even begun hiring their full team when already wild rumors about the rise of the AI apocalypse were flying around the internet. Everyone wondered where they would start. Would they train an artificial intelligence to diagnose cancer? Would they focus on nuclear fusion? Would they try to create a hitherto unimaginable means of communication? The arguments raged among specialists, each one casting bets on where gold was more likely to be struck, but Hassabis didn't have a doubt in his mind: They would begin with a game, the most complex and profound one that humankind has ever conceived.

The game of Go.

AlphaGo

I n 1997 computers became superior to human beings at chess. That year, grandmaster Garry Kasparov, the number one player in the world, was challenged by IBM to face Deep Blue, a chess-playing supercomputer, a challenge that the Russian virtuoso accepted without hesitation, as he had already beaten an earlier version of the same program a little over thirteen months before, in Philadelphia, and felt absolutely confident that computers were still decades away from anything resembling human-level chess play. The rematch was set up in New York, during the month of May, with massive billboards advertising the tournament on the city streets and a huge global audience anxious to see the contest between man and machine. Kasparov had never lost a single match during his entire trailblazing career. For over two decades he had reigned supreme, widely considered the best player of all time; he did not simply win, he crushed his opponents, with a flamboyant, creative, and highly aggressive style of play, so it came as a titanic shock when the IBM computer dealt him not only his first-ever defeat, but one that Kasparov suffered without the slightest trace of dignity. After the tournament, he experienced a profound mental breakdown, and was utterly incapable of playing for an entire year. However, what broke his mind and threw him into the deepest crisis of his adult life was not the loss in itself, but rather two particular moves that occurred during his second game against Deep Blue.

Kasparov had won the first game, but now, in the second, with hundreds of photographers and cameras fixed on him with unblinking intensity, he was on the defensive, clearly dominated by the computer. It was performing much better than anyone had expected, so the grandmaster decided to set a trap that he knew most if not all chess-playing programs would fall for, as it offered a clearly advantageous position that would seem utterly irresistible to a hard, logic-driven reasoning system such as he imagined the computer employed. But Deep Blue refused to take the bait. Instead, it made a brilliant play, leaving Kasparov to wonder if he was really facing an artificial intelligence or battling against an unseen human player, hidden behind the scenes like the Wizard of Oz, a grandmaster such as himself who could spot and avoid the snare that he had so carefully laid out, and counterattack with such style. His suspicions boiled over when Deep Blue made a shocking mistake just a couple of moves later. Kasparov couldn't understand. How could the same program play like a grandmaster and a two-bit amateur during the same game? While the audience waited eagerly for the Russian champion to make a decisive comeback after the computer's blunder, Kasparov couldn't stop doubting himself and his opponent. Had IBM brought in someone to advise them? That first move had been a stroke of genius, something that perhaps only a handful of players in the entire world could have thought up. It reminded him of Anatoly Karpov, his greatest foe. Was he behind the curtain? Was Karpov in league with IBM? Or had they brought in an entire team, a legion of grandmasters sick and tired of his supremacy, paid by that computer company's limitless pockets, bent solely on destroying him? But if that was the case, how to explain the second move, the blunder? Or had that also been on purpose, intended to throw off his suspicions, not an error in the least but a ruse, a daring gambit to hide the multiple heads of the hydra and veil the true nature of his enemy? While the clock ticked, Kasparov was unable to get out of his head and back into the game. He kept wringing his hair, rubbing his hands all over his face, and then, as the endgame neared, he simply got up and stormed off the stage, forfeiting, even though almost anyone could see that in just a couple of moves he would have been able to force a stalemate. Kasparov ended up losing or tying the remaining four games and gave up his crown. In the months that followed, he became completely despondent and increasingly paranoid, claiming that there must have been "a human mind inside the machine," and demanding that IBM give him access to the hardware and software. He insisted on seeing the machine's logs—he wanted to be able to peer into its inner workings so as to understand how the program had reached its decisions. He also wanted to see what other games Deep Blue had played. It was only fair, he argued; after all, IBM had access to thousands of his own games, and limitless computing power to analyze his strategies, openings, and preferred moves, while Kasparov had been blind in both eyes, as he had never witnessed a single match played by the computer, nor could he peer at his rival's face in search of truth. The tech giant refused, however, and even went as far as dismantling the computer entirely and scrapping the project. The Russian champion took a year off to recover, incapable of accepting what had happened to him, but he came back stronger than ever and kept on winning as before. He quit chess altogether in 2005, still ranked as the world's best player, still at the top of his game, and still obsessed with Deep Blue's incomprehensible behavior. Years had to pass before one of the IBM programmers involved in that project confessed that the flagrant mistake that Deep Blue had made during that fatal second game, which had caused Kasparov's nervous collapse, had been due to a bug in the software: unable to calculate an optimal move, the computer had simply chosen one at random.

While it is now generally accepted among the chess-playing community that the 1997 version of Deep Blue was considerably weaker than Kasparov, and that the Russian was defeated by his own inner demons, its contemporary successors, such as Fritz, Komodo, and Stockfish, have evolved far beyond our human capabilities, becoming well-nigh unbeatable. All these programs play chess in a manner that is very different from us. They don't rely on creativity or imagination, but select the best moves through sheer number-crunching and raw computing power; while the average professional player can see some ten to fifteen moves ahead, these algorithms are capable of computing two hundred million positions per second, some fifty billion in just over four minutes. This approach, in which the computer runs through every single possibility arising from each move, is called, appropriately, brute force. While a human player uses memory, experience, high-level abstract reasoning, pattern recognition, and intuition to cast his or her mind over the board, a chess engine does not really understand the game at all, it simply uses its power to calculate and then makes a decision following a complex set of hand-crafted rules laid down by its programmers. Each time its opponent places a piece on a black or white square, the computer constructs a search tree consisting of every possible future arising from that particular configuration of the board; the tree keeps on growing and branching out till it reaches the end of the game, and the computer simply selects between its many limbs the outcomes that it considers most advantageous. With each new move comes a different tree, as the game changes and evolves constantly, but with enough power, the computer can look so far into the future as to remain a step, if not several thousand steps, ahead of any human opponent.

The game of Go, however, is very different.

Its vast complexity makes brute-force search unviable. While in a game of chess you have about 20 possibilities for each individual move, in Go you have over 200. If an average chess match ends after some 40-odd moves, a single game of Go requires more than 200. After the first two moves in chess, there are 400 possible interchanges; in Go there are close to 130,000. The board itself is much larger in the oriental game—19 by 19 squares—with its western counterpart limited to a universe of just 8 by 8. Due to all of the above, the combinatorial space—the size of the tree that a computer would have to generate to see all possible game configurations arising from each move—is simply gargantuan. Also, while the total number of possible chess games is somewhere close to 10^{123}, which is a one followed by a hundred and twenty-three zeros, the number of all possible Go games is almost unimaginably larger: over 10^{700} potential games. The number of legal board positions—the unique configurations of stones that can arise from one player facing off against another—is so large that it was not clearly established until 2016:

$$208,168,199,381,979,984,699,478,633,344,862,770,$$
$$286,522,453,884,530,548,425,639,456,820,927,419,$$
$$612,738,015,378,525,648,451,698,519,643,907,259,$$
$$916,015,628,128,546,089,888,314,427,129,715,319,$$
$$317,557,736,620,397,247,064,840,935$$

If one were to consider all theoretically possible games—including ones that would never take place in the real world, since they include completely irrational, fanciful matches—the total number defies comprehension: it exceeds a googolplex, $10^{(10^{100})}$, a figure so large that it is physically impossible to write down in full decimal form because doing so would require more space than is available in the known universe.

But that is not where Go's complexity ends.

In Go, all pieces have the same value; there are no castles or pawns, no knights or rooks, no kings or queens, simply black and white stones of the same exact worth. While you can easily program a chess-playing computer to distinguish what the intrinsic value of the queen is in relation to a knight, a bishop, or a pawn, in Go the weight of each stone has to do with its position on the board, and its relationship with every other stone, as well as with the intervening spaces on the grid. Telling a good move from a bad one is highly subjective; professionals feel out positions, they use their intuition and instinct to decide where to place the next stone. They train for years to be able to oversee the entire board, to detect rising and falling patterns, and to distinguish configurations of stones that are common to almost all Go games, groupings that beginners have to master before they can even sit at the board. These formations or clusters have highly evocative names such as "eyes," "ladders," and "bamboo joints." Go players speak of groups of stones as "alive," "dead," or "unsettled." There are stones that cut, stones that kill, and stones that commit suicide. Players must be able to read the board, peering into the future with their mind's eye to determine if a group of stones will live or die. They must know how to form a harmonious position by alternating high and low attacks. They must distinguish between the thickness and lightness of their formations to decide if they need to be reinforced, or can withstand enemy attacks; they must learn to invade, to counter, and to capture; they must weigh the *aji*, the potential of each individual stone, tread the fine line of *korigatachi* to avoid being completely surrounded, and learn when to take the initiative—*sente*—or play on the defensive, *gote*; they must decide when to fight head-on and bite down on a position or to gambit and steal away to some other corner of the board, exacting *tenuki*. They must distinguish between real and false eyes. They must learn to play at the Star point, the Origin of Heaven, and at the Large, High, and Small eyes. They must develop their *kiai*, an aggressive fighting spirit that lets you control the flow of play, without giving in to irrational greed. They must learn to monkey jump, to peep, to pincer, to shoulder hit. They must learn to play *kikashi*, a forcing move that enlivens through sacrifice. All of that, and much more, must be achieved with the simple laying down of successive stones, to maximize the boundaries of your territory while minimizing your opponent's.

Played continuously for over three thousand years, Go is humanity's oldest and most studied game. Schools in China, Japan, and Korea have amassed a truly astounding body of wisdom that has been passed down through generations, encoded in a series of swift proverbs that all players know by heart, warnings for avoiding common pitfalls or amateurish mistakes, while trying to whittle down the seemingly endless possibilities that the board offers.

Don't make empty triangles.

Don't peep at a cutting point.

Don't peep at both sides of a bamboo joint.

Even a moron connects against a peep.

Play fast, lose fast.

Don't play 1, 2, 3—just play 3.

If you don't understand ladders then don't play Go.

If you have lost all four corners then you have lost.

If you have secured all four corners then you have lost.

In the corner six stones live but four stones die.

Never try to cut bamboo joints.

Strange things happen at the 1-2 points.

Strike at the waist of the knight's move.

Learn the eye-stealing tesuji.

The weak carpenter's square is dead.

Your enemy's key point is your own key point.

Greed cannot prevail!

There is death in the hane.

For centuries, Go was considered an art form more than a game. In China, it was one of the four disciplines that any nobleman had to master. Top players throughout the ages have never depended on calculation to decide their moves, but on sensibilities that border on the artistic, or the mystical. The game was considered to be too profound, too complex and labyrinthine, to ever yield to a computational approach. And then, in 2016, Hassabis and his team at DeepMind shocked the entire Go-playing world, and stunned their peers in the AI community, when they published an article in *Nature* showing that they had managed to build an artificial intelligence agent that not only played Go but had actually beaten the reigning European champion, Fan Hui. It was the first time a program had ever defeated a professional Go player, and hundreds of computer scientists started poring over the details of the paper, and the games DeepMind published online, scrutinizing every move to see if that holy grail of artificial intelligence had really been achieved, so far ahead of its time. Before DeepMind's paper, there had been a strong general agreement that artificial intelligence would need at least another decade before it could even begin to compete against human beings in Go. And yet, somehow, Hassabis and his team had done it. Their program, AlphaGo, had pummeled Fan Hui, winning all five games they played against each other. It was a stunning achievement that caused an immediate blowback: Go fans from around the world mocked and ridiculed Fan Hui, saying that he may be the champion in Europe, but he was only a 5 dan professional, and nowhere close to the world's top players, the 9 dans, who mostly lived in Japan, China, and South Korea. They picked apart the games, pointing out every single mistake that Fan Hui had made, and declared that he was not a worthy adversary, and that the whole exercise was flawed. To the people at DeepMind, it quickly became clear that their agent needed a much better opponent.

And there was no one better than Lee Sedol.

A Sharp, Sudden Invasion

Lee Sedol picked up a black stone from his bowl and placed it on the upper right-hand corner of the board.

Outside the players' room, on the sixth floor of Seoul's new Four Seasons Hotel, over two hundred journalists from all around the world watched the viewing screens, sitting alongside expert commentators who were eagerly waiting to analyze every move for the more than 100,000 people who had tuned in to the official YouTube feed of the game and a television audience of sixty million watching the seven networks from Japan, China, and South Korea that would live-broadcast the entire match. Lee Sedol was sitting in the game room—a spare accommodation with nothing but a table, two black leather chairs, some cameras, and the three judges presiding over the match from an elevated platform at the back—safely isolated from the bustle outside after walking down the marble corridors of the five-star hotel, lit by enormous golden chandeliers. Across from him, on the other side of the board, sat Aja Huang, a senior programmer from DeepMind charged with playing the moves that the AlphaGo artificial intelligence agent would select, after seeing them appear on a small computer terminal to his left; a couple of years later, after all five games had been played, after Lee Sedol had shocked the world by announcing his sudden retirement in his hollowed-out, breathless voice, Lee could not help but poke fun at Huang's uncanny stillness, which he maintained throughout the entire match, which lasted five days. "Aja Huang. Just thinking about him makes me laugh. He is truly a remarkable man. He is just a human being, right? AlphaGo is the AI. But I almost thought that he was the artificial one. Because it's not just that he had a poker face, he was like a puppet. He never once went to the bathroom, never left his seat, not once. And he would take these tiny sips of water, really tiny sips of water, which looked incredibly quaint and weird. I didn't know if it was water, because he just wet his lips, like a robot, or an animal at a waterhole. And his movements were really slow, completely deliberate, with great patience and precision. And he never made eye contact with me. Not once! I kept looking at him and thinking, *Who is he really?* It was like playing Go with a robot, an automaton, a heartless, unfeeling zombie, or a complete simpleton, a fool. Later I found out that he wasn't allowed to go to the bathroom. The people at DeepMind would not let him. He also wasn't allowed to emote or show feelings of any kind, so as not to give anything away. But even so, if you see that in a person, if someone behaves like that in front of you, you feel very uncomfortable. More than uncomfortable! I wanted to scream at him, or get up, walk over, and pinch him, just to see if he was real," Lee recalled during a prime-time television show interview, casting his mind back to the very first day of that fateful match, and the very first move made by the computer, which took an unreasonably long amount of time.

Opening moves in Go tend to be very quick. The board is empty, there are no stones at all, just the endless grid, bursting with possibilities. Commonly, a player will stake out a territory near the upper corner, and his rival will place his stone on the opposing side. There is not much to think about, it is usually just a matter of seconds, but in the Four Seasons Hotel, after Lee Sedol had laid down his opening—a slightly unconventional one meant to get away from the computer's knowledge base—the clock began to tick and Aja Huang stared at his computer screen, then at Lee's black slate stone lying there on the board, its flattened surface shining under the glaring studio lights, and then turned back to his screen, where all he could see were the lines of the grid and a tiny spinning ball that indicated that AlphaGo was still calculating to reach a decision. Five, ten, fifteen, twenty seconds went by and the anxious South Korean commentators began to make jokes about AlphaGo, while inside DeepMind's control room, situated two floors down from the game room, all twenty technicians, including Demis Hassabis and his colleague David Silver, the head researcher of the AlphaGo project, began to panic. Had the program stalled? Had it crashed? What the hell could be taking so long! Were they going to shit the bed in the first move of the game?

When almost thirty seconds had passed, Lee started making faces. Surely this had all been a mistake, a monumental waste of his valuable time. He had studied the games that AlphaGo had played against Fan Hui, the European champion, and had seen nothing special in either of them. Compared to him, Fan Hui was not even an amateur. If they had faced off against each other, it would have been as if a child (and not a particularly gifted one) had played against Go Seigen, the legendary Japanese master. Lee had also been unimpressed by AlphaGo. Yes, it could play the game, even with a certain flair that was uncommon in computer programs, but it was still nowhere near his level. Google, DeepMind's parent company, had put forward a million-dollar prize for the winner of the match, and many people who analyzed the Fan Hui–AlphaGo matches had said that it was like giving that money away to Lee. In South Korea, professional Go players joked that they were envious, that surely it was the easiest money a top-level player could ever make. Everyone was convinced that the human would win.

Lee shot mocking looks at the camera and at Aja Huang, who was sweating in his seat as he tried to stay calm during that long pregnant pause at the start, thinking, perhaps, of what Lee had said during the inaugural press conference, held in the glitzy sixth-floor ballroom that had been repurposed to house the enormous number of national and foreign correspondents who occupied every square inch of that place: "There is a beauty to the game of Go, and I don't think machines understand that beauty. I believe human intuition is too advanced for AI to have caught up yet, so I am not worried about if I will win or not. What worries me is if I will win five to zero, or four to one." After more than a minute had gone by, a white circle appeared on Huang's computer screen. The programmer picked up a stone from the bowl in front of him and set it down neatly, with a smart click, at the opposite side of the board, at the same height as Lee Sedol's stone, where almost every human player would have done so.

What followed were several plays in quick succession, and after some twenty-odd moves, nobody seemed impressed by AlphaGo's performance. Some commentators were even repulsed after a particularly uninspired white stone laid down by Aja Huang. "This program really needs a good teacher who will knock it about the head and bestow some wisdom after playing such a bad move. Everybody just knows that this move isn't good at all . . . These first white moves are obviously not optimal and look like beginner's mistakes," quipped the Chinese 5 dan professional player Guo Juan during her live commentary, shaking her head in clear disapproval. Throughout the entire opening of the game, Lee Sedol was unmistakably in the lead, but then, two hours in, Huang placed white stone 102 on the tenth line, at the middle of the board, two squares from the left edge of the grid, and everything changed.

It was a sharp, sudden invasion into Lee's territory. With a single stone, AlphaGo created several complicated positions, setting off fights across the entire board. It was exactly the type of viciously aggressive move that Lee Sedol had become famous for, and the Bigeumdo Boy could hardly believe what he was seeing. His jaw dropped and hung open for a cartoonish twenty seconds during which he remained bolt upright, with both arms dangling at his sides as if he had lost all muscle control. Completely flabbergasted, he began rocking back and forth in his chair, looking like an emaciated Playmobil toy, with his loose-fitting suit and bowl haircut. Slowly, he started to smile and leaned back, bringing the palm of his hand to the nape of his neck, where he scratched three circular moles he had there, set in a skewed triangle pattern and that look for all the world exactly like tiny ceramic Go stones. He would exhibit that same nervous tic many times during the course of the match, but on that first occasion he quickly removed his hand from his neck and then leaned forward over the board while a host of emotions washed over his face: shock, disbelief, and puzzlement, eventually leading to fear, then amusement, then something akin to sheer joy. How could a computer have played such a bold move? he would ask one of his friends after the match was done. In that moment he simply couldn't understand what he was looking at. This was a wholly different level of play. It was nothing like the AlphaGo that had beaten the European champion. But how on earth could the algorithm have improved so much in so little time? Those games had taken place only five months before. Lee thought about his next move for over ten minutes, frowning, crossing and uncrossing his feet, squinting his eyes, cupping his face in his hands, shaking his head now and again in sheer disbelief, and then becoming absolutely still, eyes fixed on the board, before placing his stone right next to the one that AlphaGo had played, knowing full well that the tide had turned, as an entire swath of territory that had been squarely in his hands was now completely destroyed. Eighty moves after that, Lee Sedol picked up a white stone—not the black ones he was using—and laid it down in the middle of the board, resigning in the politest way possible.

A Thing of Beauty, Not of This World

When future historians look back at our time and try to pin down the first glimmer of a true artificial intelligence, they may well find it in a single move during the second game between Lee Sedol and AlphaGo, played on the tenth of March 2016: move 37.

It was unlike anything a computer had ever done before. It was also different from anything that a human being had ever been known to consider. It was something new, a complete break from tradition, a radical departure from thousands of years of accumulated wisdom. The people who saw it, whether live at the Four Seasons Hotel in Seoul or transmitted via the internet, unwittingly caught a glimpse of a future that is rushing wildly toward us, for now perhaps still distant, but already affecting our present in myriad ways. It is a future that inspires hope and horror: some believe we should welcome it with open arms, while many others are convinced that we should do everything in our power to ensure that this mad dream remains safely beyond our grasp, forever inaccessible, even if its first echoes have already rung out from a slate stone laid down on a wooden board by a human hand following the instructions of an intelligence that may one day rival our own.

AlphaGo's victory during the first game against Lee Sedol stunned the world, but many players and commentators were unimpressed. Lee, they said, had made several childish mistakes and had not played to his usual standard. The machine had performed better than anyone had expected, but it had not made any truly earth-shattering moves. It was impressive, yes, but uninspired. Like its chess-playing forebears, AlphaGo was clearly efficient and powerful, but there was no beauty to its game, even if its aggressiveness and fighting spirit surprised both Lee and the Go community at large. While almost no one had the same unwavering confidence in the South Korean champion as before the first game, everybody was still betting on him to take the match, and some went as far as saying that the victory achieved by the DeepMind program had been nothing but a one-time fluke, an anomaly that Lee would surely redress during the encounters to come.

The South Korean master, however, did not feel that way.

The first game had shaken him to his core. He could not understand the incredible leap forward that the algorithm had achieved in such a short span of time. It had taken him more than two decades to develop his unique skills, and AlphaGo had beaten him, when just four months before, during its match against Fan Hui, it had played like a middling professional, someone Lee could have annihilated without strain. During the first game, Lee had followed his signature style, but now he was scared. If he lost the second game, it meant that he would have to win the remaining three in a row to avoid defeat. In the press conference at the end of their first encounter, he dialed back his bravado: "I didn't think that AlphaGo would play the game in such a perfect manner. But I have won many world championships and losing one game will not affect my playing in the future. I think it's fifty-fifty now," he said while his mentor, Kweon Kab-yong, nibbled his fingernails and paced nervously among the members of the media. On the eve of the second game, there were twice as many reporters, and Lee could feel the enormous pressure of having to represent the whole of humanity bearing down upon him. Clearly worn out from the physical and mental strain of the previous day's game, he walked out of his room wearing a loose-fitting black suit and a light blue shirt that seemed two sizes too big for him and made him look like a skinny high school student. He would only appear more frail as the tournament progressed—he lost almost eighteen pounds during preparation and play. On his way to the pre-game photo shoot he smiled at the people who cheered him on—*Go, Lee Sedol! Go fight, Lee!*—surrounded by five guards who waved the crowds aside. While he waited for the lift he kept glancing at his watch, an expensive, heavy-looking model that dwarfed his scrawny wrist and hung there like the shackle of an unseen chain, weighing on his arm. As the cameras flashed around him, he seemed to be a world away, lost deep within himself; he would close his eyes as if in prayer, then suddenly frown and pinch the bridge of his nose, as though he were suffering a splitting migraine. His young daughter ran up and hugged him before he entered the game room, burying her face in the pit of his arm. Lee knelt down and she snuggled against him, but it was hard to tell if it was her father who was consoling her, or if she was trying to give him what little strength she could. When it was time to begin, Lee's wife, Kim

313

Hyun-jin, came and gently pried them apart, so that Lee could enter the game room alone and focus solely on the board. It was his time to play white.

He used a wholly different approach, playing an uncharacteristically cautious opening. His first couple of stones avoided any violence as he sought to establish a firm base. He pondered every move with enormous care, having by then realized that his sudden changes of pace, so useful for throwing off his human opponents, were pointless against an unthinking, unfeeling machine. As was his custom, he drank coffee throughout the game, his staff refilling his cup as soon as it was empty. He was also well-known for smoking, and the organizers had set up a particular arrangement for him to be able to smoke outside the hotel, even during the game, in an open-air terrace on the upper floors, where he could pace and think by himself while enjoying a full view of Seoul's Gwanghwamun district, with its wall of towering skyscrapers and the great green mountains beyond. The stones began to build up on the board, at a turtle's pace: after AlphaGo played black 13, Lee sank deep into thought and then declined to attack a group of stones that were beginning to amass on the lower right corner, biding his time and splitting territory on the opposite side. The commentators immediately noticed his unwillingness to engage AlphaGo and criticized his attitude: "Lee seems very tense. My guess is that he didn't sleep last night," said one of the South Korean reporters as the game plodded along, adding that Lee was being overly cautious, as every now and then AlphaGo would play amateurish, or even nonsensical-looking, moves that Lee seemed to be unwilling, or unable, to capitalize on. "Those last two moves make me doubt AlphaGo's ability," said a Chinese commentator after one particularly slack move by the computer. "But we have to stay alert," he added. "AlphaGo is hard to understand." At black 15, the DeepMind computer played a "peep," a forcing move that any Go teacher would deride as crude and uninspired, but which Lee Sedol failed to respond to, continuing to proceed with the greatest caution. His previous experience had clearly left him shell-shocked and overly wary, an attitude that led several of his fans to begin to complain on the YouTube feed, writing that Lee was betraying his essence and forgoing the playing style that had made him a legend. Even his mentor, Master Kweon, had to admit that his star pupil was in trouble, saying to a reporter, "Lee Sedol is playing in a completely different style from his usual one," while also reflecting that the Strong Stone was at the center of global attention during a truly historic moment, and that while his nickname may have implied it, Lee was not made of stone. It was easy enough for outsiders to criticize Lee Sedol's attitude, but the truth is that no one really knew what was going on inside AlphaGo's strange algorithm, or what it was truly capable of. Had that last move—black 15—really been so crude and amateurish? Even the programmers at DeepMind were completely in the dark: AlphaGo made its own decisions, fully unsupervised; they simply watched it play. Demis Hassabis had explained as much ahead of the match: "Although we have programmed this machine, we have no idea what moves it will come up with. They are an emergent phenomenon from its training. We just create the data sets and the training algorithms. But the moves AlphaGo then comes up with are out of our hands, and they are much better than the ones we could come up with. The program is rather autonomous in its nature." The following fifteen moves were all pretty standard: when AlphaGo's black stones connected at 21, Lee nodded as if to reaffirm his choice to avoid conflict and play on the left side of the board. By move 30, the game remained balanced, with AlphaGo's inner evaluation function setting its odds of winning at 48 percent. The machine prevented Lee from invading a corner and extended its forces on the third line with a short fight developing and then simmering down again. AlphaGo enclosed a corner; Lee hesitated briefly and then approached his opponent's stones from below. Both sides played normally, without any upsets or excitements, until Lee placed white stone 36.

Aja Huang looked at his monitor, picked up a black stone, and placed it below and to the left of a solitary piece that Lee had just laid out near the middle of the board. It was a "shoulder hit" on the fifth line, a type of move meant to decrease the potential of your enemy's territory, but it was unlike anything seen before in competitive play. Move 37 went against everything that Go players hold to be true. You simply do not shoulder hit on the fifth line. It was so outrageous and counterintuitive that when Aja Huang played there, the commentators, the audience, and even the judges thought he had put the stone down by mistake. Because no human being would ever dare to play like that. It is not simply considered a bad move, it has been reviled and derided by the great masters and the thousands of volumes on Go written during more than three thousand years of continuous play. But you don't have to be a grandmaster or a great sage to realize that you should never shoulder hit on the fifth line—even children and beginners know not to play there, as most times it actually helps your opponent gain ground! It looks bad and it is counterproductive, but more importantly, it *feels* bad to players, as it is almost completely impossible to estimate its future consequences across the board. But AlphaGo did not care about any of that, and Aja Huang, who was a competent Go player himself, sat there after placing the stone, trying to hide the fact that he was as flabbergasted as everyone else by the algorithm's choice, and even felt ashamed of having been made to play there. Very few people were able to see its potential. All the professional commentators criticized it immediately. It wasn't like the other "slack" moves that AlphaGo would choose now and then, those uninspired stones that did little to increase its advantage and that seemed not to affect the game at all; this was altogether different, and many saw it as the computer's first all-out blunder, the concrete evidence that no matter how powerful computers became, they would never really understand the game as we humans did. The only one who immediately recognized it as something other was Fan Hui, the Chinese-born European Go champion, recently defeated by AlphaGo.

Fan Hui was the person who had the most experience playing against AlphaGo, and he was in awe of what the program could do. After he lost his five games against the machine, DeepMind had hired him as a consultant to the project. In the four months leading up to the match in Seoul, he had played against several versions of the algorithm, advising Hassabis, Silver, and the rest of the team and helping them make it much, much stronger, so strong, in fact, that he had become convinced that AlphaGo was capable of exhibiting one of the hallmarks of human intelligence: true creativity. Fan Hui had flown to Seoul for the match and was serving as one of its three judges, sitting on an elevated table that looked straight down on Lee, Huang, and the board. His intimate knowledge of the program helped him recognize move 37 for what it really was: a stroke of genius. "Black 37 casts an invisible net across the board. The shoulder hit creates potential all across the center. All the stones placed before worked together, they connected like a network, linking everywhere," he would write months later in his in-depth analysis of the game, but in the moment when he saw it for the first time, all he could do was to jot down a quick note in his logbook, after recovering from the initial shock of disbelief: "*Here?!* This goes beyond my understanding. It's not a human move. I've never seen a human play this move." After the game was done—though some people, including Lee Sedol, would argue that the game was done there and then—Fan Hui could not put his thoughts fully into words, and just kept repeating, "Beautiful, beautiful, so beautiful!" when others approached him to ask his opinion about that soon-to-be-famous move. Most onlookers remained as flummoxed as he was at first: "A totally unthinkable move," said a Korean commentator. "I don't even know if it's good or bad at this point," quipped Michael Redmond, the only western player to have ever achieved 9 dan status. Redmond was analyzing the game for DeepMind's live YouTube feed, but he did not know how to answer the questions that his counterpart, the head of the American Go Association, directed at him. He chuckled nervously and admitted that he also thought it was a mistake, but not on AlphaGo's part; he actually believed that it was the algorithm's human aide—Aja Huang—surely he must have read the monitor incorrectly before placing the stone on the board. A few people gradually began to appreciate what the machine had done: Demis Hassabis got up from the game room and ran upstairs to where the DeepMind team had set up their control room, anxious to know how AlphaGo's monitoring systems had evaluated that bizarre play. When he got there, he found David Silver just as excited as he was, already rooting around inside the algorithm, trying somehow to understand what had just happened, and waiting anxiously to see how Lee Sedol would react when he returned to the game room—as, due to one of those strange coincidences that seem to suggest that there is a hidden and slightly mischievous intelligence behind this world, the man who would have to react to one of the most uncanny moves played by anyone in centuries was the last one to see it.

Lee Sedol had just left his seat for a ten-minute cigarette break when Aja Huang placed the shoulder hit. When he came back downstairs, escorted by two smartly dressed guards, and settled himself in his chair, he scrunched up his nose and scowled in disgust with his mouth agape, as if he had just stepped in shit. After a moment had passed, he leaned forward while a huge beatific smile started slowly spreading across his face, as if he had finally seen what he himself had spent his entire life looking for: a thing of beauty, not of this world. Lee was known to be an incredibly impulsive player, one who would normally spend no more than a minute thinking before making a decision, but on that occasion he exhausted over twelve minutes of his allotted time pondering AlphaGo's seemingly absurd invention, blinking repeatedly, pinching the skin between his thumb and forefinger, with his head tilted slightly to one side, much as a dog does when it is puzzled by something it has never seen before. His thoughts were almost written on his face. "At the beginning of the game I thought it was making a lot of mistakes. It was still in charge but I was making a comeback. But it kept making more and more mistakes and I thought, 'There is a chance of winning.' I thought, 'This machine is still imperfect.' But then it made this move. In a real game, it's unthinkable, because there were many black stones, it was almost completely surrounded. You can't just drop one in there. But it made that move, move 37, and I knew that I didn't have a chance. Later I realized that the reason that it had given up spaces, given me some room in other parts of the board, is because it already had that move in mind. It was letting me win. It tricked me. With that move, I was finished, it had already won." That is how Lee would recall that game a year later, after announcing his retirement, but during the game he gave no indication of capitulating without a fight, and continued staring at the board while his clock slowly ran down, picking at his lower lip with his finely manicured nails and long, delicate fingers. "I thought AlphaGo was based on probability calculation and it was merely a machine. But when I saw this move it changed my mind. Surely AlphaGo is creative. This move made me think about Go in a new light. What does creativity mean in Go? It was not just a good, or great, or a powerful move. It was meaningful," he would say to the documentary crew who interviewed him after the match was done. Lee fought the machine for another three hours, playing long past the point where he would normally have resigned, and he continued to fight while commentators began the slow, difficult process of tallying the score, unable to accept what was already inevitable, or perhaps reticent to walk away from a game that he knew was bound to go down in history. By move 99, Lee no longer had any chance of winning, but the algorithm never went for the kill, and instead continued nibbling away at Lee's territory, bit by bit, stone by stone. Lee Sedol held on, hoping for a miracle, or perhaps expecting that the machine would somehow make a mistake, or go back to the erratic play that it had exhibited in the beginning, but the program only got stronger as the stones covered the board, and by white 211, Lee finally gave up.

The press swarmed the postgame conference room while Lee Sedol took the stage next to Hassabis looking like a broken man. A sense of sadness and melancholy permeated the entire floor, as fans, commentators, and other players could hardly believe that their national hero had been defeated, not once, but twice. Lee had been outplayed and out-smarted, dominated and kicked about like an amateur. Many agreed that if in the first game Lee had been caught off guard, during the second he had been powerless. With his frail ventriloquist dummy voice strangled by emotion, Lee apologized deeply for his loss: "Yesterday I was surprised, but today I am quite speechless. It was a very clear loss. From the very beginning there was not a moment in time when I felt that I was leading. It played a near-perfect game," he confessed as the camera flashes blinded him. Though he was deeply self-effacing and looked humbled and shocked, he made clear that he would not go down without a fight: "I may have lost the second game, but the match is not over. There is still a third game left to play."

One of the Ten Thousand Things

Lee had a day off before the third game and he spent all that time holed up in his room with four other top Go professionals, touching on every single stone of the previous matches, to try to understand how a group of computer scientists with next to no background in Go had been able to create a system capable of wiping away centuries of tradition with a single move. How had the people at DeepMind managed to program an algorithm to play like that? he marveled. The truth was that they hadn't.

Move 37 was not a part of AlphaGo's memory, nor had it come out of any sort of preprogrammed rule or general guideline manually encoded into its silicon brain. It was created by the program itself, with no human input, but what made it all the more impressive was the fact that AlphaGo knew—at least as far as a nonsentient being can be said to "know" anything—that it was a move that not even a Go master would consider. With DeepMind just one game away from victory, and media attention already at a frenzy, Demis Hassabis had to do the rounds to try to explain how such a thing was even possible. The system, he told reporters, was not hand crafted, nor had it been given a comprehensive set of rules to follow, as IBM had done with DeepBlue, its chess-playing engine, two decades before. AlphaGo was based on self-play and reinforcement learning, which meant that, in essence, it had taught itself how to play.

But first, it had to learn how to imitate human beings.

Hassabis and his team had believed that the only way to beat a top professional was to try to replicate the highly creative and somewhat mysterious ways in which human beings approach Go. To do so, they fed 150,000 games from a database of top amateur players into an artificial neural network—a complex mathematical model that mimics the web of neurons in our brains, and that is composed of several layers of algorithms connected to each other, each one designed to recognize a specific set of patterns and features; working together, they create a vast model with millions of parameters that affect each other, and that can be ever so slightly adjusted, to change the overall behavior of the network. AlphaGo's first neural network analyzed those many thousands of games and learned, little by little, to mimic, copy, and predict the moves that an amateur would play in any given situation. This first human-based data set amounts to AlphaGo's "common sense," as it equates, very roughly, to the knowledge that a beginner would derive from books and the lessons he or she would learn directly from his teachers. The people at DeepMind called this the *Policy Network*. Using it, AlphaGo could play a half-decent game, at the same level as a human amateur, but it was still a long way away from a true professional. To reach that level, it needed to develop that specific skill that great players have of seeing the entire board and achieving an intuitive grasp of how the game will play out from a particular position, that essentially human capacity to "read the board," one that young players must spend years developing, and that Lee Sedol had attained after countless hours of staring unblinkingly at the empty grid, playing out each move and its countermoves in his mind's eye. AlphaGo needed a way of estimating the value of each board position, to get a much broader understanding of the game, a way to tell—moment by moment—if it was inching to victory or staggering toward defeat. But to do that, it would have to face itself.

AlphaGo took the Policy Network it had created based on the amateur games, and played against itself, many millions of times. Learning from its mistakes through trial and error, it became better and better, stronger and stronger, no longer trying to mimic and play like a human being, but focused only on besting itself. Throughout millions of games it made billions of tiny adjustments to its mathematical model, improving for reasons that no human being could ever really understand, as the inner functioning of an artificial neural network is almost completely opaque to us, for we cannot keep track of or tally the countless effects that arise from the almost innumerable tweaks that the algorithm makes to its inner parameters while slowly building toward its desired outcome. "Initially it was terrible," Hassabis explained, "flailing around wildly on the board like a child, or an extremely clumsy and untalented human newcomer, as it had no inner representation of what the game was about, something that, to us, comes naturally, almost instinctively; but occasionally it would do clever things, totally by accident, and then it learned to recognize good patterns of play, and strengthen those patterns. Its networks worked together, reinforcing behavior that increased its possibility of winning, gradually improving its abilities." After that second training process was complete, the new, sturdier version of Al-phaGo played another thirty million games against its improved self, cre-ating a data set that allowed it to train a second neural network, which DeepMind named the *Value Network*: this one would analyze any given configuration of stones on the board and look ahead toward the end of the game, to estimate if it was winning or not, and by how much. This went far beyond what even the smartest and best-trained human beings are capable of, as this second neural network could put a numerical value on something that we can only grasp at by vague feelings and nebulous intuition. Those two neural networks allowed the DeepMind program to whittle down Go's infinite complexity and reach a hitherto unimaginable level of play. It did not need to waste its vast computing powers searching through the endless possibilities that branch out from every single stone, since it could use the common sense of its Policy Net-work to consider only the best possible moves and prune the branches of its Monte Carlo search tree that it did not consider optimal; its Value Network, meanwhile, saved it from having to internally play out the entirety of each match to come to a conclusion about whether a partic-ular move would bring it closer to winning or losing. The combination of those two systems—honed and perfected during millions and millions of games of self-play—is what allowed AlphaGo to range far beyond human knowledge and come up with radical strategies and counterin-tuitive moves like the one that it had flaunted during the second game against Lee Sedol. They also allowed it to have a precise estimate of how unlikely that particular move would seem to its human opponent.

When Hassabis and David Silver looked at how AlphaGo's internal systems had evaluated move 37, they saw that it had assigned it a prob-ability value of one in ten thousand; this meant that, according to its understanding of how we play the game, only one in ten thousand human Go players would ever consider putting a stone down in that particular part of the board, at that particular time. And yet, that was exactly the move that AlphaGo had chosen, and that was the level of cunning and ingenuity that Lee Sedol would have to reach if he was to overcome the machine and win the tournament.

The third game began at one p.m. on March 12. Lee Sedol took black and suffered from the very beginning.

Sitting atop the judges' podium and overlooking the board, Fan Hui could see Lee's hand tremble slightly as he placed his third stone down on the lower right corner of the grid. He had read that the Korean superstar suffered from insomnia, and knew, from his own experience in international tournaments, that one needed inner peace and a calm heart to play at the highest level; Lee Sedol looked so haggard and weak that Fan Hui half expected him to faint and fall headfirst onto the board, or keel over and die like Akaboshi Intetsu during the "blood-vomiting game." Before the match, Fan Hui had looked at the commentaries online: there was no one who still believed that Lee could win. Even his fans had turned against him, mercilessly criticizing his mistakes and even questioning his character, resolve, and *kiai*, his "fighting spirit." Fan Hui was perhaps the only man alive who could fully understand what Lee Sedol was going through. He had been crushed during his matchup with the machine, and knew full well just how uncanny it felt to play against a merciless, unfeeling opponent. AlphaGo did not hesitate and it never thought twice. It was immune to weariness. It knew no self-doubt. It cared not for style or beauty, and it did not waste time with any of the elaborate mind games that all professional players bait each other with. It simply did not care about what others thought or felt; all it cared about was winning. To AlphaGo, it made no difference if it won by only a single point. That explained the "lazy" moves it would play now and again, moves that seemed subpar and uninspired to everyone, till a South Korean commentator pointed out that they were based on pure calculation: each one of those lazy stones made a tiny, almost imperceptible gain toward the final goal, and their true value would only be realized when they all came together in the endgame. Fan Hui was already aware of this, as he looked at Lee Sedol trying to battle the artificial intelligence, squirming in his seat as if he were being subjected to a novel form of torture, and he wished that he could somehow help or warn him, for he knew that there was something deeply distressing about playing against AlphaGo: it could induce a sense of despair, a strange feeling of being pulled down into a void, slowly but irrevocably. "It is like a black hole," Fan Hui would later write, "sucking you in, little by little. No matter how you try to break away, you will discover that your efforts count for nothing. AlphaGo creeps up on you like a fatal yet undiagnosed disease. By the time you feel the first hint of pain, you are already dead." Lee had perhaps already realized this after his two previous defeats, for as soon as he saw an opportunity to attack, he seized it.

Before the computer's advantage became overwhelming, Lee Sedol attempted to tear into AlphaGo's territory with a sudden and unexpected attack, but he had not taken the time to build up a proper foundation, and his ambush was rash and ill-timed. "Showed his fangs too early," wrote Fan Hui in his notes, as he watched AlphaGo counter with a two-space jump that was so inspired, it became apparent to Fan that the system that Lee Sedol was facing had advanced far beyond the machine that he had played against himself, so far that it seemed to be looking down from the heavens, not only comprehending the entire board but somehow peering inside Lee's mind, anticipating every single move he made. Clearly infuriated, Lee slapped down his next stone, his face reddening as AlphaGo tore apart the Elephant's Eye formation that he had so painstakingly set up. He began losing his temper, rocking back and forth like a drunkard, glancing at the clock over and over. When he made a particularly gruesome mistake, he slapped himself on the cheek and then rested his hand on the edge of his bowl, dipping his fingers among the black slate stones as if he were physically unable to pick one up. He needed to regain his calm, but he continued attacking aggressively, without making any headway, like a boxer punching himself out. By move 48, AlphaGo's systems indicated that its probability of winning had soared to 72 percent. The game was essentially decided already, but Lee hunkered down nonetheless, and tried to dismantle the AI's Dragon formation at the bottom of the grid, to no avail. When Lee finally acknowledged that he could no longer win by playing smart, he resorted to his signature "zombie" style, a mad thrashing all over the board, a desperate, last-ditch attempt of a man who already knows that he is dead, but wishes to catch his opponent off guard with wild, unpredictable attacks. It was a foolish, almost nonsensical strategy that had let him win back many a lost game in the past but stood no chance against an opponent that could not be bullied, threatened, or confused, and AlphaGo continued to adapt to Lee's now seemingly insane moves, and secured an enormous stretch of territory on the top of the board. Its Value Network estimated that its chances of winning had already surpassed 87 percent: white was alive all over the board, while black was way behind on points. There seemed to be nowhere left to play, but in that last moment Lee found a small crack in white's fortifications, and enough breathing room to cut AlphaGo's group on the right side. A human player would never allow an opponent to live there, especially so far into the game, but AlphaGo, heaping insult on injury, did not even bother to respond; in a final show of incontestable dominance, it let him live there, in the corner, and simply played elsewhere, adding another point to its score, while reaching a 98 percent likelihood of winning. The game continued for another twenty-eight moves that were excruciating to watch. Lee Sedol fussed and twitched around in his seat, biting his nails, sighing, and murmuring to himself, as commentators derided his unwillingness to accept the inevitable. "There's no point in playing out the endgame if you know you're going to lose, right?" asked the president of the American Go Association. "I don't know how to describe the situation . . . If I were black, I would resign. We should admit that we are facing the strongest existence in Go's history," said a Chinese commentator.

AlphaGo had won the game, and with it the tournament.

God's Touch

Even though Lee Sedol had already lost, and wanted nothing more than to leave the Four Seasons Hotel, go back home with his wife and daughter, and lie down to lick his wounds, the rules of the tournament stipulated that all five games had to take place, regardless of the results. That meant that he still had to face AlphaGo two more times, and the thought that he might not win a single game was almost more than he could stand, an unbearable disgrace, a loss of honor from which he would never recover. The DeepMind team had already shamed him—albeit unwittingly—by sending a bottle of expensive champagne to his room at the end of the third game. It had been meant as a gesture of respect, for they had been informed that it was his ten-year wedding anniversary, but the timing simply could not have been more disrespectful. Lee had suffered from that lack of gracefulness (so characteristic of westerners) by himself, but if he lost the two upcoming matches against AlphaGo, in front of a global audience of millions of people, there was no way he could ever sit down in front of a

Go board again. Such a public humiliation would surely break what little remained of his formerly indomitable spirit. It seemed wholly unlikely that he could claw his way back and defeat the computer. During the press conference after AlphaGo's third straight win, Lee Sedol's voice cracked, and he was barely able to expel the air from his lungs as he apologized: "I think I disappointed too many of you this time. I want to beg your forgiveness for being so powerless. I've never felt this much pressure, this much weight. I think I was too weak to overcome it," he confessed before the cameras. At the end of the conference, he smiled bashfully as he received shouts of praise and support from fellow Go players, who urged him to recover his confidence and play like himself during the final games, but he was now far too weary, and haunted by the very real possibility of losing five to zero—the same score he had boasted that he would win by. With the match already decided, there were fewer journalists to deal with as he made his way to the game room, but there was no way for him to hide just how scared and nervous he really was. He slumped down in his chair and took his place at the board, looking thinner and more childlike than ever, and bowed deeply to Aja Huang as the DeepMind programmer glanced at his computer screen waiting for AlphaGo's first move.

AlphaGo played black and took control of the game immediately. By move 28, the commentators were already criticizing Lee's reactions as sluggish and overly cautious. He was taking too long to think, his clock winding down faster than in any of the previous encounters. AlphaGo, meanwhile, seemed to be brimming with confidence, as it was playing far more aggressively than before, looking for fights from the very beginning. That was exactly the type of game that Lee had always preferred, and when AlphaGo delivered a vicious shoulder hit, he cracked a smile, as if he were playing against a brash, mischievous child, or a younger, wilder version of himself. Was he beginning to enjoy the game at last? It seemed highly unlikely. The computer had already taken control of the entire board and was attempting to completely overwhelm him. What was even more shocking to everyone watching was Lee's total lack of response: as meek as a snow-white lamb, he allowed AlphaGo to barricade the middle of the board and seal his tiny group of stones on the left side, leaving him almost no space at all to maneuver. It seemed as if he had already given up. Only a single commentator, one of his old classmates from his days in Master Kweon's academy, who was analyzing the game for the South Korean audience, stood up for him: she was absolutely convinced that Lee was playing possum, and that he would somehow find a way to live inside that minuscule area, even if the computer's black stones now seemed to have almost complete control over the entire grid. As the game plodded along, Lee fell into a state of absolute concentration: he was no longer fidgeting or fussing with his hair; he looked focused and determined, eyes fixed on the board like a tiger stalking its prey, his body the very image of stillness. He took longer and longer before each move, cocking his head to one side, as if listening to a far-off rumble that only he could hear. By move 54, Lee's clock had just 51 minutes left, while AlphaGo's had 1 hour and 28 minutes of available time. The game inched forward, and just like before, it looked as if Lee was already on the verge of defeat; reporters began to crowd outside the playing room as the rumor that the fourth game would be the shortest of them all began to spread online. Nevertheless, Lee did not react, and played slowly, cautiously, avoiding direct confrontation, giving up almost the entire board to his opponent. "Is he not afraid to die?" Fan Hui wrote in his notes, despairing at Lee's stubborn refusal to engage with the computer. Fan was so close to him physically that he could almost hear Lee's thoughts and feel what he was waiting for, and soon he fell into the same trancelike state that had mesmerized the Korean grandmaster. By move 69, Lee was down to just 34 minutes, while his opponent still had over 1 hour and 18 minutes left. AlphaGo continued to pound Lee with its attacks, swallowing a large group on the left side, while Lee's fans despaired as they watched him waste an entire ten minutes before placing his next stone on the board. AlphaGo answered immediately, blocking off the center. There appeared to be nothing left for Lee to do; in the Deep-Mind control center, Demis Hassabis saw that AlphaGo's estimation of its probability of winning had climbed to over 70 percent. He watched a set of monitors that featured the Chinese, Japanese, and Korean commentators already calling the game for AlphaGo, as not a single one of them could see a way out of the rock-solid fortress that the computer had built. Lee remained motionless. When his clock had run down to just eleven minutes, he placed his palm flat over the edges of his bowl, then quickly picked up a stone between his index and middle fingers, and smacked it down right in the center of AlphaGo's territory.

"The hand of God! That is a divine move!" shouted one of Lee Sedol's historic rivals, Gu Li, jumping up from his seat in the Chinese webcast. Like a bolt of lightning, Lee's 78th stone tore AlphaGo's position apart, striking at the heart of the board with a wedge move unlike anything anyone had seen before. People went wild with excitement. Even if they could not fully grasp the significance of what they had just seen, or begin to compute the consequences of Lee's incredibly daring gambit, everyone recognized that it was an unthinkable move, a move no one would have considered. "That would be so cool if it works," said

Chris Garlock, an American commentator, completely stunned. "That is such an exciting move. It's going to change the whole game," said his colleague at the DeepMind YouTube feed, Michael Redmond, agog at the potential that Lee Sedol had managed to find inside his opponent's dominion, at a place where no other Go player in the world would have had the audacity to dive in. Not a single analyst or commentator had anticipated it, but as soon as Lee laid down his white stone, they scrambled to try to understand what had just happened, shouting over each other, applauding or critiquing the wedge move. Some openly contradicted themselves, lauding it and then decrying its failure, while a few simply stared dumbstruck, their minds reeling. There was a moment of chaos as the shock of the new move sank in, but not a single one of them was as utterly confused as AlphaGo.

The computer's response to Lee's flash of genius made no sense whatsoever: when Aja Huang played the program's next stone in an obviously disadvantageous position, everyone, including Lee Sedol, was surprised, but nobody dared to point out the obvious blunders that AlphaGo began to make from then onward, as the previous games had left them wary about critiquing what they could not understand. Lee Sedol himself hesitated before capitalizing on the clear advantages that AlphaGo was suddenly gifting him. Was this a new strategy? he wondered. Was the computer laying another trap for him? The only ones who knew that AlphaGo had lost its mind and was simply playing nonsense were the people up in DeepMind's control room.

When he saw what was happening, Demis Hassabis snuck away from the players' room as quietly as he could and ran up the stairs, storming into the control room just in time to watch the head programmers huddled in front of a screen, where AlphaGo's probability of winning had just fallen off a cliff. "Did anything strange happen before it started acting this way?" he asked them, and when everyone replied that, just a few moments before Lee Sedol played his wedge move, everything looked normal—hell, better than normal, AlphaGo had been massacring Lee—they had nothing else to do but hunker down and try to contain the sinking feeling in their stomachs, as they realized that their worst fears were now coming true: AlphaGo had become delusional.

It was not the first time that they had witnessed this type of behavior. Every now and then, in very specific board configurations, AlphaGo went mad, suddenly losing all sense of position and value, to the point where it would think that it was alive in areas in which it was very clearly dead, as if it had become blind, unable to distinguish self from other, black from white, friend from foe, life from death. They watched as Aja Huang tried not to betray his feelings before the cameras, although they knew that he understood just how far AlphaGo had fallen, and how deranged its systems had become: "I knew after move 78, after like ten or twenty moves, that AlphaGo somehow became crazy, but I didn't realize why," he would later recall. In the moment all he could do was faithfully translate what he saw on the screen to the board, even as Lee Sedol gawked at him, begging for some type of explanation. Back in the control room, David Silver, Aja Huang's counterpart as head programmer of AlphaGo, saw that the computer had searched over ninety-five moves ahead after Lee's astounding move, developing endless lines of probability branching out from each one of those possible moves: "I think that something went wrong," he said to Hassabis, who was pacing frantically from one side of the room to the other. "That's the longest it has searched during the entire game. I think it searched so deeply, that it lost itself."

"What's it doing there!" Hassabis screamed as he saw the next move that the computer was considering.

"Maybe it has a master plan . . ." joked one of the younger engineers.

"No, it doesn't. It doesn't even think it has, does it?" replied a bitter Hassabis. "It knows it's made a mistake, but it's evaluating it the other way. I mean, look! Look! Lee is confused. He's like, *What's it doing?* That's not an *I'm scared* look, that's a *What the fuck is it doing?* look."

The entire DeepMind team watched in despair as the international commentators started demanding answers. "What's going on!" cried Kim Myungwan, a Korean 9 dan professional, after AlphaGo continued to stumble blindly across the board. "This could be that it can't find a way through, like it looked far enough ahead to see that it doesn't work, and now maybe it's . . . on tilt? . . . I don't know . . ." answered one of his counterparts.

"Are you *kidding* me?" David Silver groaned as he watched one of AlphaGo's inner monitors, holding his face in both hands. "This . . . this move, literally, this next move we are going to play . . . I think they're going to laugh. I think Lee is going to laugh."

Aja Huang picked up a black stone and as soon as he laid it down, the entire audience outside the playing room burst out laughing.

"Oh, that is ridiculous!" shouted the female host of one of seven South Korean TV stations that were broadcasting the match live. "Is it a mouse mis-click from Aja Huang? No, that's the move. These are not human moves. It's inexplicable. Those are mistakes, clear mistakes. For the first time in four matches, we have seen AlphaGo make mistakes. I think Lee Sedol found a chink in its armor. He found the weakness in the system," she added as everyone watched the champion stare at the board, clearly as confused as everyone else. It took AlphaGo more than twenty moves to recover its sanity, but by then it had completely lost control of the game.

Lee's clock had run out, and from then onward he was playing under *byoyomi*, a time constraint that forced him to make his moves in less than a minute each. Ahead for the first time, he could not afford a single mistake, and played on without betraying a smile, even as a horde of reporters who had left early when AlphaGo's lead seemed incontestable started piling back into the hotel and filling the press room to capacity in anticipation. Lee sat up straight as AlphaGo began playing a series of last-ditch attempts that no self-respecting human would consider, mainly out of a sense of dignity that the computer lacked, as they were easy enough to counter and even allowed Lee to increase his already considerable lead. They were not bad moves per se, simply pointless. When AlphaGo's internal networks indicated that its probability of winning had fallen below 20 percent, a message appeared on Aja Huang's monitor:

The result "W+Resign" was added to the game information

AlphaGo resigns.

Aja picked up a stone from his bowl, laid it down on the edge of the board, and bowed to Lee Sedol.

Professional commentators screamed, clapped, and burst out laughing from sheer delight. The onlookers inside the game room erupted into applause and several of Lee's best friends rushed forward to greet him. Outside in the hall and in the streets of South Korea, perfect strangers who had been watching the game hugged each other, while others were moved to tears—it was as if Lee Sedol had just won a victory for our entire species. The press room lit up with excitement as cameramen and foreign journalists began to jump up and down, cheering wildly, all objectivity thrown out the door, but Lee himself remained perfectly still, moving stones around the board and analyzing alternatives as he had done at the end of all the previous games, not even smiling to himself, despite the fact that he could clearly hear the voices of many hundreds of people shouting his name, and see that the only female judge of the match was beaming down at him from her podium, with tears welling up in her eyes. "I heard people were shouting from joy when it was clear that AlphaGo had lost the game," he later said. "I think it's clear why: People felt helplessness and fear. It seemed we humans are so weak and fragile. And this victory meant we could still hold our own. As time goes on, it'll probably be very difficult to beat AI. But winning this one time . . . it felt like it was enough. One time was enough." He remained seated and did not look up from the board or smile until Demis Hassabis walked over to him and very gently tapped his hand on Lee's shoulder, nodding to convey his congratulations and respect. He stayed there, picking stones from the board, as Fan Hui descended from the judges' podium, bent down to his eye level, and gave him a massive thumbs-up before leaving him there, alone, his chin resting on his hand, while he pondered the entire game, almost as if he were afraid to stand, because to him, as to so many others, it seemed as if he had witnessed a miracle, a moment in time so precious as to never be forgotten.

When he entered the press room, the applause was so thunderous that one might have thought the massive chandeliers would suddenly crash down onto the journalists who chanted *LEE-SE-DOL! LEE-SE-DOL! LEE-SE-DOL!* at the top of their lungs. Lee made his way to the podium as serious as he had been at the end of the game, almost indifferent, but when he finally looked up from his shoes, his expression changed in an instant, as if he had just snapped out of a trance. He began to smile, then beam as he bowed his head again and again in appreciation, while the room was flooded with cheers, hooting, and applause. At first, it was hard for him to understand, he later said. After all, he had lost the match and this new result did not change that at all. "I didn't expect it to be like that. It was unbelievable, unbelievable!" he would recall, but in that moment he could hardly contain his emotions. "Thank you very much," he said, chuckling to himself. "I've never been congratulated so much for winning one game! I couldn't be happier, after losing three in a row." He had to stop speaking as cheers erupted once again. "I wouldn't give this up for anything in the world." Completely drained after five hours of play and emotionally overwhelmed, Lee took just a couple of questions and then retired to his room amid deafening applause.

Outside the hotel, Lee's fans were running out in the streets of Seoul, chanting and celebrating their hero's victory. Even the team at Deep-Mind, who had lost, rather embarrassingly, were amazed at Lee's stunning ability to create something out of nothing. How could a man, however smart, defeat a computer like AlphaGo, able to calculate over two hundred million positions a second? Surely it was a feat that would go down in history, as it showed the true measure of Lee Sedol's creative genius, something that all mankind could truly celebrate. Demis Hassabis, however, could not lay his mind to rest.

He needed to understand what had gone wrong with AlphaGo, and he gathered the members of his team in the DeepMind control room.

Just like Lee Sedol had done, they went over the entire game, and quickly confirmed that it was move 78—as everyone suspected—that had thrown AlphaGo into madness. Lee would later confess that he had wanted to find a move that the computer could not anticipate, however much it calculated, but that his own thought process had not been rational at all: the move had come to him out of sheer inspiration. He had not foreseen or planned it, and when he was asked about it during the press conference, he admitted so quite frankly: "At that point in the game, it was the only move I could see. There was no other placement. It was the only option for me, so I put it there. I am quite humbled by all the praise I am getting for it." Hassabis and his team huddled around the main terminal, prodding the system to see exactly what had happened, but due to the nature of AlphaGo itself, it was exceedingly difficult to unpack the choices the program had made, and why it had let the center of the board, which had been squarely under its control for almost the entire game, crumble away like it had.

"We were winning before this," said Aja Huang as he pointed to Lee's wedge move, but nobody in the DeepMind team could really judge its true worth, as they did not have a sufficiently profound understanding of the game. Finally, David Silver had the idea of running the entire match through AlphaGo's systems, making it play Lee's moves and its own moves, to see how the Value and Policy Networks would assess "God's touch." "Would we have played it?" he asked as they fired up the computer and saw it apply its boundless computational powers to sort through the endless lines of probability. "What chance does it give that particular move?"

"Zero point zero zero zero one," a junior researcher replied.

There was silence. One in ten thousand: exactly the same probability that AlphaGo had assigned to its own groundbreaking move 37 during the second game, the one that had made the entire Go community recognize its potential. As it turned out, AlphaGo's networks agreed with Gu Li, the Chinese professional who had christened Lee's move: it truly had been divine, a touch from God's hand—only one in ten thousand human players would have considered it. That was the reason AlphaGo had been incapable of dealing with Lee's wedge move: it was too far from human experience, and past even where AlphaGo's seemingly boundless capabilities could reach.

Facing each other, Lee and the computer had managed to stray beyond the limits of Go, casting a new and terrible beauty, a logic more powerful than reason that will send ripples far and wide.

Game Over

Lee lost his final game with AlphaGo.

During the fifth encounter, there was no hand of God, no blinding flashes of inspiration that could have allowed him to defeat that unnatural, behemoth intelligence. There were more journalists than ever before, over two hundred million people following the game worldwide, and major international networks like CNN and the BBC reporting live from the Four Seasons. For the last game, Lee had requested to play black, even though that meant giving the machine a slight advantage that no one really thought he could afford. But Lee had won playing white, and he wanted to prove, perhaps only to himself, that he could also do so with black.

The press room overflowed as more journalists flew into Seoul to be firsthand witnesses of the final game between the man and the machine. Never before, in all of Go's three-thousand-year history, had such attention been paid to a single game. On the South Korean networks, the excitement was almost unimaginable; there was no other news that mattered that day.

At first it seemed that Lee had more than a fighting chance, as the computer began playing moves that no one approved of, leading one commentator to joke that perhaps the algorithm hadn't recovered from the previous day's defeat. Hassabis fretted in front of the control room's monitors, as it looked like AlphaGo was once again short-circuiting. "Why's it playing there for!" he shouted when Aja Huang placed a stone in a position that seemed completely useless and out of place, even though the program's inner evaluation function was 91 percent certain that it was winning. "Because it's incorrect again," answered one of the technicians. During the entire game, the DeepMind team was convinced that AlphaGo was wrong in its judgments of the board, playing weird, slack moves that appeared to do nothing to further its own score, even though everyone thought they could see several options that were more solid and robust. Hassabis, Fan Hui, Aja Huang, David Silver, and the others on the DeepMind team were absolutely sure that it was going to turn out to be another huge embarrassment for them. But they were all mistaken. None of them knew Go well enough to judge AlphaGo's merit. However, others did.

"White is winning now," said Kim Ji-yeong, a top-level player commenting for the American audience, after seeing the computer make another apparently nonsensical throw-in.

"I don't know," his broadcasting partner replied, confused. "Perhaps this is what 10, or 11, dan play looks like? It looks weird, it looks ugly, it just doesn't make sense to us."

AlphaGo continued playing its strange moves to the very end, and some analysts began to point out that there was indeed a different kind of thinking behind its decisions. Normally, a human player would judge a player's strength by the amount of territory that he or she controlled; by that simple, straightforward logic, the more territory one had, the bigger one's chances of winning were. But AlphaGo could do something that no human was capable of: it could calculate, with unerring precision, just how much it needed to win, and do no more than that. To the computer there was no difference between winning by a landslide or a hair's breadth. Why should it gobble up vast expanses of territory when it didn't need them? The match stretched out endlessly, over five hours of play that led to an excruciatingly complex endgame. Lee and AlphaGo played a total of 280 moves, almost completely covering the board in black and white stones, before Lee finally gave up and resigned. It was almost impossible to tell who had won just by looking at the board. When the experts finally tallied up the score, they found that it had been by far the closest of all five games: AlphaGo had beaten Lee by just two and a half points.

During the award ceremony, Lee Sedol looked dignified but shrunken. "I've grown through this experience," he said. "I will make something out of it with the lessons I've learned. What surprised me the most was that AlphaGo showed us that moves humans may have thought creative were actually conventional. I think this will bring a new paradigm to Go. I'm thankful for all this, I feel like I've found the reason why I play Go. I realize that it was a really good choice, learning to play this game. It's been an unforgettable experience." The packed press room had fallen into a deep and solemn silence. Demis Hassabis sat next to Lee on the podium and could not hide his excitement, despite the fact that he was very keen not to gloat, and tried his best to respect the dignity of the fallen idol at his side. Lee was nervously fumbling with the earpiece they had given him for the simultaneous translation of the final press conference, and had to ask for help from an assistant to fit it in his ear. "I'm kind of speechless," Hassabis said. "This is the most mind-blowing experience of my life. It was an incredible game, very exciting and incredibly stressful. At the beginning it seemed that AlphaGo made quite a big mistake with a stone-killer tesuji that it played wrong, but in the end it came back and it was very, very close. We saw some incredible games of Go these past five days, and I think there are some moves, like move 37 in game two, and move 78 in game four, that will be discussed for a very long time to come. This is a once-in-a-lifetime thing. For me it's the culmination of a twenty-year dream. I would say it's the most amazing thing I have ever experienced." Lee gnawed on his lower lip and apologized once more to his fans and to the world at large for having been so powerless, so utterly helpless, convinced that it had been his own personal weakness, and not the computer's fundamental superiority, that had led to his ignominious defeat. "I don't necessarily think that AlphaGo is superior to me," he said. "I believe that there is still more that human beings can do against artificial intelligence. I feel regret, because there is more that I could have shown. Go is a game that you enjoy, whether you are an amateur or a professional. Enjoyment is the essence of Go. And AlphaGo is very strong, but it cannot know that essence. My defeat is not mankind's defeat. I think that these games clearly showed my own weaknesses, not humanity's weakness."

When Lee Sedol finally bowed to everyone present and stepped down from the stage, Demis Hassabis and David Silver stayed on to receive, on behalf of their entire team, a certificate from South Korea's Go Association, awarding AlphaGo an honorary 9 dan ranking, the highest level a grandmaster can achieve, a title reserved for those players whose ability at the ancient game borders on the supernatural. The citation on the certificate—the first one of its kind ever produced—carried the serial number 001, and stated that it was given out *in recognition of AlphaGo's sincere efforts to master Go's Taoist foundations and reach a level close to the territory of divinity.*

Calculate, Abandon Instinct

During the months following his defeat against AlphaGo, Lee Sedol won every single tournament game that he played.

When he was asked for his secret, he replied, "Do not rely on instinct. Calculate with the utmost precision." His series of consecutive victories and his new style of play made it look like he would extend his already illustrious career for several years to come, but in November 2019, Lee shocked the world by suddenly announcing his retirement.

At first, nobody understood his decision. Famous Go players usually compete well into old age. In Japan, professionals often play tournaments until the last day of their lives, and Lee had just turned thirty-six. There was a public outcry for him to take back his decision, but he explained that he had dedicated his entire life to Go, having thought of nothing else since he was five years old, and now it was time for something new. As brave as ever, he decided not to play his farewell match against his longtime friend and rival Gu Li, or the cocky rising star of the international circuit, Ke Jie, but against HanDol, an artificial intelligence software developed by South Korea's NHN Entertainment Corporation.

HanDol had already defeated South Korea's top five players that year, and Lee started his first game with a two-stone advantage granted to him by the organizers of the event, to level out the playing field. "Even with a two-stone advantage, I feel like I will lose the first game to HanDol," he told the press, leading everyone to think that he had lost his fighting spirit, but in what has to be one of the most uncanny of coincidences, he managed to win that first game after his 78th move threw his artificially intelligent rival into utter confusion, just like during his bout against AlphaGo. While Lee regarded his move as nothing out of the ordinary, many experts said that it had been unthinkable, and the team behind HanDol declared that they were astounded at Lee's ability to find bugs and weaknesses in what had previously seemed to be a totally flawless software architecture; they had to bear witness when HanDol began to make completely irrational moves and nonsensical throw-ins, resigning just fourteen turns later. Lee Sedol became front-page news once again: he was the only human being alive to have defeated two advanced artificial intelligence systems in a tournament setting. No other player in the world had even come close to doing so. Nevertheless, during the following game, which he played without any type of advantage, HanDol crushed him.

The tournament was held not in Seoul but in El Dorado, a five-star resort in Sinan-gun county, just thirty kilometers from Lee's home island of Bigeumdo. The posh, high-class hotel was a veritable world away from the humble home where Lee had played his first matches against his brothers and sisters, most of whom had become professional players like him, raised under the strict tutelage of their father. His whole family showed up for the game, and many of his old classmates and teachers from elementary school took the ferry to see him; they crowded outside the lavish beachside hotel with hand-painted signs to showcase their support, eager for a chance to see the Strong Stone, the Bigeumdo Boy, with their own eyes, as they could hardly believe that the small, timid child they had seen climbing trees and fishing with the other boys had become a national hero, won tens of millions of dollars in prize money, and turned into a legendary figure in Go. They cheered throughout the first twenty minutes of the match and only quieted down when hotel officials came and told them that their racket could throw Lee off his game. Everyone wanted him to go out with a bang, to demonstrate the sort of gameplay that had made him a legend, during this, his swan song, but after five hours of grueling effort and 181 stones, Lee resigned.

"I used to have this sense of pride," he said a couple of weeks later, after losing his third game against HanDol, when he was interviewed on a popular talk show that recapped his entire career. "I thought I was the best, or at least one of the best. But then artificial intelligence put the final nail in my coffin. It is simply unbeatable. In that situation, it doesn't matter how much you try. I don't see the point. I started playing when I was five. Back then, it was all about courtesy and manners. It was more like learning an art form than a game. As I grew up, Go started to be seen as a mind game, but what I learned was an art. Go is a work of art made by two people. Now it's totally different. After the advent of AI, the concept of Go itself has changed. It is a devastating force. AlphaGo did not beat me, it crushed me. After that, I continued playing but I had already decided to retire. With the debut of AI, I've realized that I cannot be at the top, even if I make a spectacular comeback and return to being the number one player through frantic efforts. Even if I become the best that the world has ever known, there is an entity that cannot be defeated."

The God of Go

Shortly after Lee announced his retirement, a strange player appeared on the international online Go circuit.

Under the moniker Master, it began racking up one win after another. Seemingly unbeatable, it won fifty consecutive games against the world's top Go players and when it finally lost one, DeepMind's people confessed that they were the ones behind Master, and that it was a stronger version of the artificial intelligence that had defeated Lee Sedol, explaining that the single loss Master had suffered had been due to an internet connection time-out.

Once again, DeepMind's researchers decided to pit their program against the strongest possible player, to see just how far it had advanced: they chose to challenge the Chinese prodigy Ke Jie, the world's highest-ranked player, at the Future of Go Summit in Wuzhen, China, the country where the game had originated over three thousand years before. Ke Jie was only nineteen years old and even more boastful than Lee

Sedol. He had risen to the top spectacularly and had heavily criticized Lee for the games that the South Korean had lost against AlphaGo, saying that Lee was no longer at the top of his game by the time he had faced the computer. Ke was absolutely sure that he would do better, bragging before the matchup that he would show the supremacy of Chinese Go and restore the hegemony of the human race.

Master annihilated Ke Jie, winning all three games.

The teenager cried during the final press conference, taking off his thick-rimmed glasses and wiping tears from his eyes as he tried to convey the feeling of helplessness that had overcome him during the games, saying that, as soon as he had started playing against Master, he had begun to sense something that was new, and deeply unsettling. When he was asked to explain what made Master different from AlphaGo, he could not help but lapse into the type of language that we usually reserve for conscious beings: "To me, he is a god of Go. A god that can crush all who defy him. I've never doubted myself. I have always felt I had everything under control. I thought I had a very good understanding of composition, an intimate knowledge of the board. But Master looks at all this and he is, like, 'What's all this rubbish!' He can see the whole universe of Go, I see only a tiny area around me. So please, let it explore the universe, and let me play in my own backyard. I will fish in my little pond. How much more could it improve through self-learning? Its limits are hard to fathom. I think the future belongs to AI."

With both Lee Sedol and Ke Jie defeated, Demis Hassabis and the team at DeepMind could climb no higher, at least not by playing against human opponents. While he had reached a fundamental milestone in his quest toward artificial general intelligence, Ke Jie's final question— *How much further could the program evolve through self-learning?*—continued to gnaw away at Hassabis, even as he celebrated DeepMind's complete dominance over a game that had once been considered mankind's bastion against the machines, the pinnacle of human intuition and creativity. Just *how* far could they take their self-learning algorithm?

Hassabis and the DeepMind team made a radical departure: they stripped Master, AlphaGo's successor, of all its human knowledge—those many millions of games based on which it had first learned to play, and that formed the cornerstone of its common sense, the program's unique ability to judge the value of an individual position, to estimate its chances of winning, and to see the board as a human being would, and left only its bare bones. Their aim was to create a more powerful and much more general artificial intelligence, one that was not restricted to Go in its learning capabilities and that did not rely on human understanding and knowledge as a crutch during its first formative baby steps. They took their algorithm and wiped it clean, leaving no human data from which it could learn, depriving it of its only direct connection with mankind.

The results were terrifying.

The new program defeated the version of AlphaGo that had pushed Lee Sedol into retirement one hundred games to zero. But it was only getting started. When they applied that same algorithm to chess, it proved to be just as strong: after two hours it had played more games against itself than have been recorded throughout all of history; after four hours it had already become better than any human; after eight it could defeat Stockfish, the reigning AI chess champion. "It plays like a human on fire," said Matthew Sadler, the English grandmaster who was first exposed to it. Sadler described its style as extremely aggressive and reminiscent of the manner that Garry Kasparov used to play in, an opinion that was later ratified by the great Russian genius himself. After conquering chess, the system took on shogi, a Japanese game that is somewhat similar to chess but with higher complexity, as pieces are not fixed, and can be swapped from one army to the other, creating multiple variations that would never occur in chess; the new algorithm mastered shogi in under twelve hours, and beat the world's strongest program—Elmo—in 90 percent of the games they played.

For all these games, it considered no human experience: it was simply given the rules and allowed to play against itself. At first, it made completely random moves, but in next to no time it had evolved into an unbeatable force. It has now become the strongest entity the world has ever known at Go, chess, and shogi.

Its name is AlphaZero.

This book is a work of fiction based on fact. I would like to thank Constanza Martínez for her invaluable assistance in helping me shape it. I also owe a debt of gratitude to the authors who inspired this work and served as sources for these stories: first and foremost, George Dyson, because his wonderful book *Turing's Cathedral* introduced me to von Neumann's life and ideas, and Fan Hui, Gu Li, and Zhou Ruiyang, for their expert analysis and commentary on the matches between Lee Sedol and AlphaGo. Other important sources were Marina von Neumann Whitman's memoir, *The Martian's Daughter*, Norman Macrae's biography, *John von Neumann: The Scientific Genius Who Pioneered the Modern Computer, Game Theory, Nuclear Deterrence, and Much More*, and the documentary *AlphaGo*, directed by Greg Kohs.

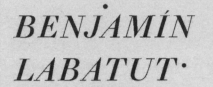

Pushkin Press